# HOW TO LOOK, DRAW & PAINT

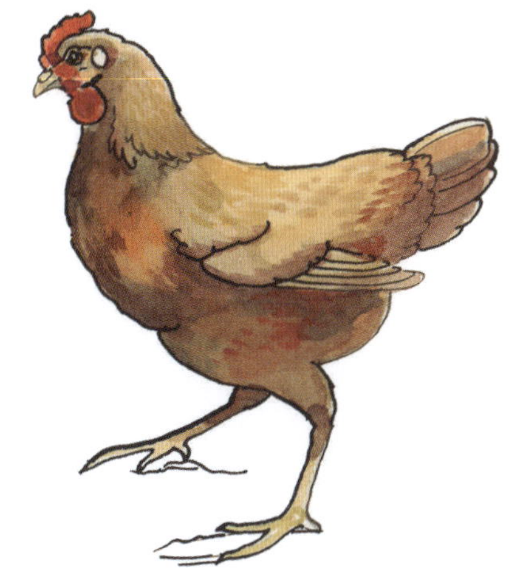

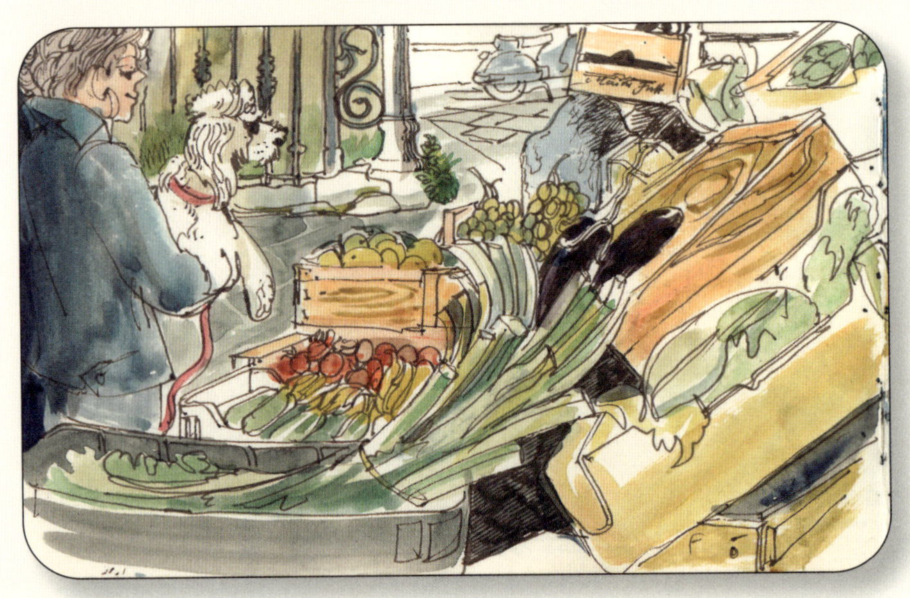

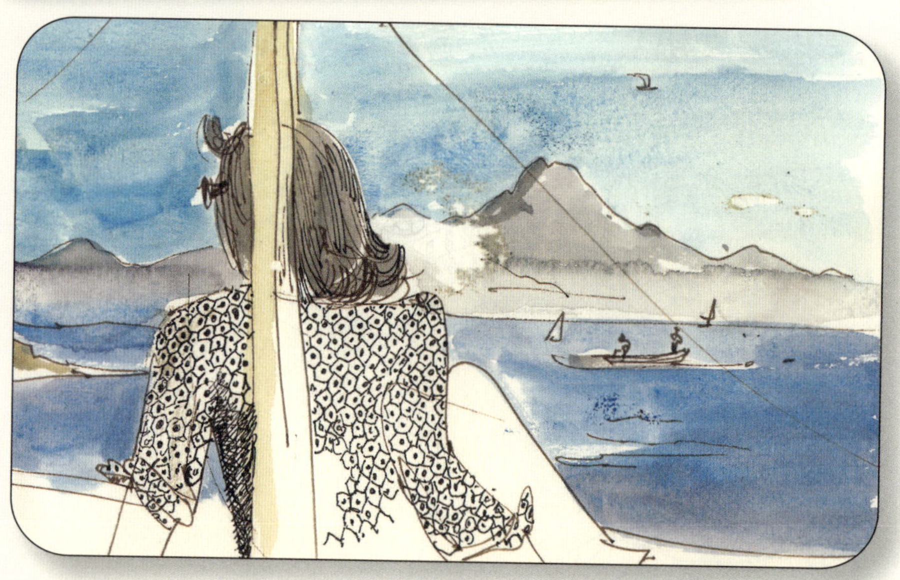

*This book is dedicated to Louis Marsh Cross*

# HOW TO LOOK, DRAW & PAINT

MATTHEW RICE

ilex

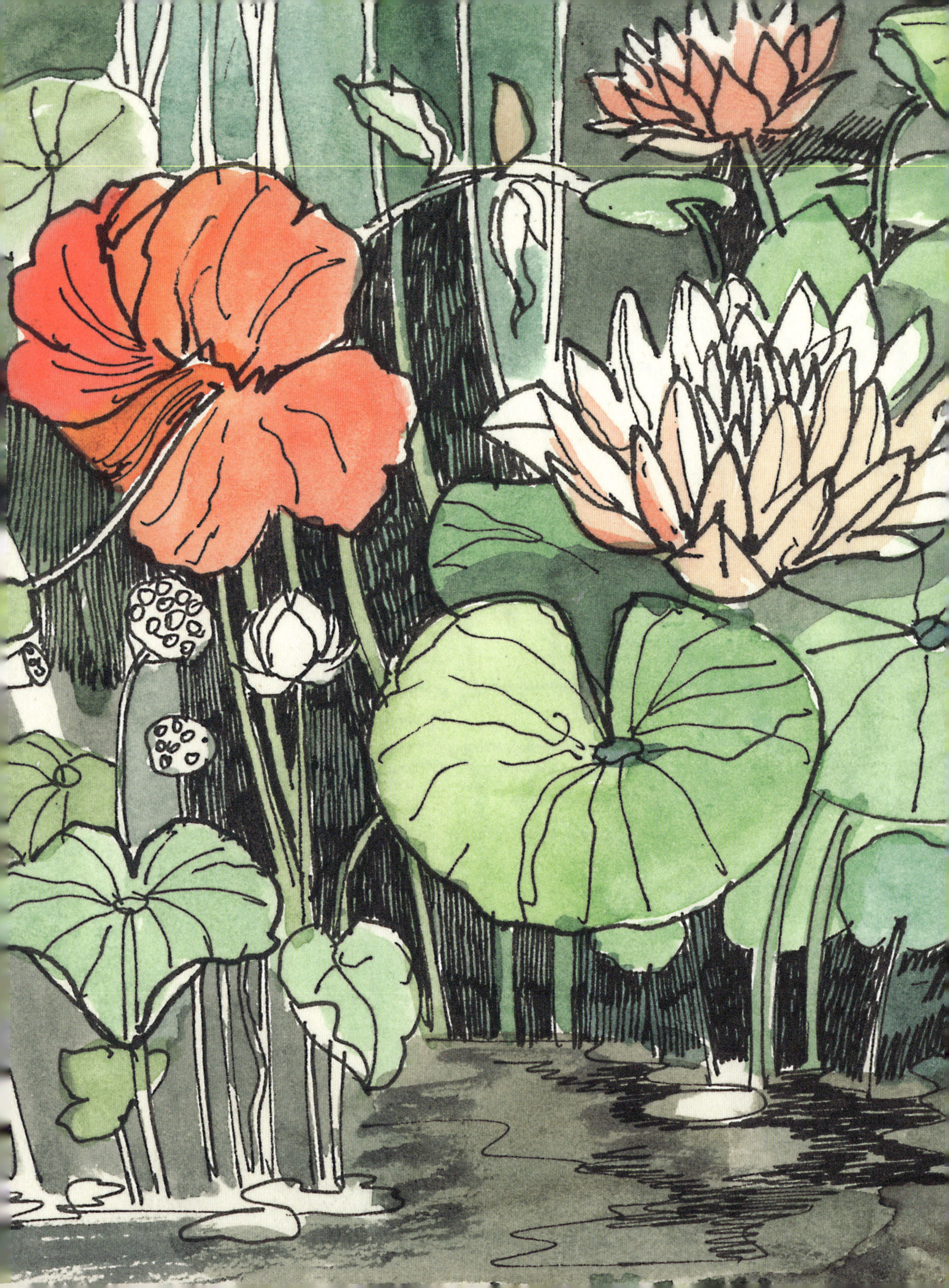

# Contents

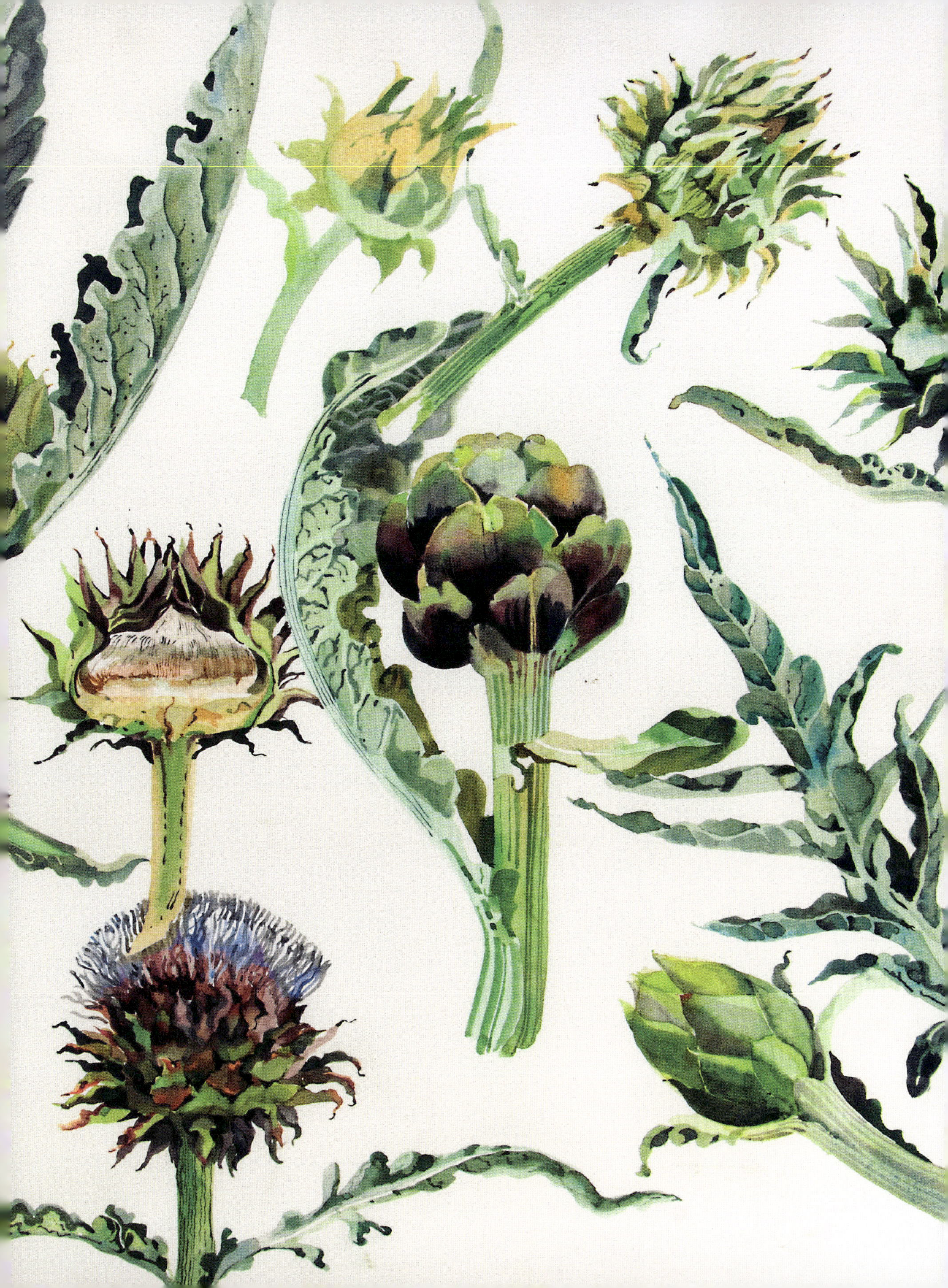

To know how to draw you need to think about how to look, because to draw is to look and report on what you have seen. This report may be dramatic, whispered, assured and confident, or tentative. It may tell all or imply more than it states directly. But if the report is actually *wrong*, then not only is nothing explained but the process of creating it is dispiriting and futile. When we learn to count, we aim for accuracy. The spelling bee winner misses no letters, and as we learn foreign languages, we try (hard) to learn the correct tenses, genders and declensions. It is the same with drawing. There are many styles, but the basic aim remains the same: to express what you see in a way that explains that to others. As we learn to draw better, we also learn to understand, to analyse, and to explore and understand our world and its inhabitants. This exercise is more than an expression of a desire to decorate or to kill time or amuse. It is, in fact, a vital and near-universal mode of communication: a cube or a duck, a cone or a tree, are instantly recognizable and allow us to speak to those who find our written or spoken language inexplicably alien. Conversely, drawing that is wrong is obviously so to any viewer: a curve too steep or angle too acute are equally out of kilter in Japan, Mexico or in your home town.

# WHO AM I?

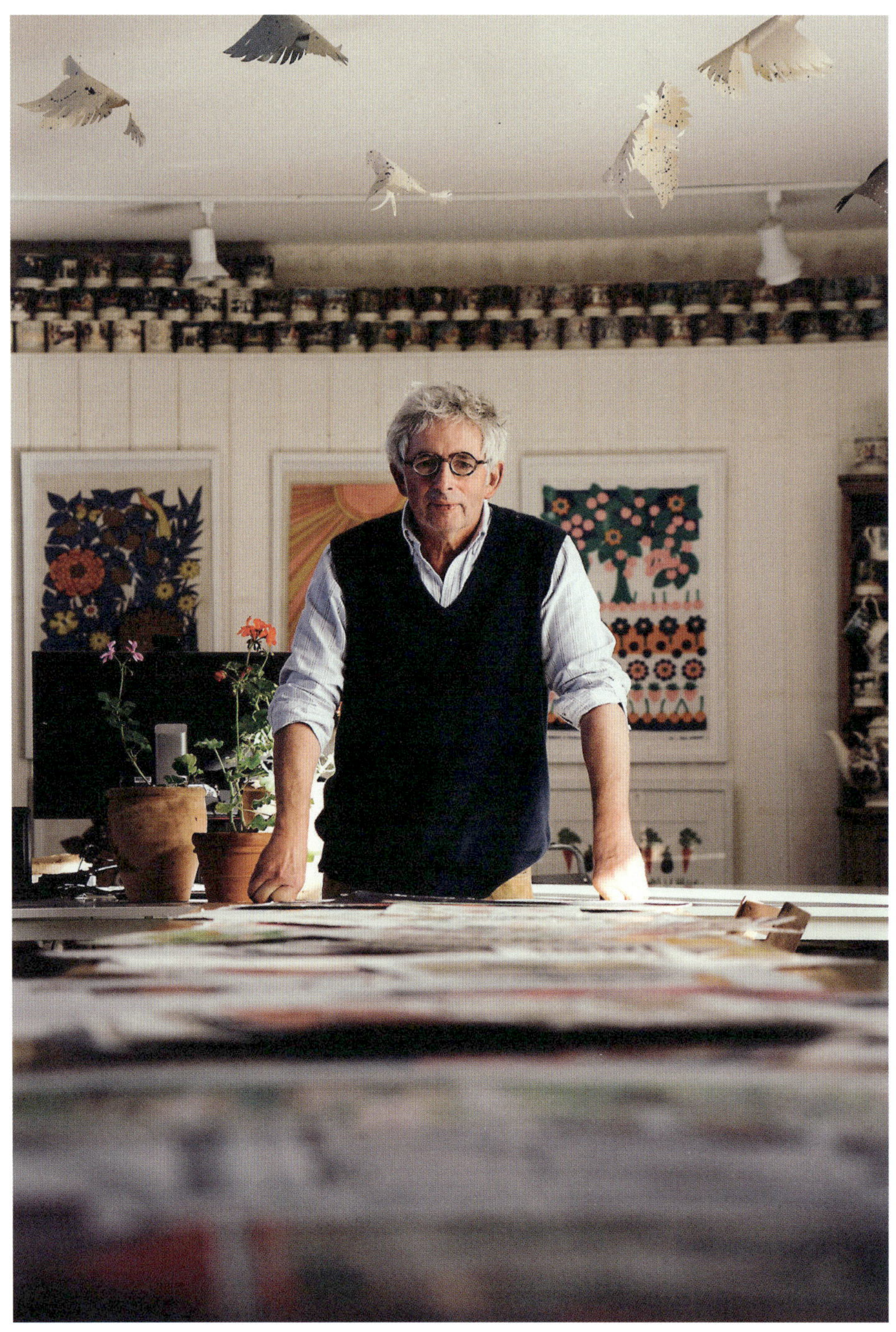

A self-portrait is worth avoiding at all costs! But here, in writing and for once without a drawing, is some kind of explanation of my work. I am a draughtsman, a painter and a designer (also, I guess, a gardener, writer and teacher). My working hours are flexible, often beginning uncompanionably early, especially in the summer, and continuing into the evening, but rarely after 10 p.m. I work sitting or standing and usually with two or more dogs on a bed or sofa nearby. I am lucky to have a lot of room and to be able to leave work and materials out and not have to clear away to make a kitchen table for supper. I work alone, but with a book being read to me via my phone as company.

I grew up in a family that drew – for work and for pleasure. My parents were both accomplished draughtsmen, although my mother sometimes let her naturally iconographic expressions draw her away from genuine accuracy, while my father's more academic discipline meant that simplistic child-art never felt good enough (at least to me). Drawing was the principal activity on family holidays and, in one form or another, in the evenings or at weekends. From the age of 13, I had a marvellous and totally engaged teacher who helped my drawing grow up. His faultless drawing allowed him to explain errors and weakness simply and kindly. He taught me to *look*.

My work is varied: sometimes I paint the plants and flowers around me; at other times I work on commissions or produce designs for the pottery company founded by my ex-wife Emma Bridgewater. Inspiration and subject matter are largely provided by my immediate surroundings and, where possible, with the fruit or flower placed on a sheet of white paper on my desk. Watercolour is almost invariably my medium, so I know it quite well. I use pans, not tubes, and love the way that supersaturated colours are so intense and bright on the white Arches paper I favour. I don't think my work is that different now from its younger self, but when I look back, I see that there is an agonizingly slow but traceable improvement in my drawing, which I hope will continue.

My influences are many and varied, but the watercolours of John Sell Cotman, David Hockney, Edward Burra and Patrick Procktor are important, as are the drawings and paintings of Samuel Palmer and Stanley Spencer. Travelling has been a really important part of my painting both in terms of subject matter (predictably, Venice is something or somewhere to which I always return) and also, more importantly, as stimulation to change and grow. Sometimes an exhibition can really jolt one's work (*Anglo-Saxon Kingdoms* at the British Library and *The Great Mughals: Art, Architecture and Opulence* at the Victoria and Albert Museum both made me stop and stare), and often a gallery visit makes me lean away from designs towards painting, although those visual stimulations are really important in terms of design as well.

Drawing may be work for me, but there are times when it plays another role. Drawing makes escape routes. You can draw the world you want – the way you wish things were or might be – and even if the world around you is your model (and for me it is endlessly full of subjects and models), there are always improvements to be made.

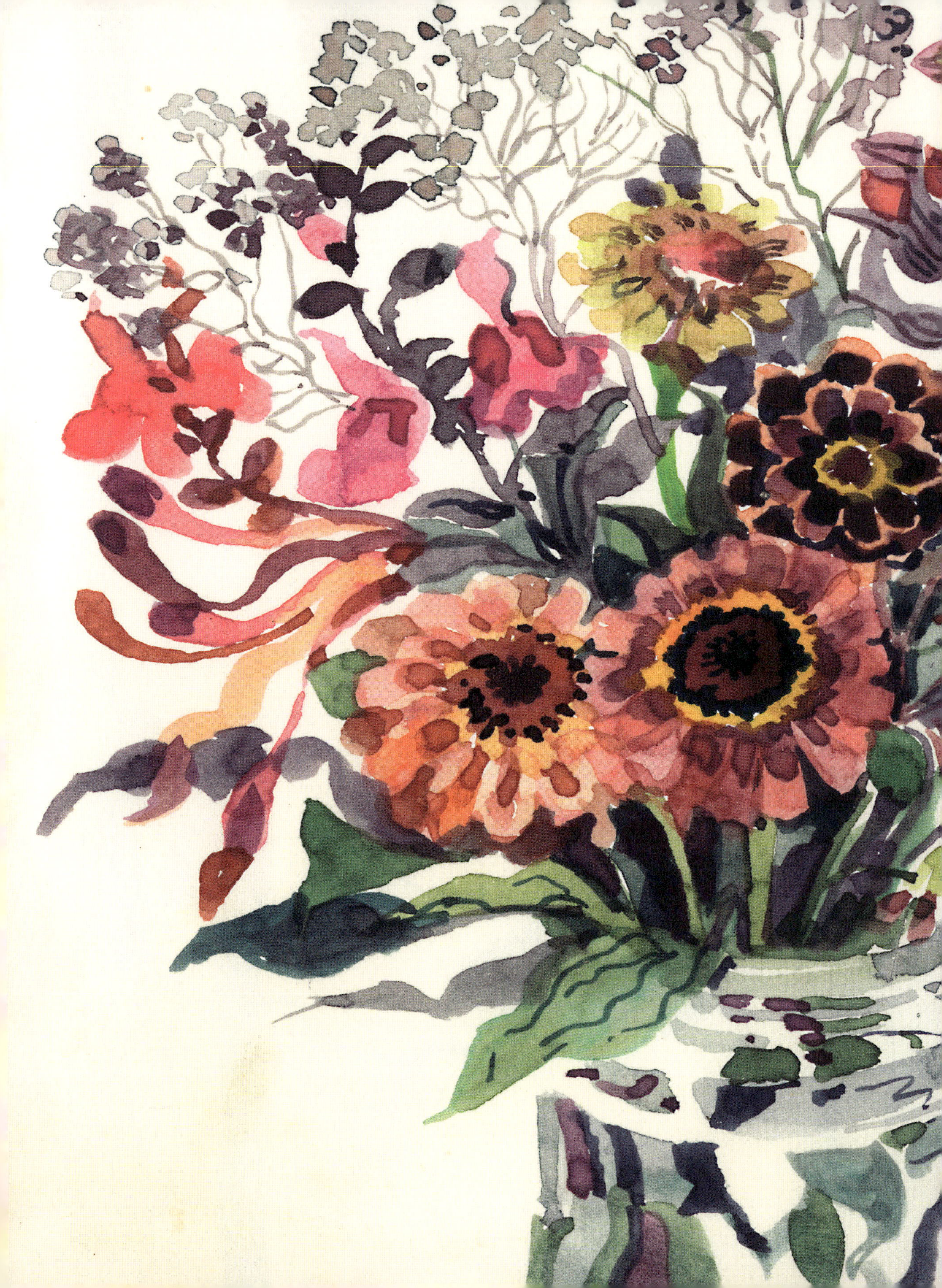

# HOW TO USE THIS BOOK

This book is a very basic companion for a rather complicated journey. It would be silly and untruthful to say that drawing is easy. Fun, absorbing, beautiful, calming and personally stretching, *yes*, but easy... not really. If you are looking for easy, then go for colouring in. It's not surprising that this has become something of a pastime for creative adults in the last decade. There is tremendous skill in carefully colouring in a complex image, and also judgement and inspiration in choosing which colours and tones to employ as you do so. But it is still, in essence, far easier, as the drawing has been done. In fact, some of the lessons in this book, for example the section on directional light and shading or that on how to use watercolour, might be usefully employed in a colouring project.

But this book is really about looking and drawing – both natural and universal habits but both (if they are to help you grow and learn) difficult. Teaching drawing on and off for a long time – to students at art school or university, in schools or indeed in my own studio – has shown me that I can be a bit bossy and critical. I hope that the format of a book and the comfort of your own home will insulate you from that! But if some of that tone does break through and you find me a slightly fierce taskmaster or one whose suggested exercises are a bit testing, well, that is probably an indication that something is working.

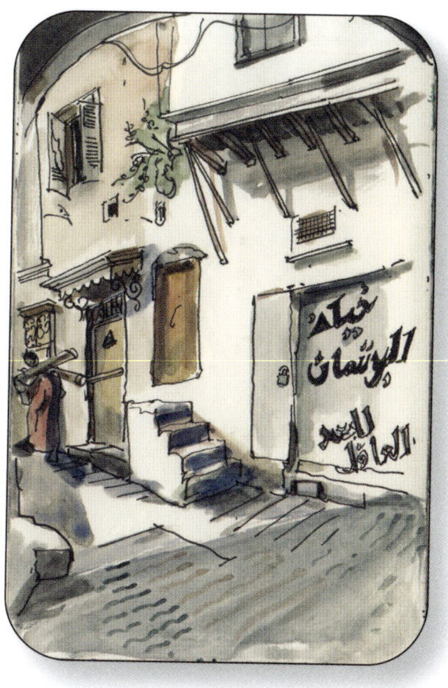

Perspective is the hardest aspect of drawing if you are unfamiliar with the approach. It requires the most sustained attention and focus. We are taught early on about the rules of one- and two-point perspective, vanishing points and horizons, and they are all really important. I have included a bit of that in this book because some very simple rules are useful, but my inclination is always towards measuring rather than employing rules because I am as interested in looking as in drawing, and measuring requires that above all.

The work of an artist or designer seems now pretty universally to be described as their *practice*. This is fairly new – it was not common currency 40 years ago when I began to work.

But I have come to like the label, as drawing does require practice. The repetition of tasks, measuring and resolving the uncertainties that a pianist or even an acrobat must do both to learn and then to retain their skills is in fact needed for a drawer as well. Practice may not make perfect, but it does fix new learning and make new skills familiar. So, this book is about learning a practice.

This book is also a series of exercises that are fun but progressive. Each one addresses one element of the job, and most might usefully be done several times using a different subject. Because if you draw only once a week, then, like playing the piano, it's hard to get any better.

Lastly, this book is about having fun. Drawing isn't a chore or an insurmountable peak to climb. It's a total joy and one way to be more in your own world – to understand what you see around you and to explore the detail, the form, the structure and the colour of your environment.

## DO AS I SAY

My first-year tutor at the Central School of Art and Design in London was the distinguished theatre designer Pamela Howard. She was emphatic and authoritative and taught us brilliantly and made us work hard. Her welcoming advice as we began the year was, paraphrased, that she would teach the way *she* worked – her techniques for and ways of designing sets and costumes for an opera or play. She was generous, proffering solutions and routes along which to go to resolve the many questions raised by such a complicated design process. It was not, she most clearly emphasized, the *only* way, but it was *her* only way, and if we wanted to get the most from that year, we would do well to learn her methods. If later they were useful and could be employed in a more universal way, that was good, and if not, that knowledge was banked for reference.

Perhaps that is the only way one can really teach drawing. There may be some basic laws that are a form of rightness from which one might subsequently choose to diverge, but another approach altogether would not be invalid. There are, however, *conventions*, and these allow us to concur to use a common visual language. And I do think there is a generally accepted way of drawing that is perceived as *right*. Not one particular style or technique (these are endlessly variable) but perhaps more a visual language that, pared down, is understood by all and which is the basis for further creative work.

So, as you follow the exercises and ideas in this book, try to stick with me, follow my occasionally bossy suggestions and, when or if you feel you have exhausted those lessons, you can either use them as a framework for your own practice or move on to a freer and more expressionistic approach. Good luck!

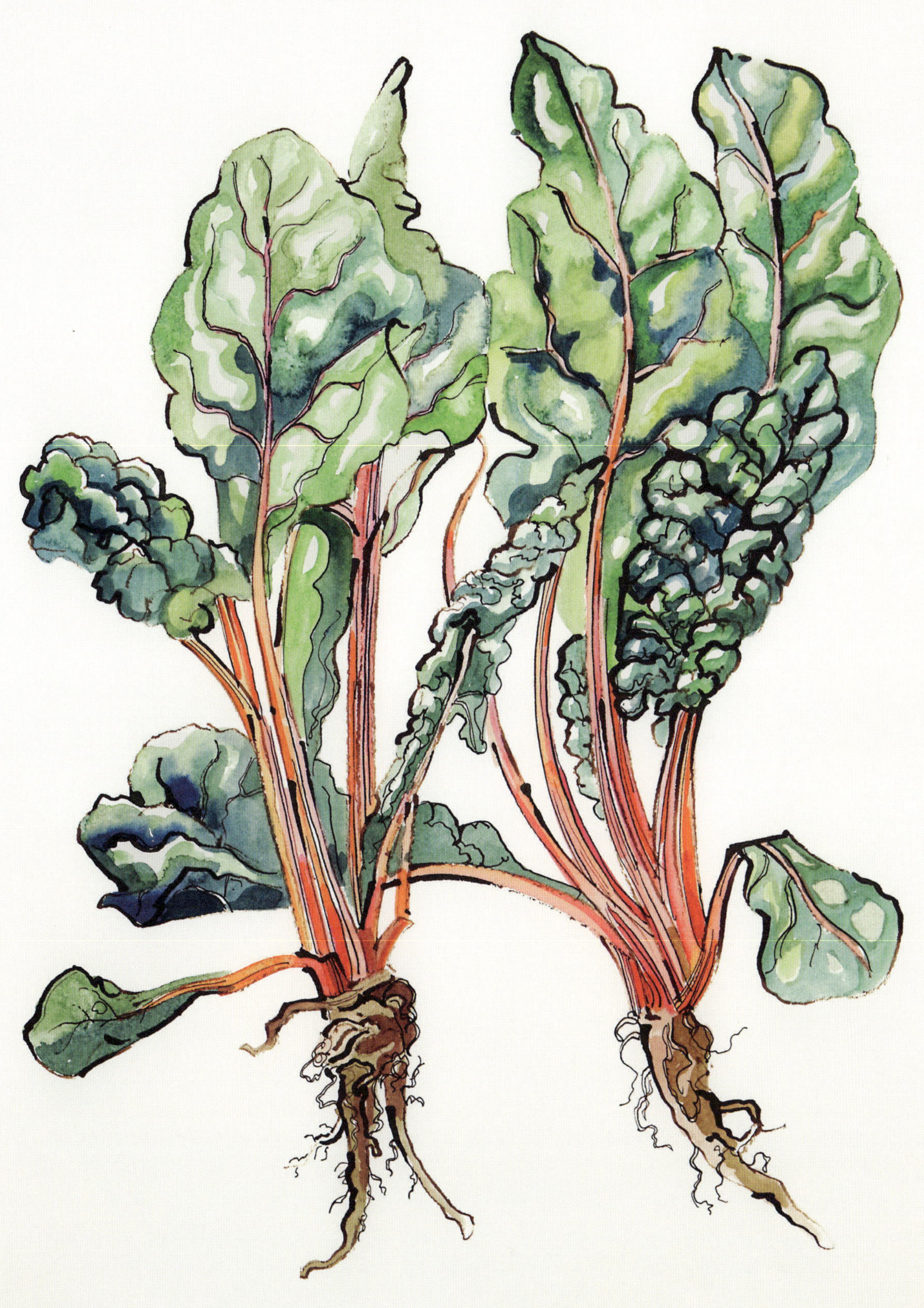

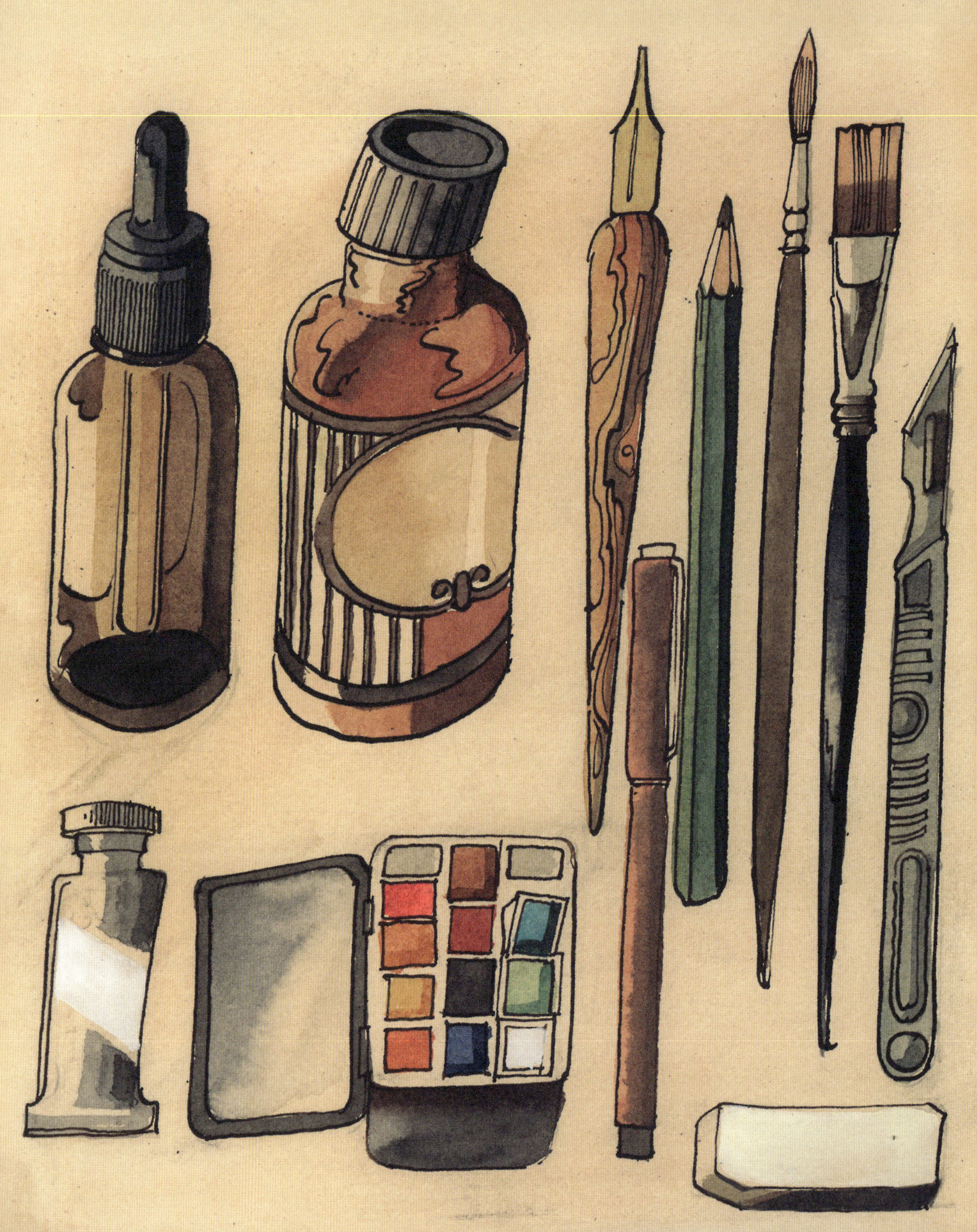

# Getting started

# WHAT DO YOU NEED?

Prehistoric humans made astonishing drawings with burnt earths, water and sticks as brushes. Stranded on a desert island, incarcerated or bored in a meeting, it is possible to make do with even the least promising materials. But if you want the best results, it is far easier with good tools. That said, I find the fewer different things you have, the easier it is to make sure you have enough of them and that they are in good condition. I don't like too much kit, so here is what I work with...

## PAPER

I am always excited by new paper arriving. The blank sheet doesn't scare me; it makes me incredibly excited, as does breaking up the sheets into smaller pieces

A sketchbook is invaluable when drawing initial ideas or studies, as loose sheets tend to disappear and are impossible to find when you want to use them as reference. My sketchbook is made of quite an absorbent cartridge paper in a deep ivory and is A5. Shiny white can also be nice, but this is what I use. A landscape (horizontal) format is easier to hold and put on your lap or table, and I therefore find it more useful than portrait format.

A larger pad of heavy cartridge paper is useful if you want to be more expansive. As long as it is of high enough quality, it can usually take watercolour or coloured inks as well. Bear in mind that they will not behave as washes, as the surface is not absorbent enough. As my sketchbook is quite small (A5), I use A3 pads.

Now there are some terms to deal with. Proper watercolour paper is sold by the sheet and identified by weight and type of surface. Imperial weights (in pounds) refer to the weight of a ream of that particular size and thickness of paper (e.g. 200lb), while metric weights are the weight (in grams) of a square metre of the same (e.g. 425gsm). Papers are then divided by surface: *rough* is self-explanatory, while *not* means it is 'not hot-pressed', and is not rough but has enough texture in the surface of the paper to hold on to larger washes of colour. Hot-pressed paper is super smooth and suits more detailed work.

The thicker paper (which is really a card) is good because if you carefully fold and then

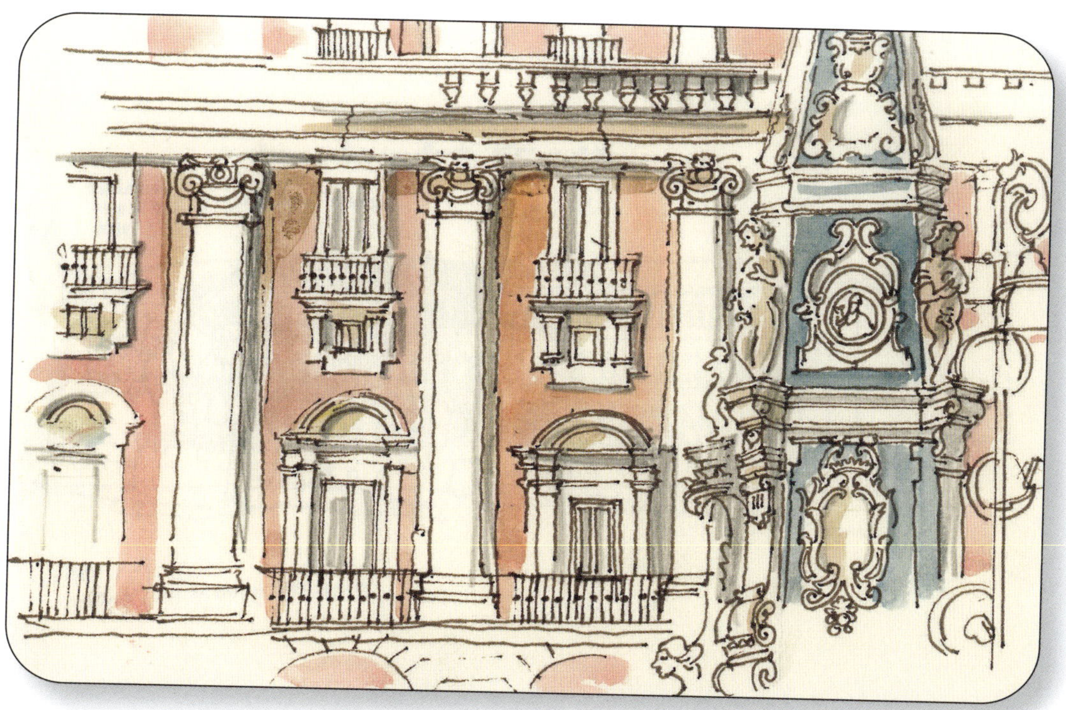

crack it into pieces, it will have a nice deckle (feathered) edge. I often crack a sheet into as many as a dozen pieces for easy use. Some papers are very much too hard, and the paint seems to float over the surface, and conversely some are as absorbent as blotting paper.

When I was 14, I inherited two quires of heavy rough-textured Whatman paper made in the 1950s. (A quire is a very big pack of 25 sheets; 20 quires make a ream.) The paper smelled very strongly of rabbit-skin size, but its combination of rough surface, glaze and absorbency really affected how I learned to paint in watercolour. My parents used Kent 90lb not (and those words are hugely redolent of my childhood), often stretched on a drawing board. I went through a phase of Saunders 200lb (425gsm) but now am settled (I think) on Arches 300lb (640gsm) hot-pressed.

## PENS

You may, of course, use any pen you like to begin drawing, as long as it is watertight and can withstand watercolour paint being laid over it. For years I have used a series of fibre-tipped fineliner types, and really you must try to see which you most enjoy and which produce a good, regular flow of ink. To complicate matters, I also like to use sepia-coloured ink for its slightly more forgiving and softer effect.

In my childhood, my father, a theatre designer, used a Rotring pen. These maroon plastic pens had hypodermic nibs in graduating sizes from 0.2 to 0.8 of a millimetre in diameter. So thick was the ink that the nibs were always prone to blocking and needed endless washing and then, before use, a vigorous shaking to release the bearing that produced the ink flow. In my mother's studio, a floor below, an invasion of plastic-, felt- and fibre-tipped pens began their own colourful takeover in the 1960s. She was a textile designer and had originally used pen and ink to produce fine linework and to express form with cross-hatching. But the products of Pentel and Stabilo, Caran d'Ache and Micron proved quicker and more convenient, and by the time I began to draw seriously at the end of the 1970s, nibs were an archaism.

And so, for 40 years I have used the fibre- tipped pen. If I use up four per week, that would make a pile of 8,000 dead pens. I fear that is a terrible undercalculation. They are the most decadent of single-use plastics, a phrase unknown a decade ago. Of course, the waste is tiny compared to the great polluters, but it is still worth addressing, and there we find the role of the nib pen.

If there was one reason to think about changing to a nib, it would be the quality of the line. Cursive, elastic and responsive, the brass nib glides across the paper expressively, making each line or mark intrinsically attractive. It is true that some materials – charcoal, bamboo pen or even a stick dipped in emulsion – can by their very limitations bring something to the party. Conversely, the apparent convenience and ease of use of the fibre-tipped pen might in fact rob the drawer of that advantage, bringing a slightly mechanical consistency to the line where

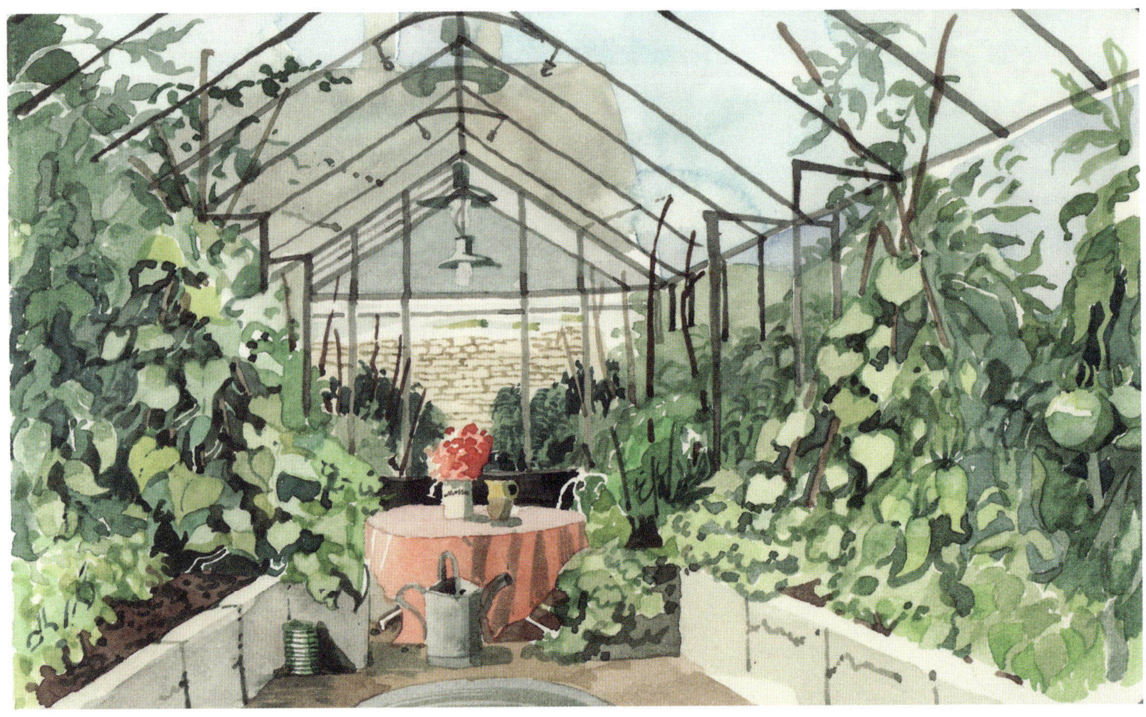

something more fluid and freer might make even the tightest drawing breathe.

I am no zealot. I shall continue to use both nibs and fineliners, but my eyes have been opened, and I now see what is lacking when (to avoid bringing ink in bottles, using better paper and other inconveniences) I take out my 0.3 and start to draw.

Aside from the choice of pens, the initially confusing choice of inks begins. If you are to add colour washes, it must be watertight. Some are more treacly or shiny with shellac; others flatter and more matt. I am very keen on one called Antiktusche, which is an acrylic shellac but treacly, smooth and delicious to use. There are many good ones including tempting bottles of walnut inks and other natural formulations. But buyer beware! Do check first that they are genuinely watertight (inks for fountain pens often are not).

It is also worth bearing in mind that some papers that are fine for fineliners may seem suddenly too flimsy for the ink overload they are now receiving, but if you are using heavy cartridge and watercolour paper, there will be no need to change. The need to transport ink is obviously an extra thing to consider. Mine travels in a small bottle with a pipette through which I squirt enough to fill a tiny lid. This is deep enough to dip my pen into easily. If there is some left at the end, I suck it back up with the same pipette and squirt it back into the bottle, wasting none.

I think the nib versus fineliner debate is a little like the digital versus analogue discussion. It is quite possible to draw on an iPad. Hockney has proved that with great brilliance. The technical brilliance of the stained-glass backlighting of the screen is thrilling and perhaps also the ease of having

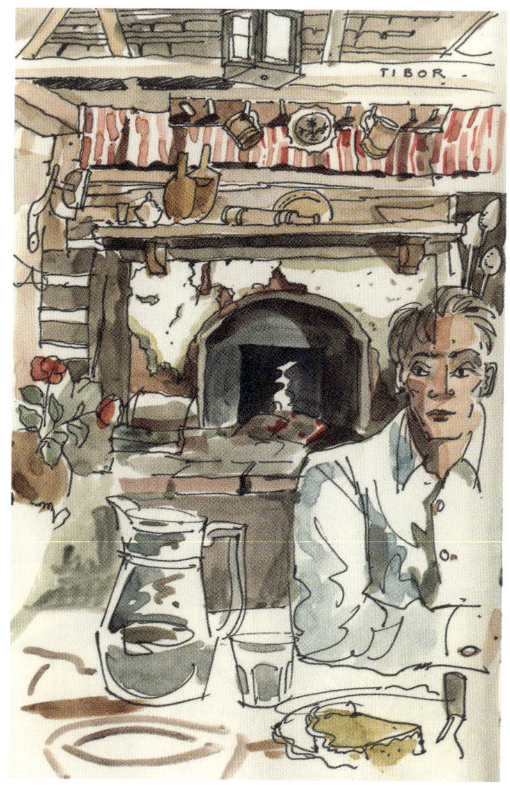


*Don't forget to change your painting water: a sludgy jam jar will make muddy colours on the page. Clean water makes for bright colours.*

no materials. There are clever tools, virtual brushes and pens and pencils – all brilliant in their way – but for me they are a filter between real life, the actual experience and the drawer.

In the age of AI and digital processes, and when the services and products we consume seem increasingly to be automated, there has been a converse interest in the analogue. To eat olives from a bowl a potter has thrown, turned and sponged by hand, and decorated in a way unique to that piece, seems to elevate the experience. Cooking from fresh or from scratch – that is, not relying on ingredients that have been super-processed – has similarly been elevated as an idea. Perhaps this move to nib is yet more evidence of the same desire as we try to relocate these foundational skills in our rather sanitized lives.

## PENCILS

My pencil tastes are vanilla: HB only, and the more expensive the better. I have always used a 10A Swann–Morton scalpel blade to sharpen mine (it wastes less than a pencil sharpener, and you have more control). But really only you will find what your armoury will be, and this will change with discoveries of new colours, papers and pens until you refine your very own personal selection.

*You may, of course, use any pen you like to begin drawing, as long as it is watertight and can withstand watercolour paint being laid over it.*

## PAINT & BRUSHES

Choosing your materials is an exciting challenge. I have often waited at the till of an art store while a keen student lists a bafflingly long list of what their course has prescribed. My advice is to keep it simple. On pages 52–5 I have suggested some watercolour colours you might like to start with, and have limited this to 15 (they are so expensive!), but you may well want to experiment further and find that you have different needs. I am, however, quite clear in recommending Schmincke colours, as they are so saturated and bright. I also use Gallo for some colours, and they mix together well. Winsor & Newton makes a nice cerulean blue. Half pans (little blocks of solid colour) are nicer to use than wasteful tubes, but when I use gouache as body colour that does have to come in a tube.

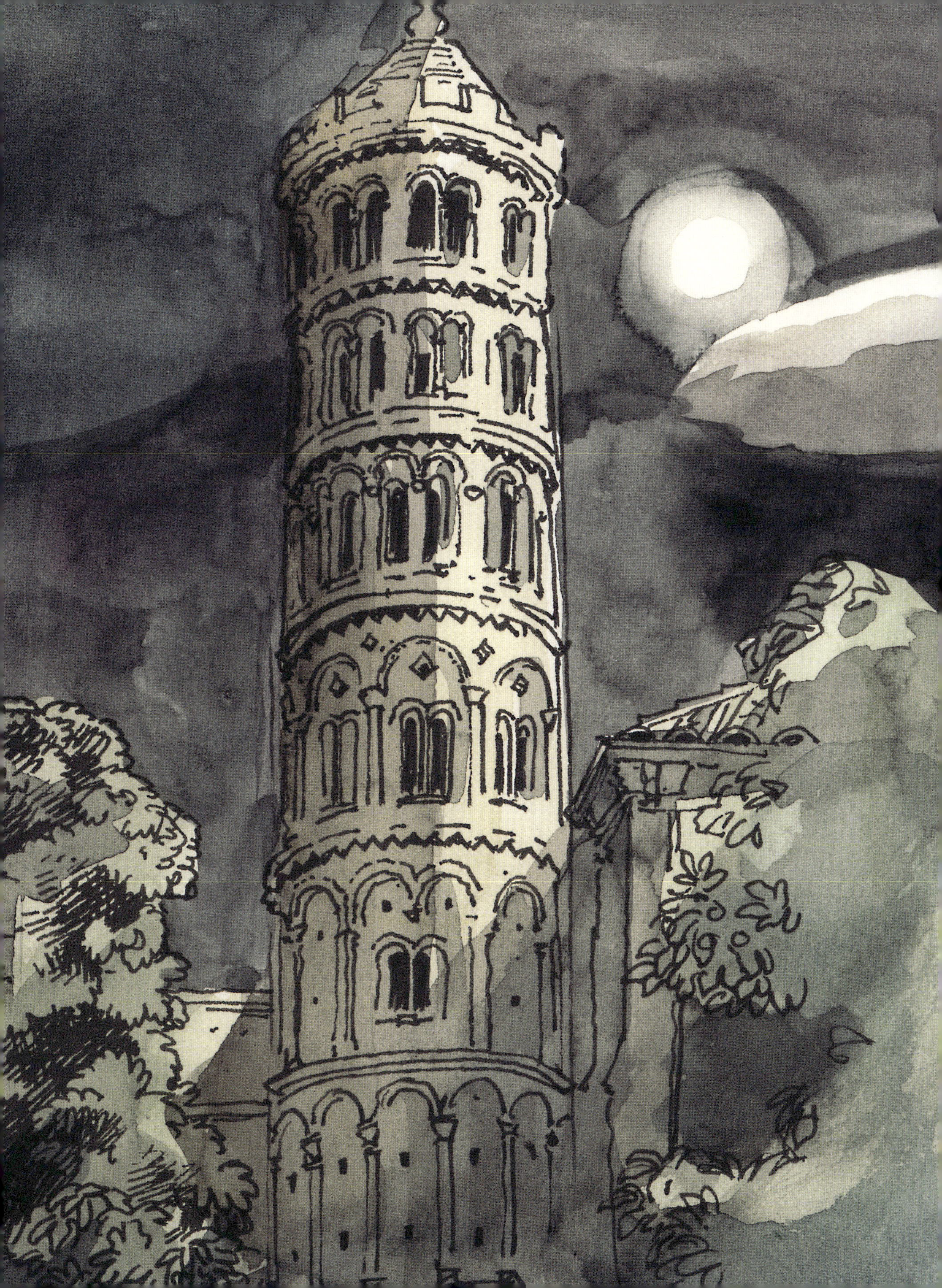

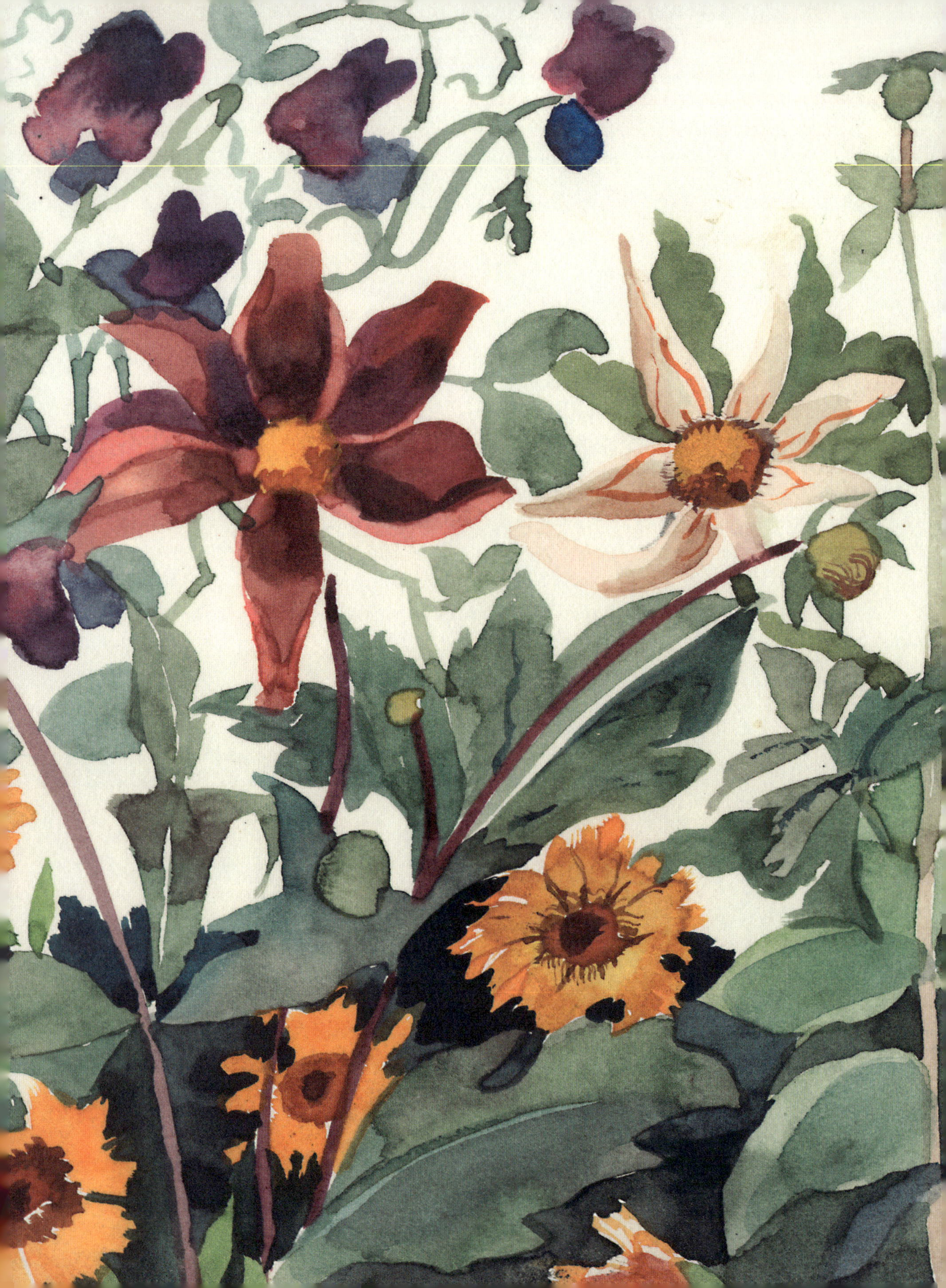

*The success of a drawing is due as much to the process of a careful analysis and assessment as to clever and experienced painting techniques.*

## TIDY UP!

I am only *quite* neat. My father spent nearly as much time tidying his studio as working in it. His job as a theatrical designer meant he had much more stuff: the materials and tools needed to make 1:24 models, annotate costume drawings, make ground plans and make and paint props. There were bottles of coloured varnishes, every kind of paint and glaze, every single shape and size of brush, thickness of board and shape of balsa wood.

I have less excuse, but I do still try to put my more modest mess in order, at least between individual tasks. That means sorting pens and pencils into favourite mugs (a good use for those separated from their handles) and a hardening of hearts towards scraps of paper that will never in truth be used. A tidy studio or just a tidy kitchen table is the foundation of a better drawing. I'm as sure of that as I am that we cannot all be Lucian Freud, whose studio was famously an encyclopaedia of accumulated brush cleanings and colour tests, of dirty rags and old paint tubes.

## COMFORT

Comfort has an underestimated role to play in the drawing process. Working in awkward physical circumstances would seem to add a quite needless layer of difficulty, but it is surprising how often I see somebody crouching on their haunches, paper or sketchbook awkwardly balanced on a knee and paints only just in reach on the ground.

Of course, it's possible to draw on a train or rocking boat or perched on a wall whose one recommendation is its being in the shade on a hot day, or in the sun to keep one's fingers alive in the winter chill. Getting everything one needs together before you start is a kind of comfort as well. It is certainly good practice and avoids tiresome dashing back to your desk (if indeed you are at home) to find a rubber/eraser or a scalpel to sharpen your pencil with.

Comfort may not be essential, but discomfort is something one can do without!

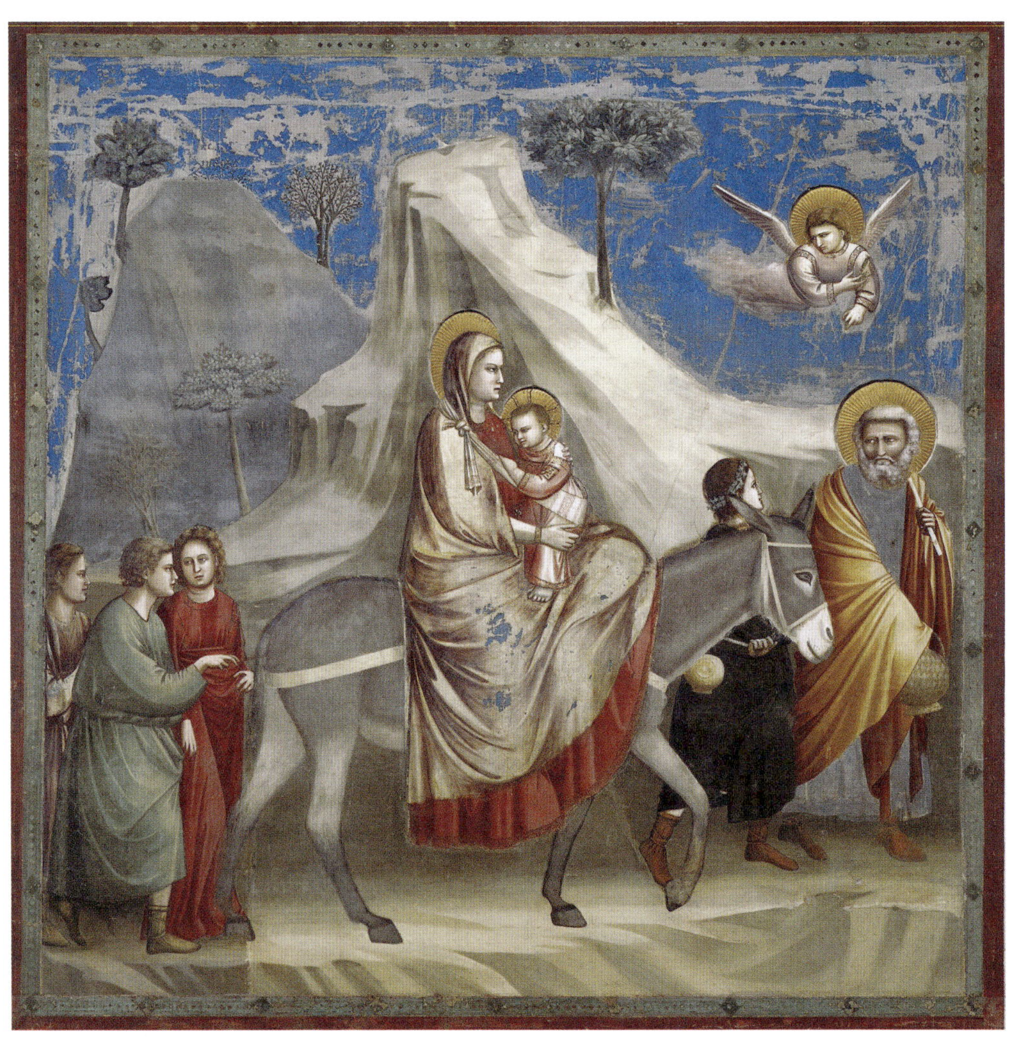

Giotto di Bondone,
*Flight into Egypt*, fresco,
*c.*1304–6

# OBSERVATIONAL DRAWING VERSUS ICONOGRAPHY

This is no sort of value judgement, and the world of icons is one of skill, moving emotion and decorative brilliance, but it does rely on a form of communication that is directly opposite to drawing from life. Icons, whether a smiley or frowning face, an iceberg or indeed a peach or aubergine, are part of modern life as they pepper and otherwise spice up the conversations on our phones. Similarly, religious painting in the pre-Renaissance era used a language of preordained symbolism and simplification to engage the viewer immediately in the subject. The earliest painters in the caves of Lascaux or Altamira used a pared-back visual language that spoke clearly and directly to the viewer with simplified shapes that still say *bison* or *horse* to awestruck visitors 5,000 years later.

When a child draws a tree, it has a straight, brown trunk and a dark-green cauliflower of leaves on top and sits on a band of green grass and below a band of royal-blue sky. Few trees actually have brown trunks (they normally seem a green-grey); the sky is rarely dark blue and reaches down to the horizon, and so on. But parents, friends and teachers understand what the child is expressing: an idea of a tree in a field on a sunny day.

The same language but in a different dialect is used in early Italian painting, such as Giotto's *The Flight into Egypt* (*c.*1304–6). The trunk may be grey, but it casts no shadow, the way of expressing the greenery is leafier and more even, and it has some shadow to imply a rounded form. But there is no attempt to say 'these are beech trees'. They grow on a craggy hillside but one where pattern defines the rock forms, not shadow, and the sky is a glorious plane of gold leaf burnished to a shine that is the glory of God.

In the foreground is the Blessed Virgin Mary. Everything about her appearance shows us who she is. A crisp, gold disc of a halo describes her sanctity, her cloak is blue and her dress red. In her hand is her floral symbol, the lily, and perhaps her birdly insignia, the goldfinch (its red face a symbol of the blood of Christ). Mary is wonderful and powerful, but she is not real. She dominates the picture, but she does not seem to actually be riding on an actual hillside beneath a Middle Eastern sky.

That is iconography. Sophisticated or simplistic, it is a language of symbols. The schoolchild with frayed brush and cheap poster colours and little skill speaks this language, and the icon painter with egg tempera and gold leaf also. Neither is attempting to communicate the specific. Both are expressing themselves with fluency and both are communicating but using a generalized and formalized vocabulary and even a formulaic grammar and syntax where the arrangement of components follows a preordained systemized plan.

In the other corner of the ring is the observational drawer, using skills that come from the Renaissance. It is an enlightened language where line and form, colour and detail, composition and narrative are all drawn directly from the real world. Nowhere is this better illustrated than in Albrecht Dürer's astonishingly detailed study of a small part of his lawn, as shown opposite.

At the core of an observational practice is the sketchbook (see pages 144–52), in which the drawer records what they see – buildings or plants, trees or birds, planes or cliffs (or indeed a woman of great beauty whose magical aura of holiness seems almost to be a visible emanation). The sketchbook is a convenient collection of notes where you can record the musculature of the cockerel, the form of the hollyhock, or the topography of the mountains from the train window.

Albrecht Dürer,
*The Large Piece of Turf*,
watercolour, 1503

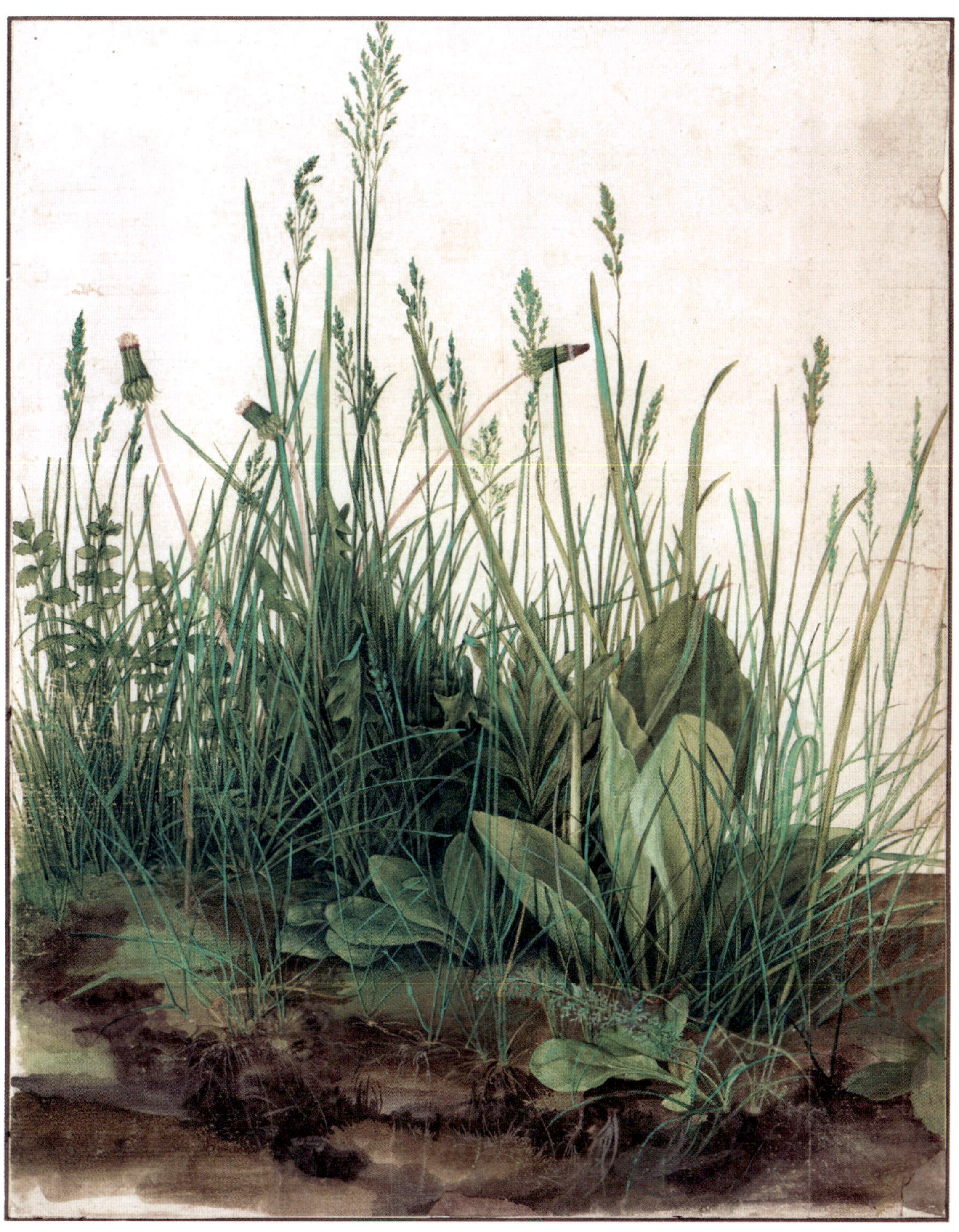

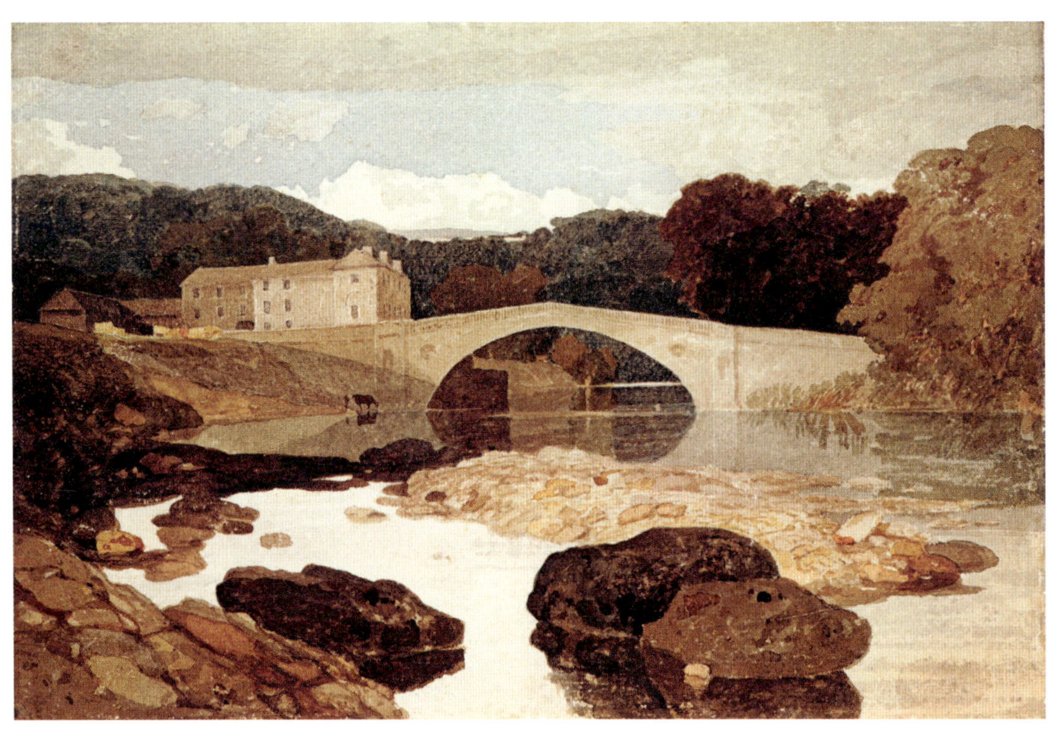

John Sell Cotman,
*Greta Bridge*, watercolour,
1810

*In this artwork, Cotman works in broad areas of strong tone and colour. There is very little detail in the trees or building, but great strength in the light and dark values. This is one of the world's great watercolours.*

Let us take the floral example. We know a hollyhock to have a tall spire of pink or salmon flowers, with large, irregularly round, pale-green, slightly furry leaves in a rosette below. The flower gets progressively smaller towards the tip. Perhaps not a spire, like a lupin, but still tall and with a point. That description is a basis for an icon. I could draw it, and you might say 'hollyhock'.

Or with the flower right in front of you, preferably in comfort and your subject lying on a table, you might begin a more sophisticated visual analysis. As I write this, it is February and the hollyhocks are not out and so I cannot begin that process. But the method is the same whenever or with whatever; looking carefully at the subject and breaking it down into its component parts, what shape is the stamen, the petals? If you cut the stem, what would it be in section? Now the leaves. How are they arranged? What do they spring from? Then there is texture – what shines or tickles? What is furry or tough?

But before this dissection, visual or even actual, what does the whole plant look like? Is it powerful and tree-like, top-heavy or waving in the wind? Does it sit securely on its root? Is it leathery, strong, delicate, thrusting with spring energy or fading and desiccated as autumn calls? None of the above is drawing, but it is a series of decisions and observations that so totally inform the drawing you will make that it is intrinsically linked to the drawing process. It is why this book is called *How to* Look, *Draw and Paint*.

Correctness in drawing went out of fashion in the 1970s, and the ability to teach it followed swiftly. Freedom of expression, mark making and naïveté (space for iconography...) were more loved, and a feeling that accurate drawing had become unmodishly academic and retrograde in tone was ubiquitous. Happily, the tide has turned, and a real appetite for drawing is returning, both among viewers and drawers.

## WORKING FROM PHOTOGRAPHS

Now here is a tricky one. Many brilliant painters have used photographs for inspiration and information. The great American artist John Singer Sargent worked with dashing bravura, often using photographic reference, and his brushy and dynamic paintings seem to owe little to their photographic origins. Others use photographic elements as a shortcut in compositions when time doesn't allow individual sketches to be made from life. But the custom, much used in school examination art, of simply copying a painting from a photograph is reductive and rarely makes something much more interesting than the original reference. There is, of course, great skill to be employed in creating an exact and precise copy of anything, whether in painting, drawing or indeed photography, and that process is an end in itself, but to learn and observe is a different matter.

At its simplest, this is a matter of being able to look around the back of the subject, to understand its structure and its underlying three-dimensional reality. To look at a photograph is to look at a flat image that cannot really yield any more than a first glance provides. Grids and rulers will let you transfer dimensions from original to new work, but they are the measurements of a two-dimensional image and not of its subject, and the project of transferring one to the other is simple but uninformative. Or, perhaps more optimistically, it is a good way to produce a superficial but convincing copy. This is useful in itself: very quick, easy and, while limiting, yielding a speedy result. I do use photographs for reference when I want a shorthand. It genuinely speeds up the process, and the reference is readily available on our phones, but it is not serious research. For that kind of analysis, it is the very change from reality to the two-dimensional drawing that tests and thus informs us.

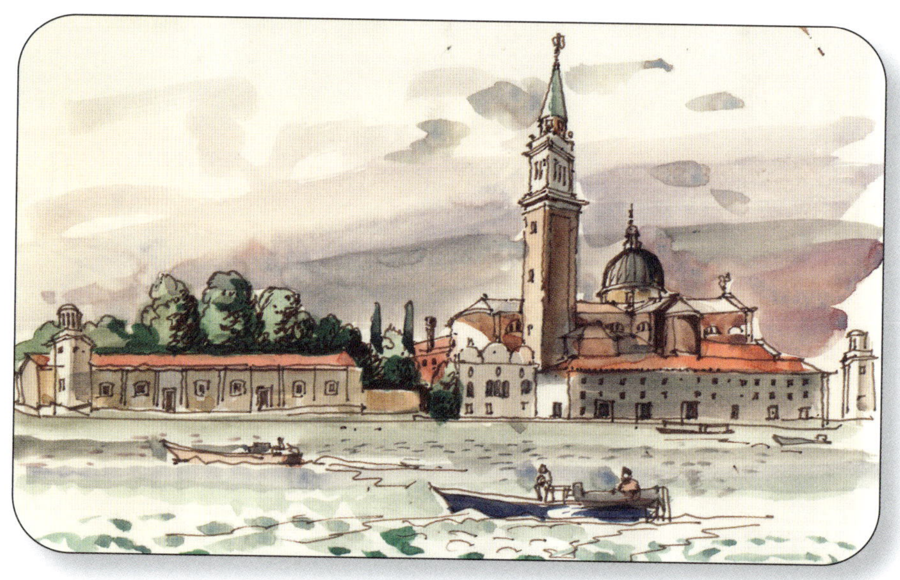

The exercises in this book all tackle that transformation, a process that attempts to convey the form, character and essence of a plant, place or person, and one through which we can understand the subject more thoroughly and deeply. If this were, in fact, a book about working from photographs, I would emphasize more the techniques to be employed, the design or composition, and the process of elimination or editing that might, making use of photographs, create a picture. I would be writing about making pictures but not about drawing.

## GOING OUT TO DRAW

Working out a realistic plan of a drawing trip can help avoid subsequent feelings of failure – partial or total. If you are in a busy group on holiday, you'll need to carve out the drawing time, even if that does occasionally mean skipping a drink or an ice cream, or even a visit to some unmissable site of interest or exhibition. Tiny, quick sketches have a value: vital memory jogging or lightweight information grabbing. Often, they are just more productive than a set of photographs, as you have to look harder, even if briefly. But it is the action of sustained observation that both imprints an image on one's mind and that lets one explore the subject. I am a quick drawer, but I still need half an hour; most people might say an hour. Either should be easyish to accommodate in one's timetable, whether on holiday or at home.

When at home, early morning (if you are that person) or evening (if it is summer) is good, as it feels easier to escape at either end of the day. The lower light is also more directional and casts useful shadows which make drawing, and in fact looking, so much easier. The clarifying properties of shadow are not to be underestimated: the obscuring darkness edits out information and, in simplifying the image, makes the drawer focus on what is more telling.

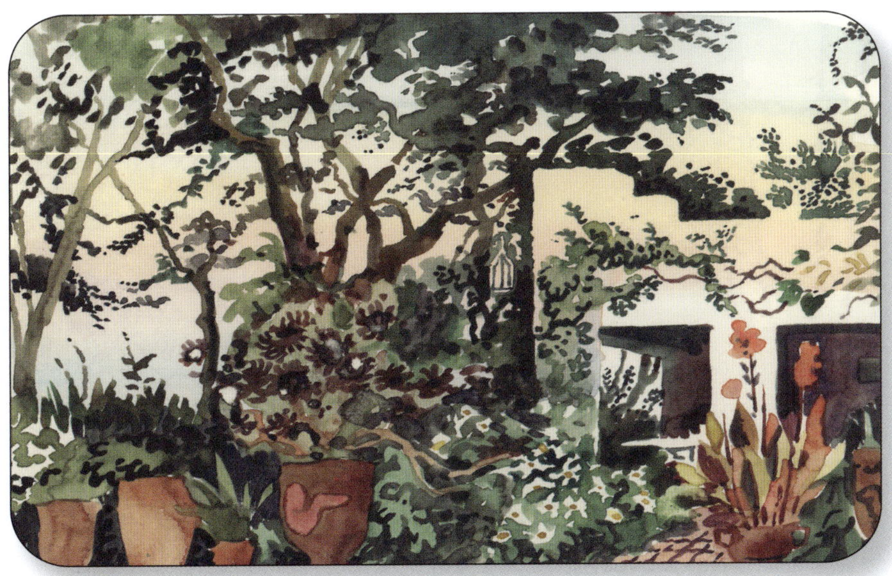

Regularity (or, more truthfully, frequency) is probably the most significant influence on drawing better. Practice, of course, makes perfect, but it is *regular* practice that really earns the dividends. If you don't draw for a week, you lose your 'fitness' and your hard-won skill of drawing what you see. Even the most accomplished drawer can quickly become rusty relying on skills learned many years before that in some ways have become fossilized.

Drawing is a skill to be developed, an internal conversation about the world around us. Go quiet for a few days and you lose the thread. Conversely, keep at it, giving yourself regular exercise, and an automatic process will begin to be established, and it is then that, with the process in the main de-risked, you can allow yourself the freedom that will make your drawing really develop.

Among the many disturbances that break the thread and that lose your focus, at least one thing can be controlled and thus edited out of the process. That is the need to find more pens and pencils, ink or paper. Get all the things you will need *before you start*. Apart from anything else, it means that you have no excuse to divert attention from the job in hand.

I am not a devotee of the sketching stool. They seem to position you too low and also to put you at a different level from your materials, but these things are all personal and for some people a tidy aluminium-framed stool with nice, stripey canvas seat may be just the thing. When I'm in the garden, I use two kitchen chairs. One for me and one for the materials. It means they are at the right height for easy use. I will admit to working in the car, especially if it's cold, but it is far easier if you cross to the passenger seat where there is no steering wheel to hinder you, either from putting your paper flat or from moving your hands easily. I had a Land Rover for some years and the glovebox between the seats had a splendid flat surface, and I haven't had another car that even approached it as an ideal conveyance for artists (it didn't have good heating, however).

One more thing: whether away from home or in the garden or house, once I have stopped work, I stop looking at my drawing for a bit. That distance, even of half an hour, gives me an objectivity, and almost always in a positive way. One is so often surprised to find it's not as bad as one imagined!

*Always pick a view or subject with articulation – that is, with angles, curves, pattern and colour changes – on which to focus. A simple form is often the hardest.*

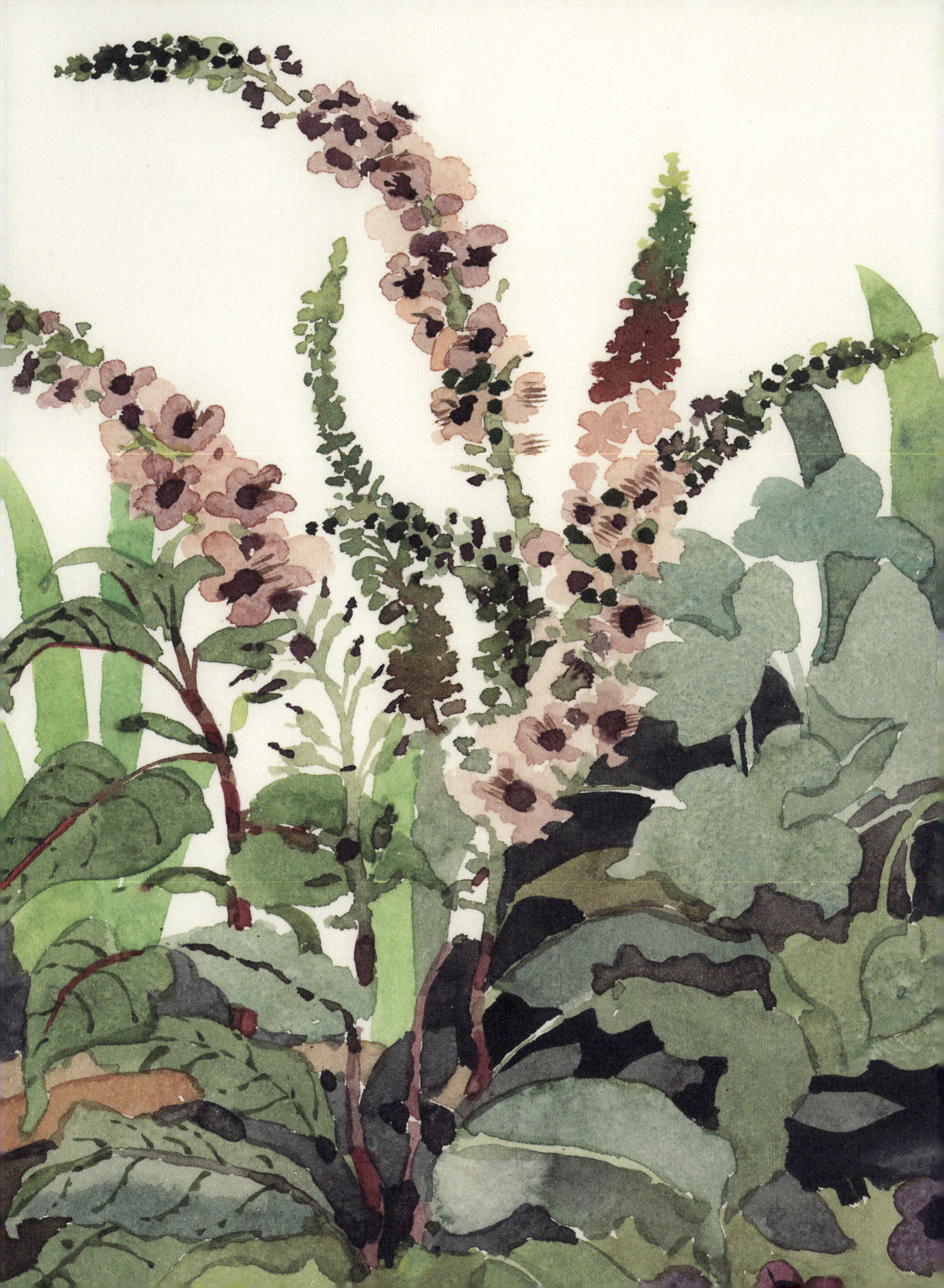

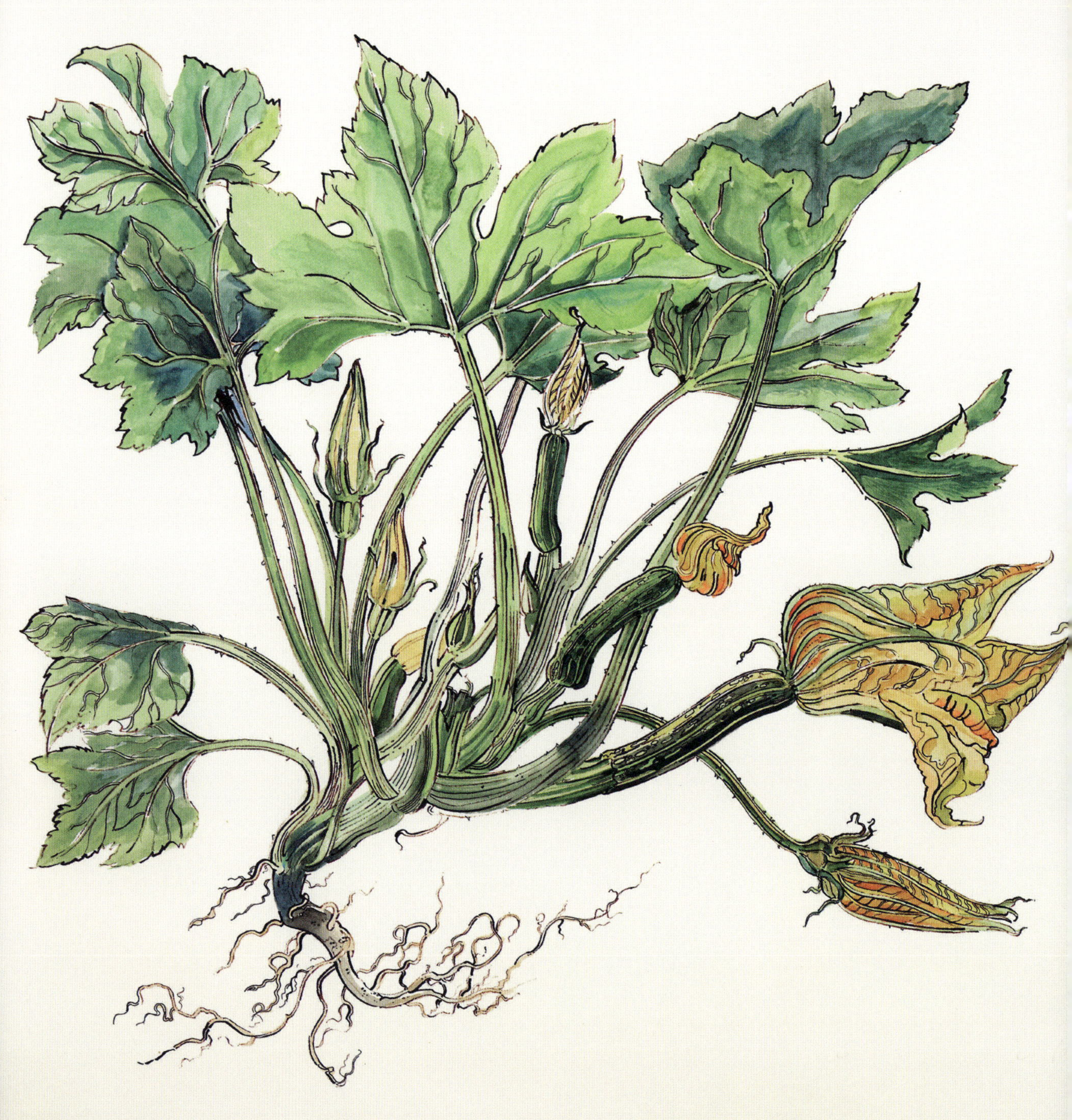

# THE WILD PLEASURE OF BOTANICAL DRAWING

We think we have looked. We *know* we have seen (and the older we are, the more times we have seen) peonies or violets or indeed potatoes or artichokes. We can do a cartoon drawing of most of these, an iconographic representation of each subject. But the degree to which secrets are revealed when we stop and draw is always astonishing. Details that are so obvious once you begin to look, and which have previously usually been *over*looked, are often quite important features: the section of a stalk, the format of the stamens and pistil, or the way the leaves join the stem at a node... all these come into focus once we begin to draw. As we record, we learn.

A few years ago, I painted a potato. The potato is the most familiar and frankly least poetic vegetable one could tackle. I began gradually to explore its structure, the box-section stalk and the glossy green leaves, and eventually the lavender-to-mauve flowers, little trumpets with waxy yellow stamens. As I drew, this everyday companion became a glamorous stranger and every bit the South American subtropical arrival in the garden that so amazed sixteenth-century Europeans. As I arranged the component parts of the plant in a way that at least slightly looked like potatoes in the garden, I found my own view of the formerly unfeted tuber subtly change.

I am a little unsure about the whole cult of botanical illustration. The practice of producing what is almost a graphic dissection of a plant can sometimes produce a drawing that is accurate but unlike the actual experience of looking at the subject growing. It is like carefully parsing a Latin verse and in the subsequent meticulous translation inadvertently losing the poetry.

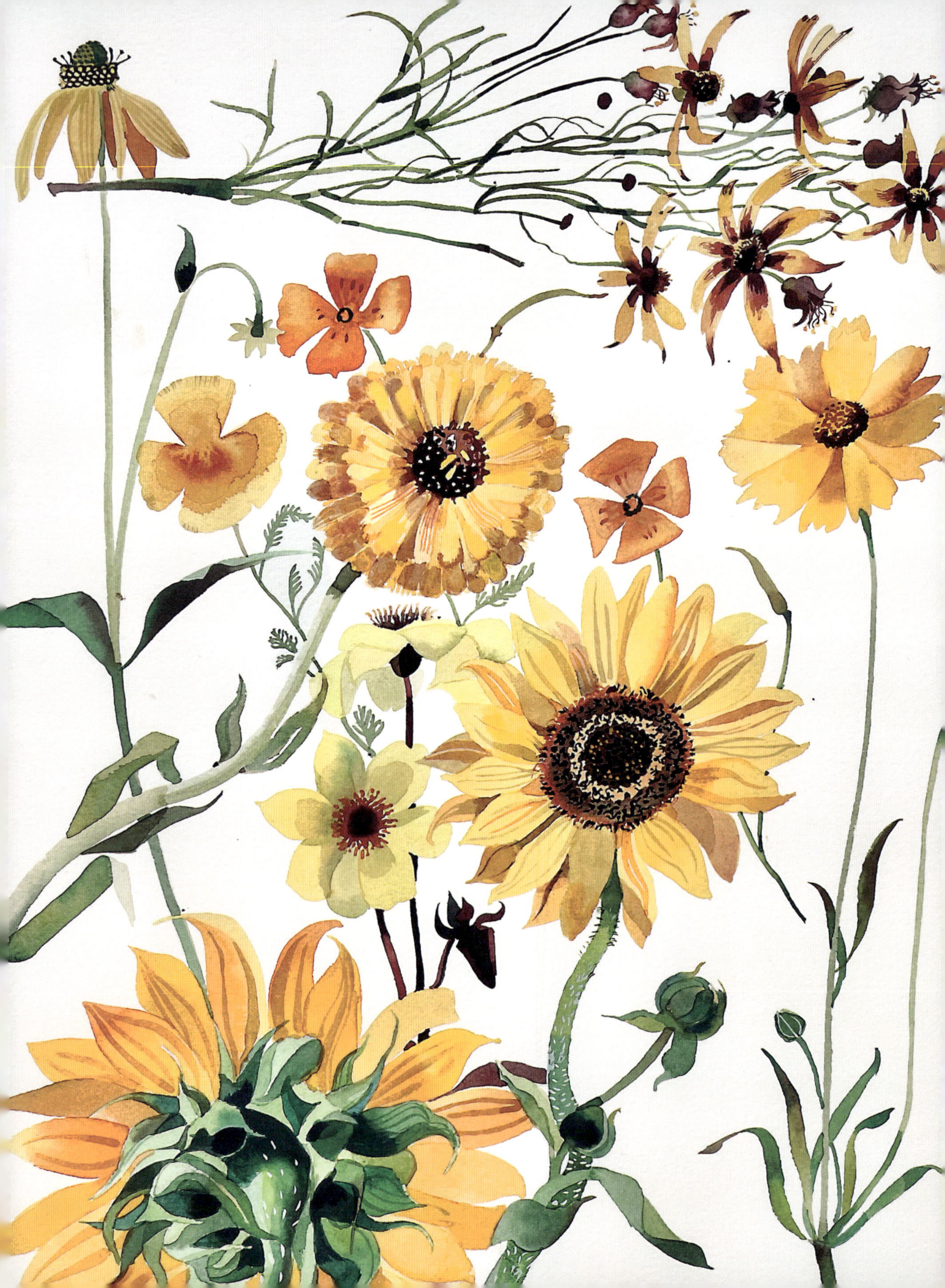

Plants are in essence joyously alive, and their root can sometimes be so complex that to draw it in every curly, twisting detail can so distort the plant's portrait as to make it virtually unrecognizable.

So, perhaps when setting about a plant portrait, the drawer should decide which are the particular features that most characterize the plant in question and then focus more on those – not leaving out the less interesting but privileging them less in the hierarchy of the painting. A geranium has a root, but it means less than nothing to most of us. And you can easily paint an onion without its (very lovely) flower. The botanical drawing I am interested in, the botanical portraiture that I think works best, is that which shows what a plant *feels* like as well as what it *looks* like. That said, while it is not a scientific record, it should be scientifically correct and should illustrate the plant's taxonomy as well as its colours or particular textures.

Sometimes I fill a page of my sketchbook with small flower portraits, arranging them without much care but, I suppose, with a degree of designing on the sheet. I frequently kneel down so I am *right among* the flowers, almost as if I am one of them. I look carefully at how they grow and, with pen and wash, try to make a fairly accurate record of what I see in that particular meadow or perhaps on that particular day. These are good reference, of course, but mainly the act of drawing them is their main purpose; a glancing conversation with a whole cocktail party of orchids and coltsfoots, daisies and trefoils that populate the turf. The flora changes depending on time and location, and there is always something new to see and to understand and to draw.

As I have said, my mother, Pat Albeck, was a textile designer, and in her long career she must have drawn a hundred thousand flowers. Often, these were much simplified and schematic, but very rarely were they so different from their appearance in the garden or greenhouse as to be unrecognizable. And when employing a strawberry plant in a wallpaper to cover a bathroom, or a rose to curtain a window, her particular knowledge of how plants grew and what made them their particular selves was carried on throughout her work, whether illustrative as on one of the over 300 National Trust tea towels she designed, reduced to a minuscule sprig on a fashion print, or formalized into a near-geometric design for a tin tray. Her ability to look carefully and draw observantly made her work more engaging and evocative; it made it *resonate* more clearly to her customers, and so made it sell.

# DIRECTIONAL LIGHT

Nothing is more useful to the project of making your drawings look three-dimensional than strong, directional light. It can be real, or it may have to be imagined, but a clear idea of where the sun is shining from will show you where the light and shadow will fall. Of course, there are many gradations of tone in any view, but a good basis is to fix on three tones – light, mid-dark and black – and to know that every face or plane in your picture must be in one of these. As soon as you work out what goes where in that tonal jigsaw, the outline will come to life and have form. If that works, you can always elaborate.

The normal terms and conditions apply. Think before you put anything on paper. Ask yourself which of those tones it is and then slowly proceed. Rushing will cause mistakes. The project is the same whether you are using watercolour or cross-hatching or all-over areas of pencil tone (or, indeed, cut paper or any other technique).

The light is directional in the morning and evening but, when the sun is overhead, it creates a dull shadow and with that comes a flattening of the picture. There are really only bright light and dark shadow, so for best effect (and to best express the three-dimensional form of an object or place) work at either end of the day. This is the case with so many looking-based activities (e.g. visiting gardens, churches or sculpture parks): go early or wait until the end of the day and the softer but more directional light will throw the subject into more descriptive focus.

Sometimes the analysis needed to break an object down into that tonal division is hard or

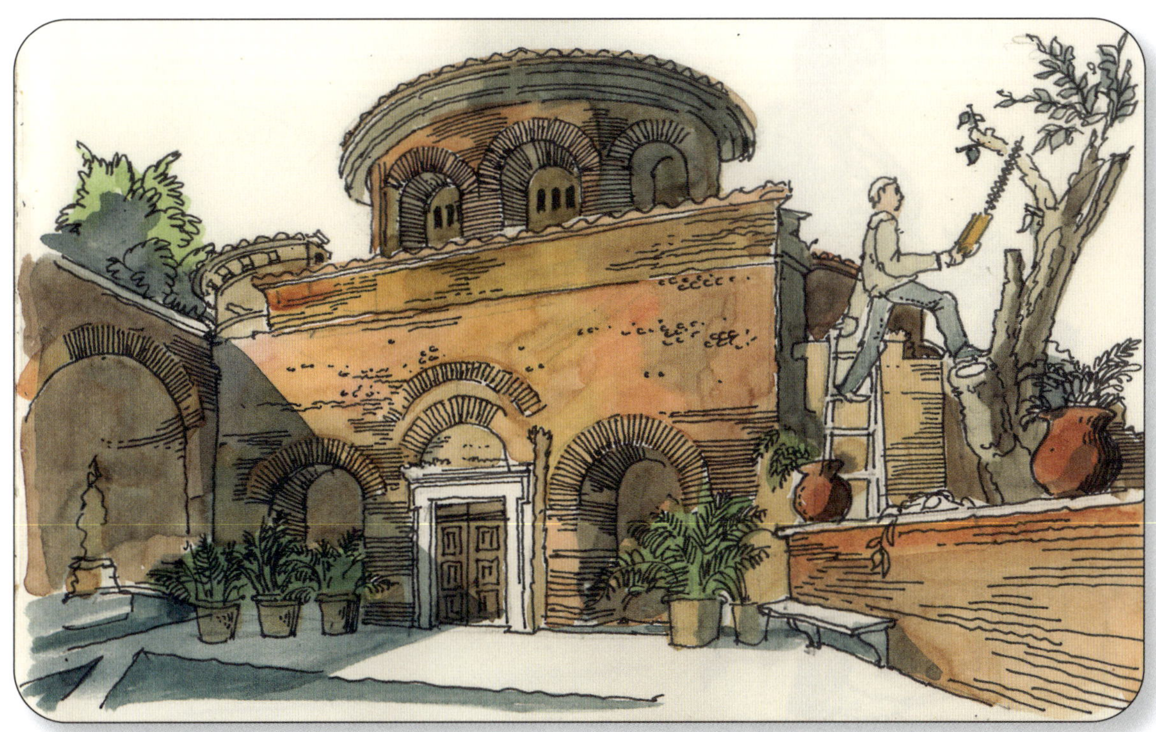

confusing. This is particularly the case when something you *know* to be pale in colour proves to be mid in tone. A good illustration of this is the distant wooded hillside, which you know must be green and yet appears to be blue. If you are confused, half close your eyes and let the reduced information you are receiving bring on a useful editing that reveals the truth. The half-closed eye is an essential part of the draughtsman's toolkit. It helps define what is most important in a view, which elements of a composition dominate, and what can politely withdraw to a backroom entity. So often what is intellectually the most significant component becomes visually subordinate in the terms of your drawing. It is also a helpful way to see where a framing beam or branch might leap into an important dramatic role.

Most importantly, the half-closed eye can eliminate chatter – the visual clutter that muddles and confuses the viewer. Drawing is as much a process of leaving out as it is of recording, and separating the chaff from the grain is sometimes as important as doing the drawing. Look carefully and work out what you see as important, which things might be in tighter focus, and which will recede even if their actual place in the picture remains.

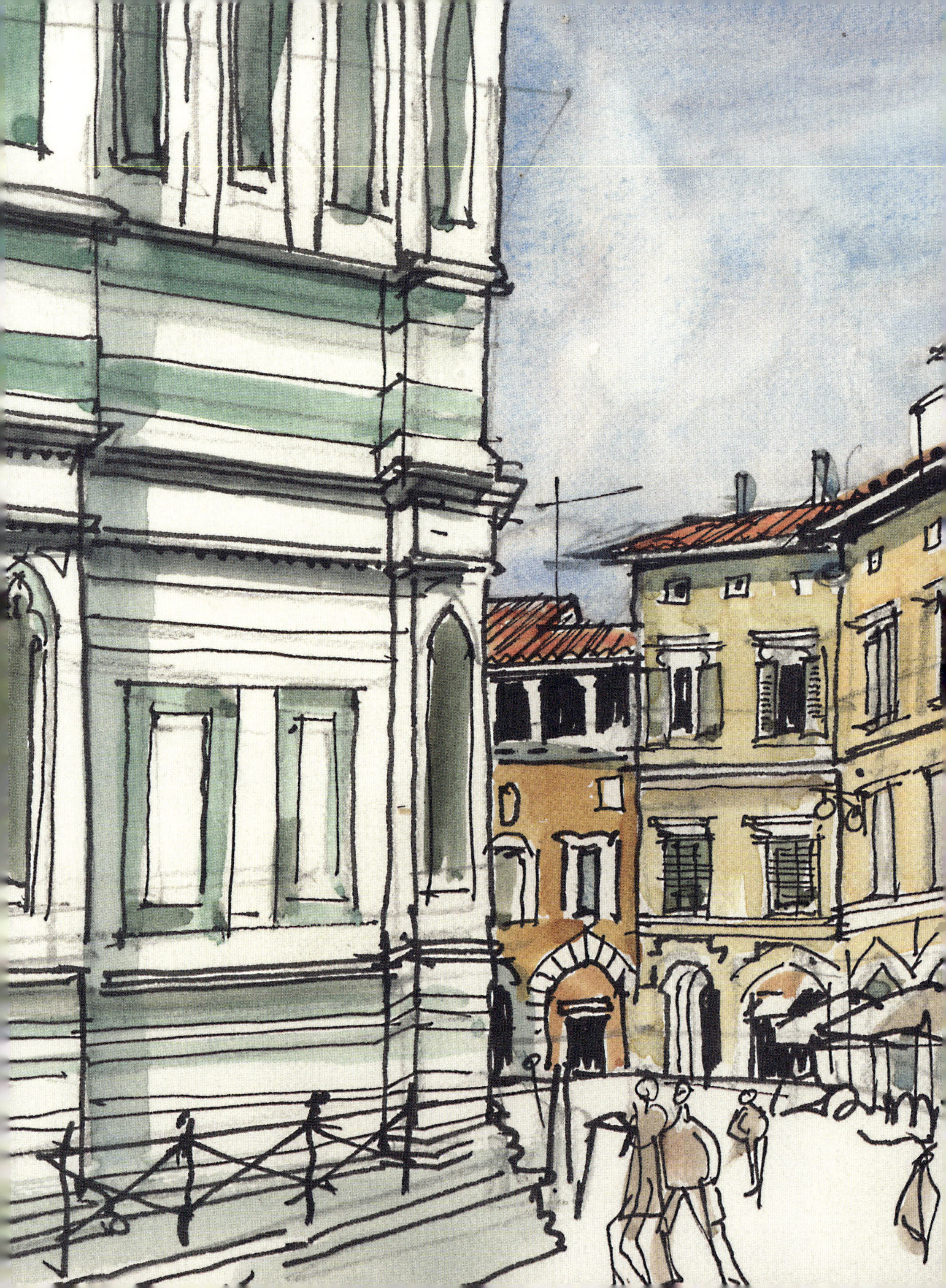

# The basics

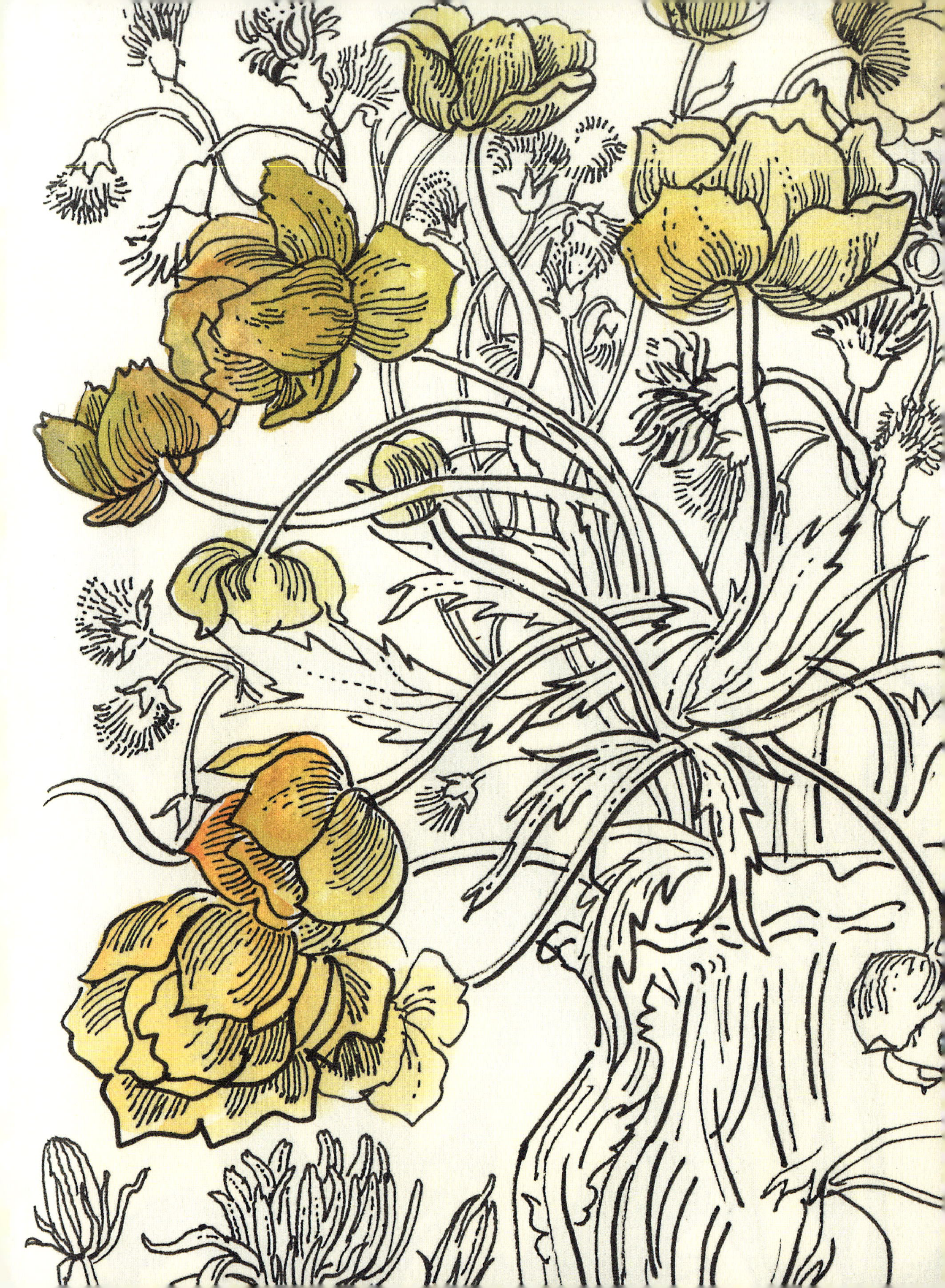

# DRAWING

When drawing from life, one must address a few issues, among them:

1. line
2. form
3. colour
4. texture
5. pattern.

To give a drawing a lifelike credibility you can put aside 3, 4 and 5, but 1 and 2 are essential and go hand in hand.

## LINE

It is incredibly easy to rush a line and therefore to rush a drawing. There can be excitement and dynamism in speedy execution (think of brilliant draughtsmen like Oskar Kokoschka or Jean Dubuffet), but in the hands of most artists speed just leads to mess, and expressive lines drawn in a hurry are simply inexpressive. Most of us have to make time for drawing in a life full of other imperatives. So, when you are in front of a subject with pen and paper, it is worth slowing down a bit and really making each line count.

At its most basic, this means making intentional marks, and that means knowing, when you start a line, where it will end. If you aren't sure, pause and think and then make the journey. That convinced confidence makes one more economical with lines and eliminates scribbled approximation. Most importantly, it allows you to know what you are looking at properly, because only careful exploration can give the discoveries that make drawing fun.

This neatness (which can also be bold and beautiful) is just as important in cross-hatching or the foundation lines of a drawing. Every line counts, and the better and stronger (that doesn't mean heavy, just certain) they are, the better your picture will be. It is useful to practise with a new pen or pencil and just to draw neat grids and stripes. They are a kind of drawing warm-up to keep your lines fit.

## FORM

To deal with form is to give a drawing three-dimensionality, and this is usually achieved by using tone to express light and dark. To throw shadow onto an image is to make it real, to give it plastic form.

A simple way to tackle this is to imagine a series of shades of grey from black to white. They might, in descending order, be called: black, dark grey, mid-grey, pale grey and white. As you look at an object you begin to analyse its tonal values by dividing them into those gradations. It is, of course, a simplification, but one that will usefully convert into a readable image. If you find it hard to work this out, it can be useful to squint slightly, and those imaginary changes of tone will become easier to read.

How you handle shading in your art depends rather on what drawing implement or implements you are using. With watercolour or ink, wash is the solution, but with pencil or pen and ink it is a matter of hatching and cross-hatching. The little drawings that come on the following pages illustrate how you might use those techniques and materials in your work, and although tackled differently, all do the same job. The watercolour example uses black tones only – that is, a series of greys. This is sometimes called grisaille (on a computer screen: greyscale). The pencil versions show pure tone (in which you can barely see the marks) and cross-hatching (discernible lines), and the pen relies on orderly hatching and cross-hatching. You can also use black dots in increasing density, but this is incredibly slow by comparison. When hatching, practise making your lines parallel. It is more visually restful and so makes the drawing more expressive in terms of form. Keep the lines consistent and the angle of the tool consistent as well.

The essential first step for any shading exercise is to be clear on where the light is coming from. Sometimes this is easy to see, but in more muted conditions one is sometimes required to amplify an almost imaginary directional light, as without this the drawing (however good) may appear flat. It is important that the light falls in the same way on every component in your drawing. As ever, all the information you need is in front of you, but there is technique here and a trained eye will identify where those darker tones should fall with increasing ease.

*If in doubt, keep looking. The answers to all your questions are in the subject in front of you.*

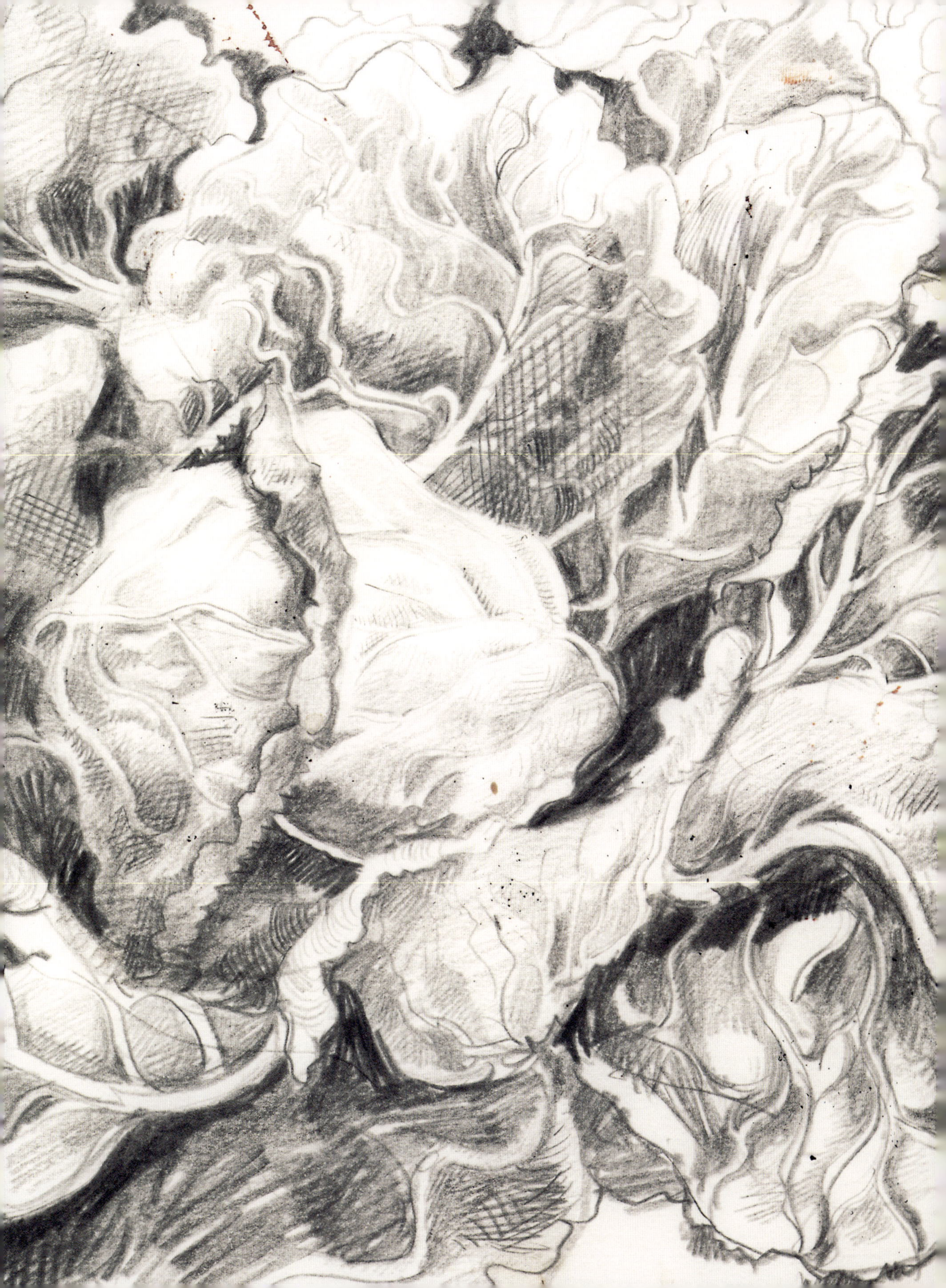

## SMALL ROUND-TOWERED CHURCH – INK CROSS-HATCHING

### STEP 1

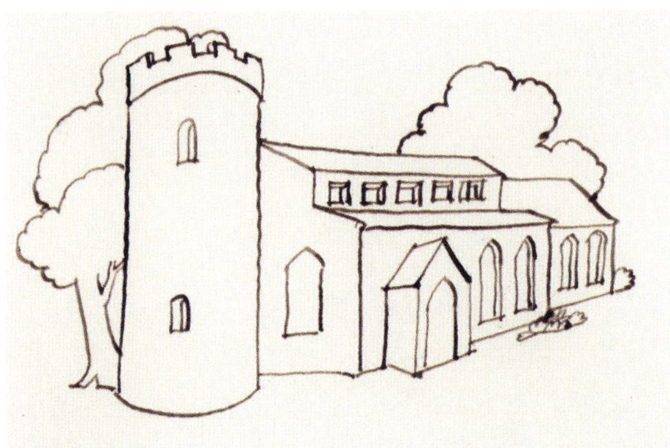

Begin with a careful line drawing. Observe the directions of all the lines – allowing the most correct perspective will be the easiest on the eyes. If a line seems wrong, measure, look and then redraw. If the initial line is wrong, then no amount of shading will correct the original errors. The line is the skeleton on which to hang the drawing. See the exercises on pages 105–11 for more on measuring.

### STEP 2

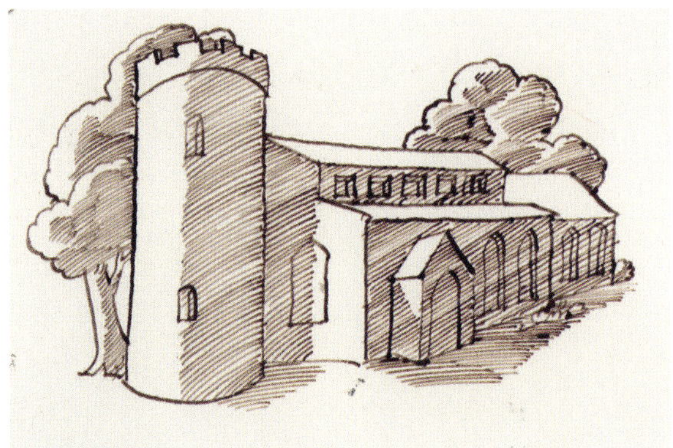

Where does the light come from? If it is not immediately clear, look for something with a steep change of direction and see which facet or edge is dark and which is light. The shade is on the side opposite the light's source. When you have sorted this out, you can begin the first layer of hatching. Think of this as the 'pale grey' component of the image. Make sure your lines are well spaced and parallel.

### STEP 3

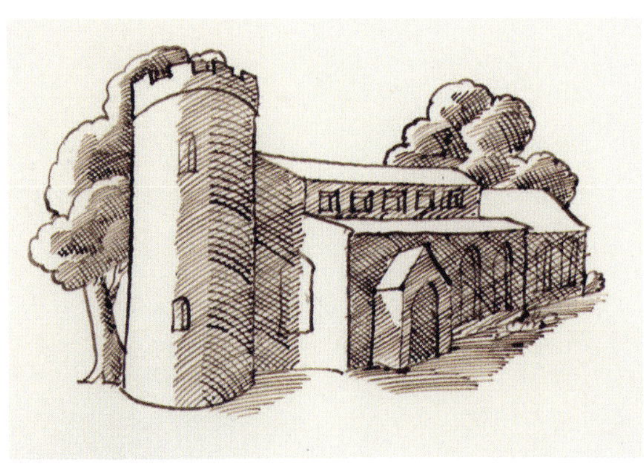

Make your second attack with lines set at a clearly different angle. These are very nearly the opposite angle of the initial application. In most of the areas, I have persevered with straight lines, expressing form only through light and dark. But for the tower, the lines are curved to emphasize its cylindrical form.

## STEP 4

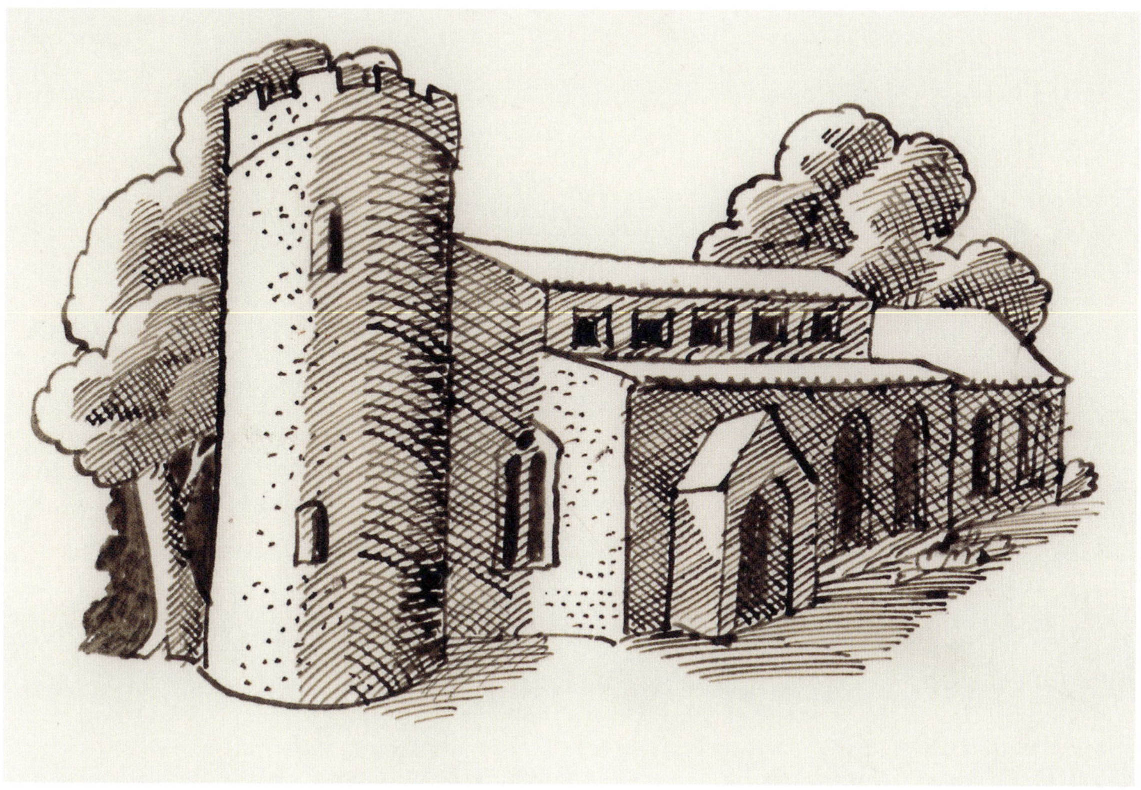

In the final stage, I have added a third layer of hatching to express the darkest grey shade. I have also added a few dots to imply the flint of the tower, and also to show that even the brightest bit of the building is darker than the sky.

## A GROUP OF TREES – PENCIL HATCHING

### STEP 1

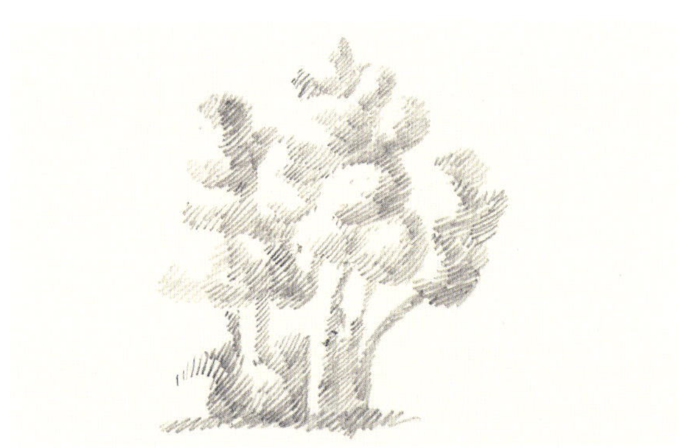

As before, the initial step is to draw each tree, deciding which elements are essential and which are needless detail. You cannot get everything in and identifying which branches and clumps of foliage best characterize the group is the essential first stage.

### STEP 2

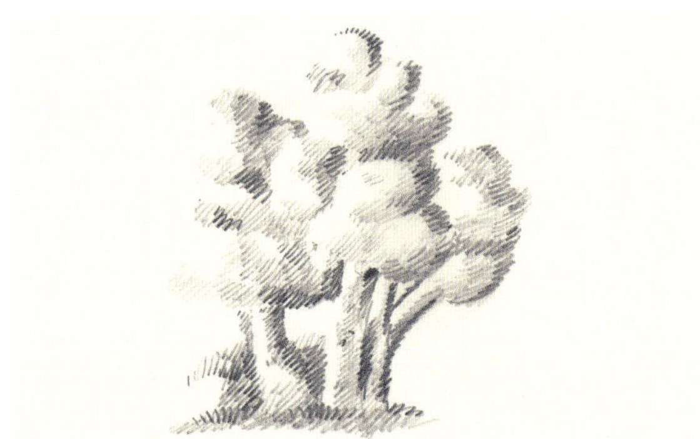

Trees are every bit as constructed as a building. There is form and skeleton and a series of three-dimensional shapes that go together to make the whole. A frequent mistake is to think of them as fluffy and freeform. In fact, they have their own geometry and architecture. And as such the light and shadow will help emphasize their shape.

### STEP 3

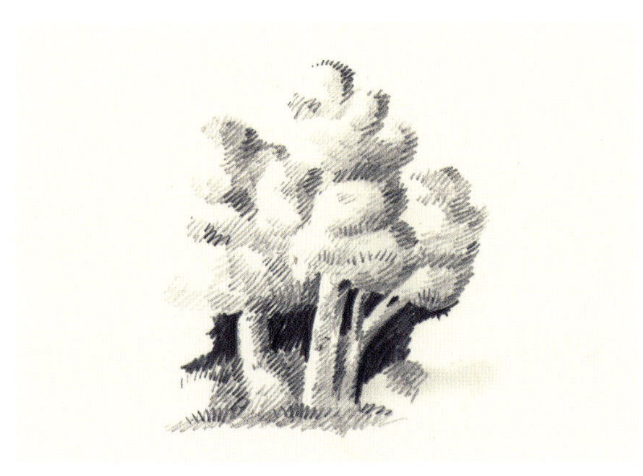

Now work in a larger area of darker tone, which will throw the trunks into focus and define their light side, as well as the shaded dark. You can also add some more bushes.

## A TUSCAN VILLA – PENCIL SHADING

### STEP 1

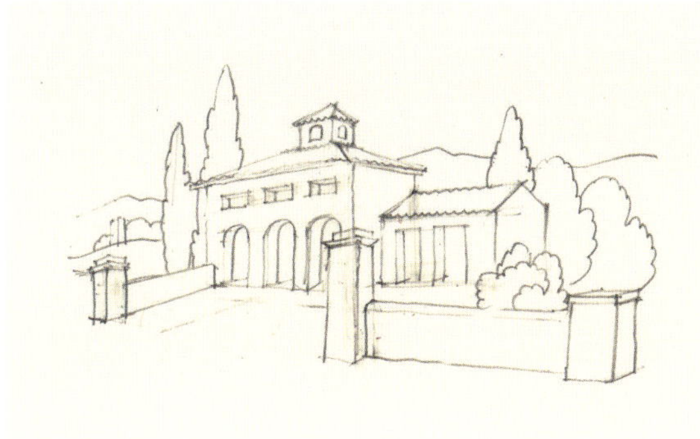

This is an invented view, with a composition that has plenty of angles and shapes that require shading. The cypress trees are bold – dark forms to send the building into sharper focus. The shapes are geometric and will catch the invented strong Mediterranean light well. I have included a context with distant hills as a further challenge when filling this in.

### STEP 2

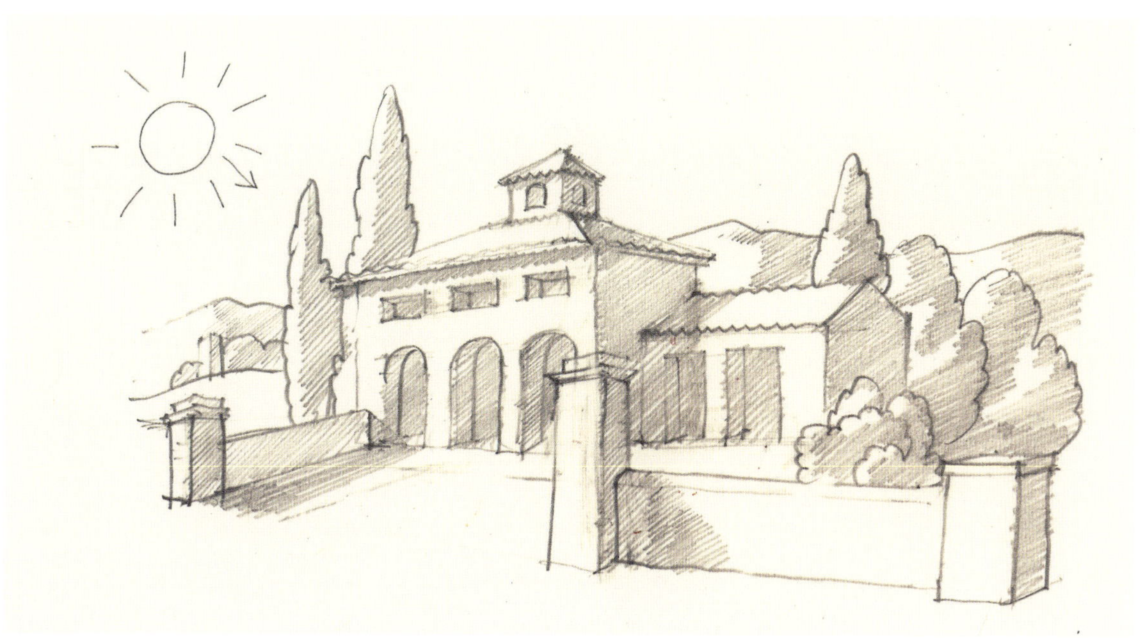

As the building is invented, so is the light source, and so I have drawn a cartoon sun in the sky to clarify my plan. I have identified the front face of the building and the tower as the brightest areas, and the arched recesses as the darkest, but have initially concentrated on the less strongly contrasting elements of the composition, using a gentle pencil-angled hatching to build up the pale and mid-tones.

## STEP 3

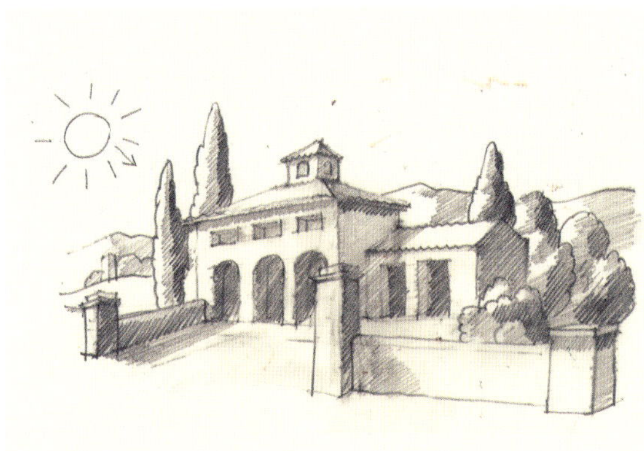

Now I am building up areas of higher intensity, adding the dark-grey parts of the building, leaving the strongest contrasting areas until last (it is easier to get darker than softer).

## STEP 4

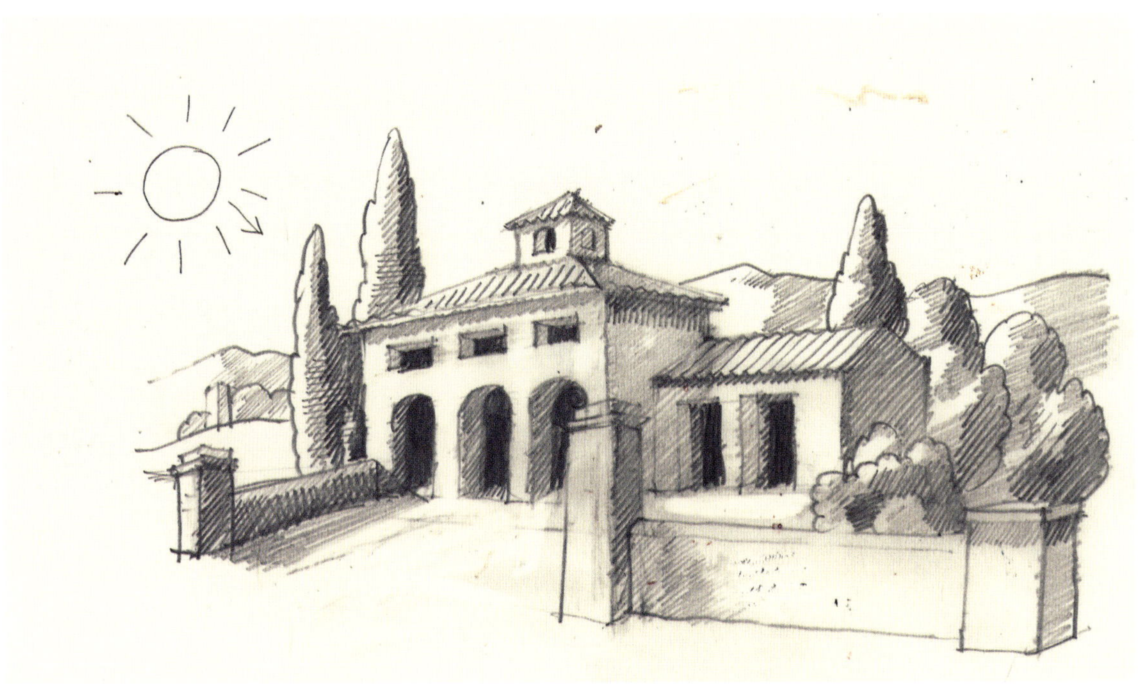

Finally, the darker areas, windows, arches and the sides of the cypress trees are strengthened. These punchy black elements seem to throw the whole drawing into a sharper focus. Remember that the sun (even the imagined sun) shines everywhere and that not only does the building have areas of light and dark, but the building itself also sheds shadows onto the ground.

## TWO TREES – NIB PEN & WASH

### STEP 1

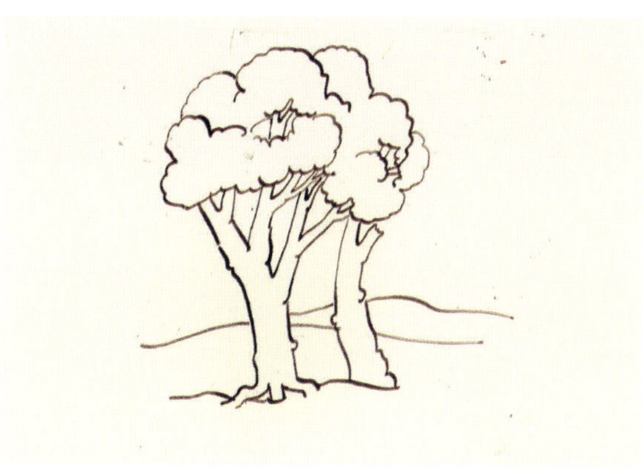

Begin with a simple drawing in hyper-opaque shellac ink. There should be little or no detail; the line is bold and expressive in itself. Make sure it's properly dry before you start step 2.

### STEP 2

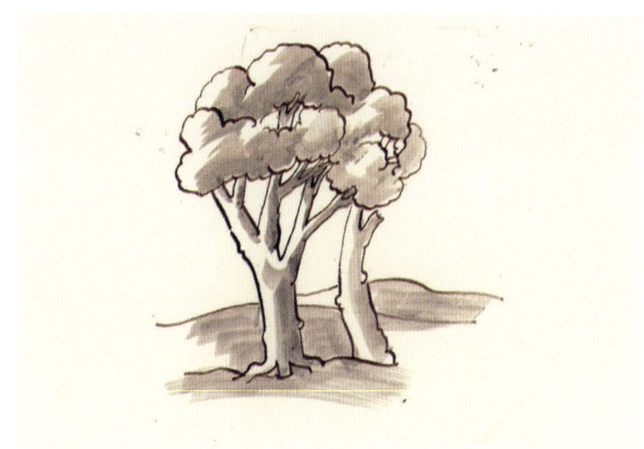

Having mixed some black watercolour in your palette, begin with the paler tones. As you fill these in, the lighter elements will shoot forward. Paint in a shadowy side to each clump of leaves.

### STEP 3

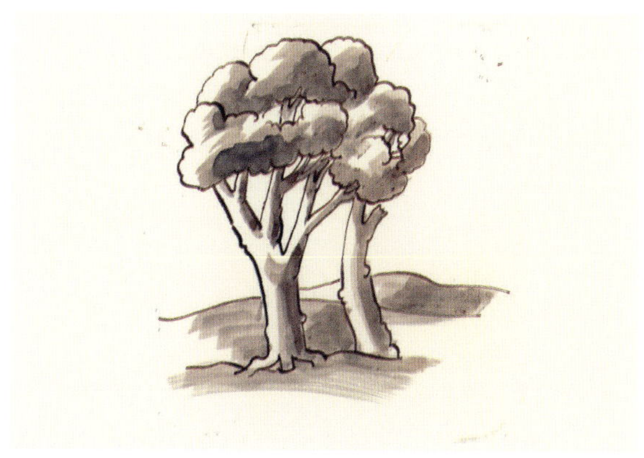

Begin to build up the darker areas with increasingly robust washes. Let each wash dry before adding the next, and make sure you approach the defining line of each area carefully.

### STEP 4

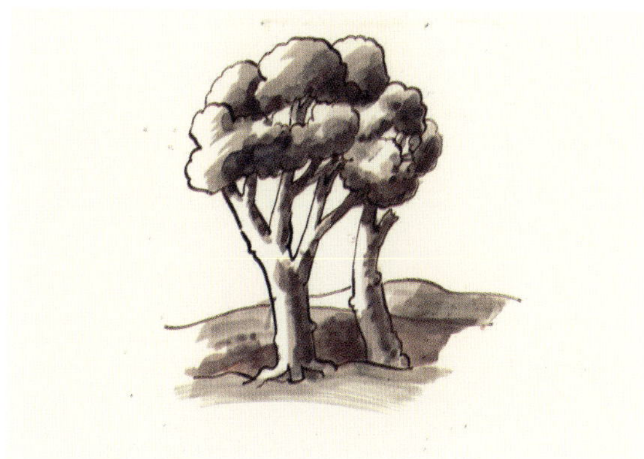

Now add the strongest wash of all. Although this is a line and wash drawing, this final stage has reduced the prominence of the line and produced a consistent weight throughout.

# WATERCOLOUR

Colour, and how to use it, does become second nature to experienced artists, and most painters develop a series of colours that, in combination, work best for them. Establishing that range of components in your paintbox does not require a 'right and wrong' selection, but there do seem to be a number of useful directions.

1. A huge box of colours is not needed to create the almost endless spectrum seen in the natural world. If one does have that view when you open your paintbox, it is a good guess that a proportion will seem rarely, if ever, to be used. As well as wasting money, this inclines the painter to indecision or at least to having to consider unnecessary choices. Honing this down to a smaller number of pans might, in fact, speed things up. I think the 15 colours shown on these pages are a good start.

2. You can make quiet and natural colours from the bright ones but not the other way round. Mixing bright yellow with a number of contrasting agents will quickly produce the sludgiest of ochres, while chasing the wild alchemy of producing a bright kingcup yellow from ochre is a fool's errand. This means that, if you are trying to find a tight collection of colours, you are better using *brights*.

3. Mixing colours can be easy. Every child is taught to make orange with red and yellow, green with blue and yellow, and so on, and in those simple recipes lie the secrets of making colours. That is, that *opposite* colours have a dramatic effect on each other. The colour wheel opposite shows you what those are and indicates that, for example, green will send red brown. Experimenting with some of the $a + b = c$ examples on the hopscotch page (page 57) will push this a bit further.

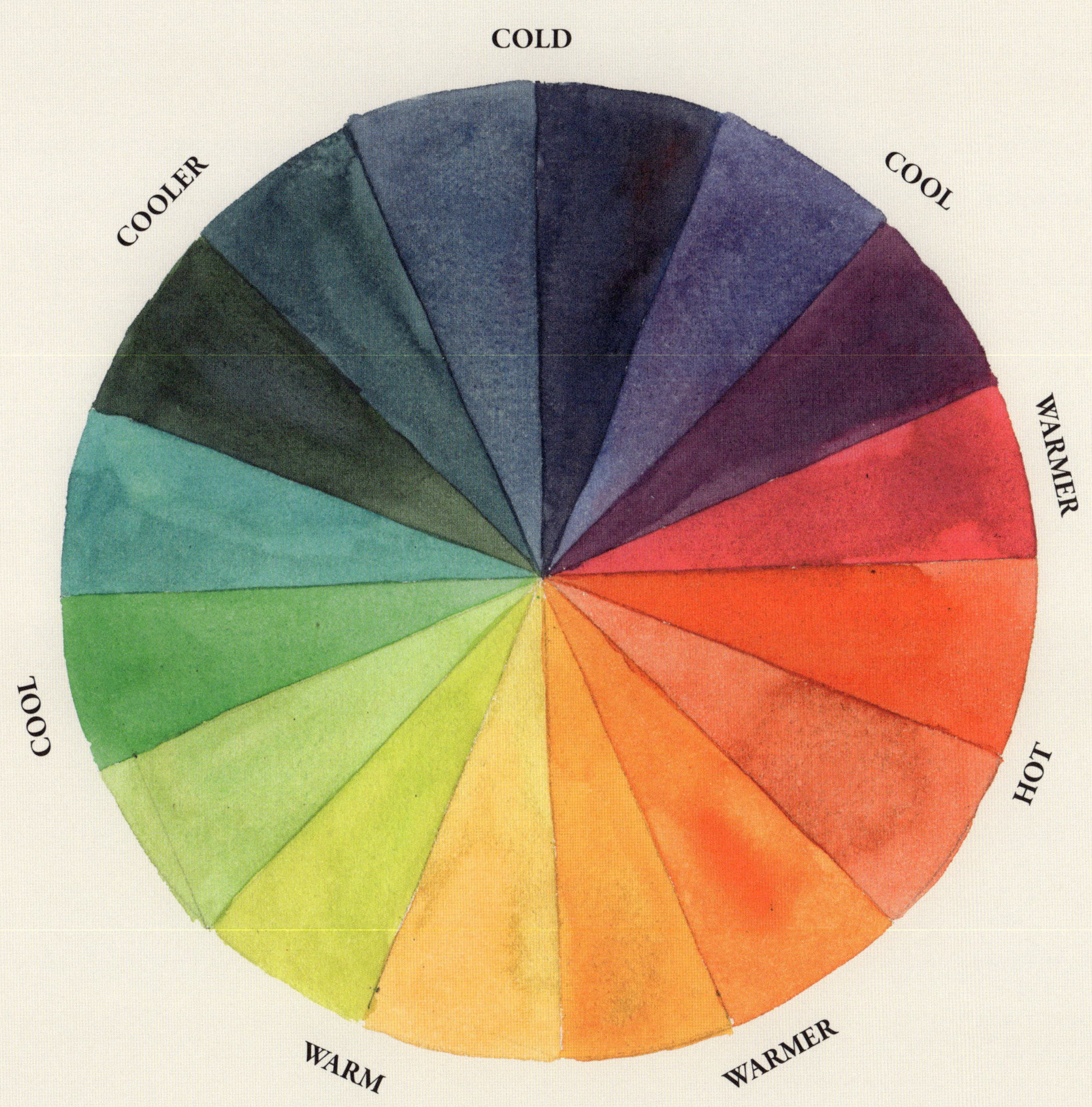
COLD
COOL
WARMER
HOT
WARMER
WARM
COOL
COOLER

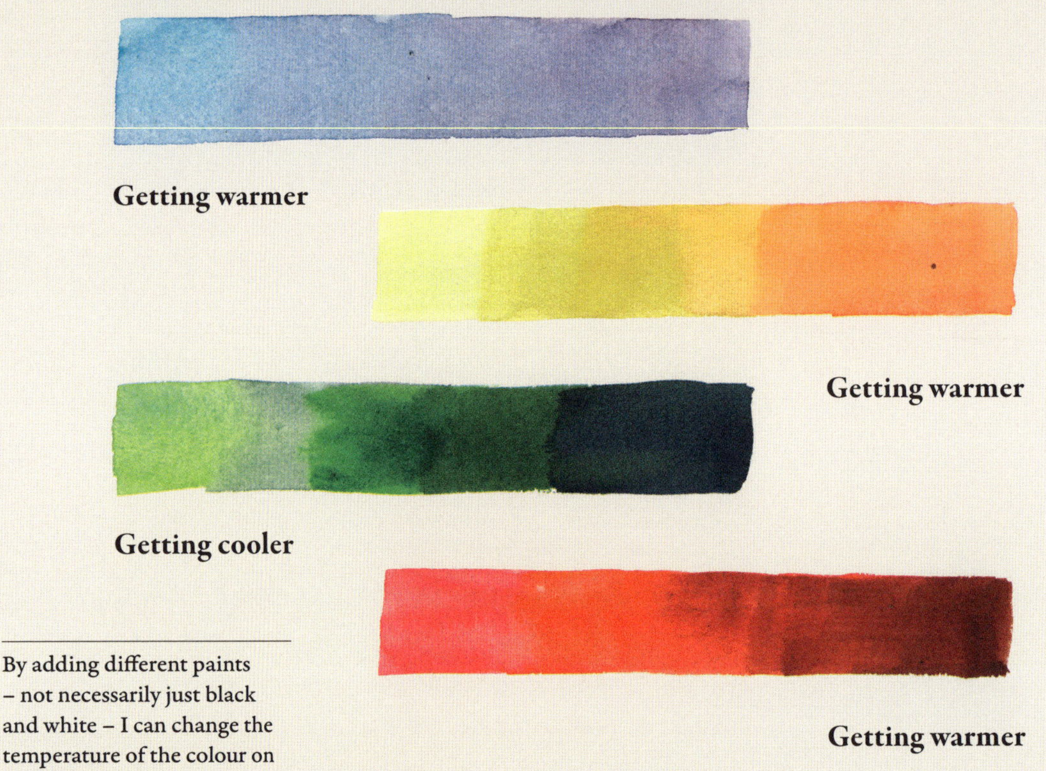


By adding different paints – not necessarily just black and white – I can change the temperature of the colour on the page.

## CHOOSING YOUR COLOURS

The colours you choose to use will come to define your work, and while one might sometimes think that a trip to Venice might call for Indian red and burnt sienna, in fact these are easy to achieve with simple, bright colours used in combination. This method will also help keep a happy brightness in even the more muted shades.

Even within this rather tight group of 15 colours there is a graduating scale of brightness. In descending order, opera rose, the yellows and cobalt turquoise are more powerful than geranium red, cobalt azure or permanent green. At the other end of the scale, deep red, phthalo blue and black are the agents of dark.

You will notice the inclusion of black and the absence of white. For me, white has no place in the watercolour box. White is in the paper beneath (with its bright china-clay glow), and it is with dilution that clear colours can be made brighter and paler. White in any form has a chalky opacity that deadens the colour by making a pastel and not a pale colour and reduces the transparency, which is the joy of watercolour and central to the system of laying one wash above another.

White gouache, a chalk-medium-based paint (in a tube) can be very useful in making bright-white overpainted lines (perhaps a stamen or a branch or even a highlight), but it is a last resort. Not a last resort of desperation, but the last application of paint on the picture, as further washes will disturb the white gouache line, making a milky mess of the painting.

Some purists are against black. They suggest that black is not a colour, that using black to darken a colour is an admission of failure – why not use dark blue or brown? These are strictures once commonly heard on the lips of teachers. But, in fact, black watercolour is very useful and powerful, particularly when deep contrasts or heavy shadow are required. It is indeed not a colour, so absent from the colour wheel, and does lead to dull, inert shadows in mid-tone areas of colour, so it is to be used with care.

Black paint also makes your water so dirty. My mother used three water pots – warm, cool and black – and while she changed the water regularly, it was important to her not to pollute a colour even with the dilute agent in the brush-washing water. I don't do this, but I wash my brush regularly to keep brightness.

This, for me, is the ideal colour collection, and I do not need more than this. You may find you wish to supplement, or subtract, once you get started.

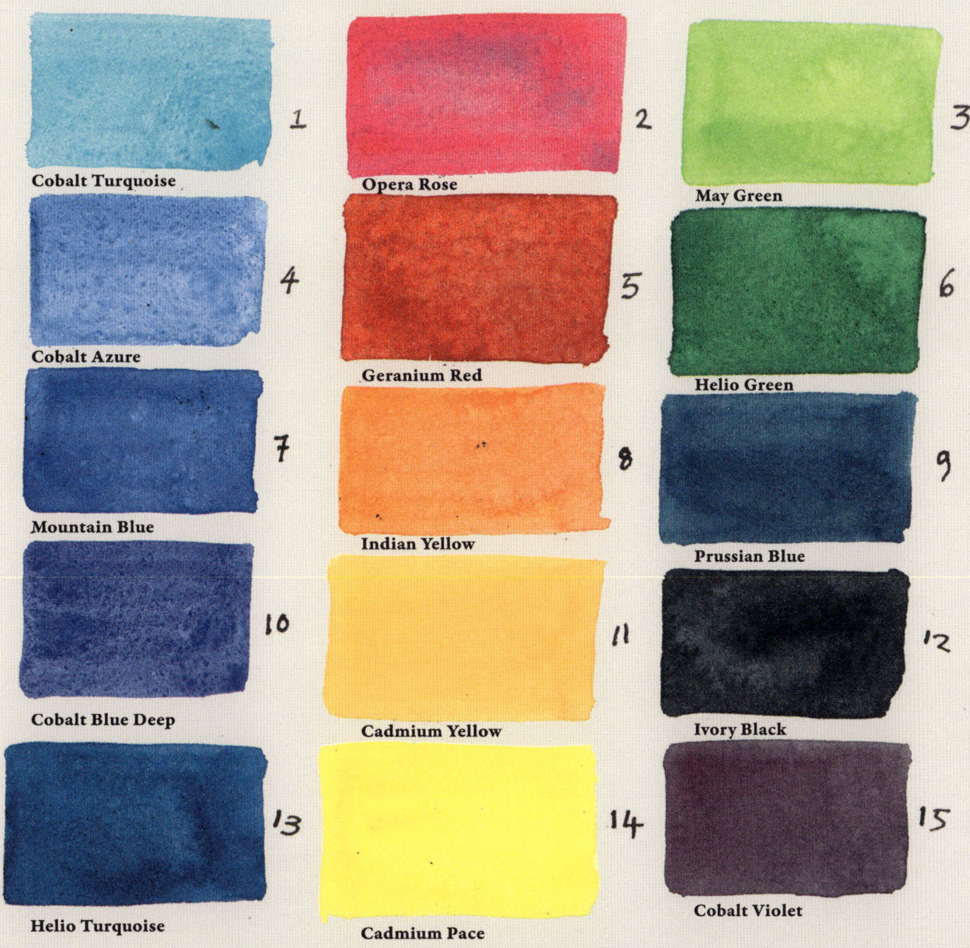

## EXPERIMENTING WITH COLOUR

I have used at the centre of my hopscotch diagram opposite a tile of opera rose pink. This is a rather magical colour, whose clarity and cool strength move other colours to great things. It sends yellow into a happy, bright orange while heating up cool blues into lush violets and ultramarine into deepest purple. But I might easily have started with a bright cadmium yellow or emerald green and showed different but equally dramatic results. Opera rose is a colour enhancer. It is to other colours what sugar or monosodium glutamate is to so many foods: an agent that makes a yellow even yellower or a bright red more intense. I rely on it for a lot of what is most joyful and bright in my work.

These pages show areas of very bright colour, in highly saturated washes and the brightest intensities. I have also included one picture showing that these same compounds and pigments can produce subtle and gentle washes while retaining a basic brightness and clarity. Muddiness is simply muddy.

Phthalocyanines are a group of pigments created to make extra-powerful and transparent paints. You will notice the abbreviation *phthalo* on several colours. These don't have the Folies Bergère glamour of opera rose or the familiar domesticity of May green or geranium, nor yet the Mediterranean allure of azure and ultramarine, but look out for them. They can be very useful.

## A NOTE ON PIGMENT

Chemical components, bromides and chromiums, encapsulated grains and powders are outside the remit of this book. In medieval Venice, the guild of spice merchants embraced the city's colourmen: an indication of the commercial and cultural significance of imported pigments made from rare minerals, metals or natural materials such as shells and beetle wings. These colours stained bright the glamour of the antique world: Tyrian purple, lapis lazuli, carnelian and cinnabar, madders, orpiments and red leads. And in either dilute forms or faithful imitations, and alongside (for some) the gentle earth colours (naturally occurring ochres and burnt soils), they fill our paintboxes today.

In this diagram, I started with opera rose pink and experimented with combining colours. Trial sheets like this can be very useful to refer to when you are getting to grips with mixing colours in your artworks.

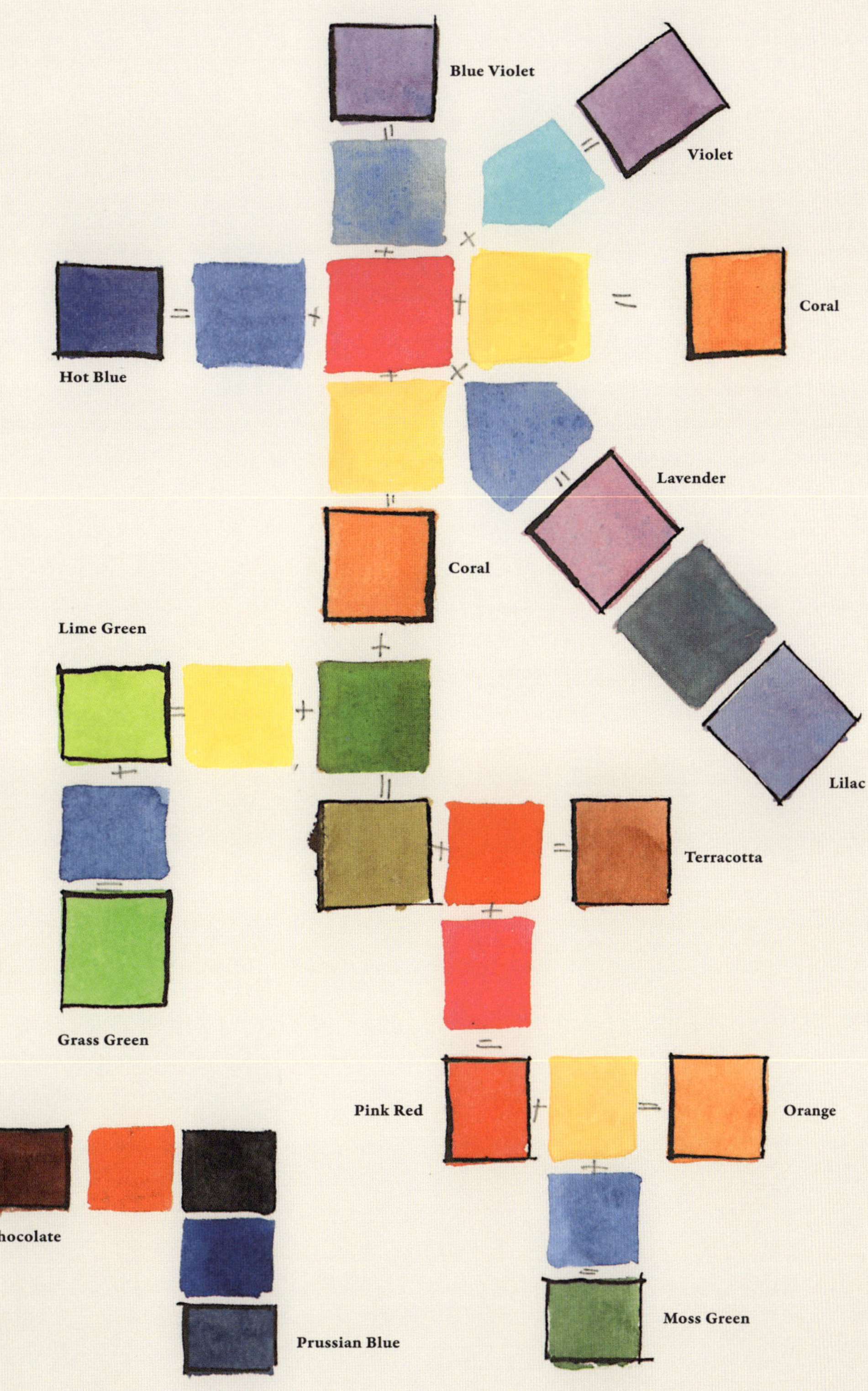
Blue Violet
Violet
Coral
Hot Blue
Lavender
Coral
Lime Green
Lilac
Terracotta
Grass Green
Pink Red
Orange
Chocolate
Moss Green
Prussian Blue

# GETTING COMFORTABLE WITH WATERCOLOUR

The following exercises are really just playing. The idea is to use intense, dense colour, to keep the colours bright and clear, and to keep each block of colour, each wash, clean and pure. In some blocks I have moved from one colour to another, blending them carefully. I have tried to make that even and again to keep them bright.

To get a pure colour, I suggest mixing the colour neat, or a simple mixture of two colours, with water in your palette. I usually test it, or even mix it, on a piece of white paper. Make sure you have enough colour and enough water (the clue is in the name!) and then really load your brush before laying the wash, the area of colour, on the paper. A wash should be a little puddle of colour wet enough to move, dry enough to control, and saturated enough in pigment to give you the desired intensity of colour. The larger the brush, the more paint it will hold, but also the more it will use and waste. I like a no. 6 or 7 for most things, but I have enjoyed a chisel-ended brush as well, which is a quick way to apply a wash. The bigger the area you want to cover, the more useful a large brush is.

Try some practice washes using your brush to literally pull the puddle of colour across the paper, but all the time keep the colour strong. I never 'wet' the paper first unless I am stretching and tinting a whole sheet. I just mix the colour I want and pull the wash as above, almost like pulling a sheet up over a bed.

By letting each block of colour dry for a few minutes I am able to put two washes completely abutting one another with no running or blurring. This is worth practising, and the time it takes to dry will depend on how warm your room is. It's slower outside – unless it's a hot day! Draw some finer stripes and see how good your brush control can

1A

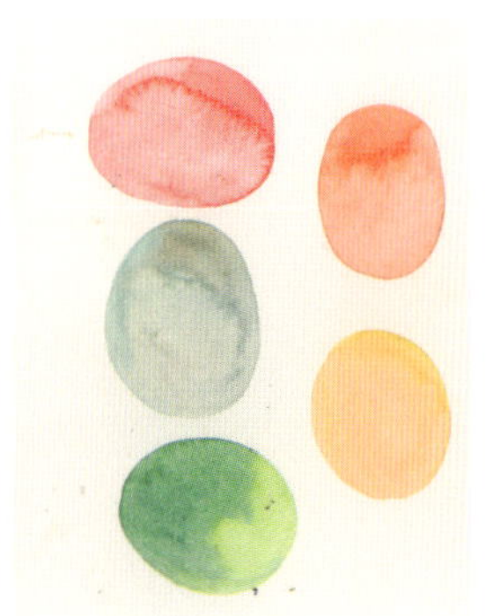

1B

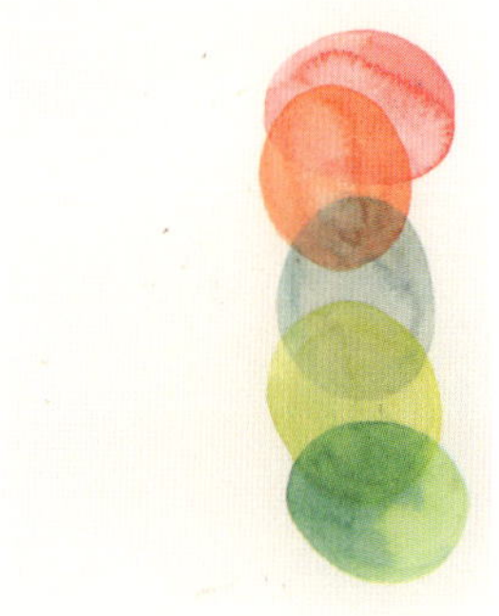

1C

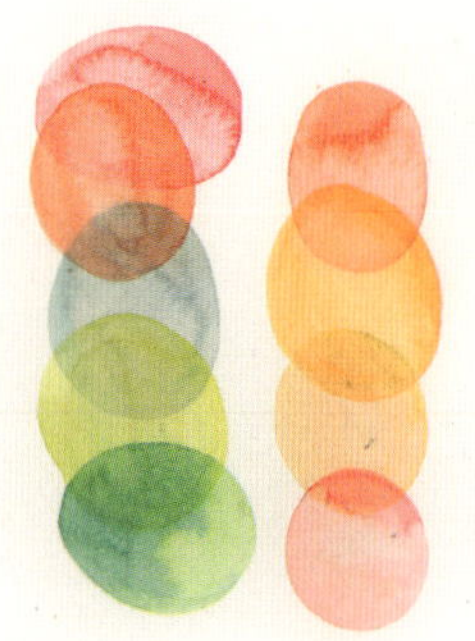

1D

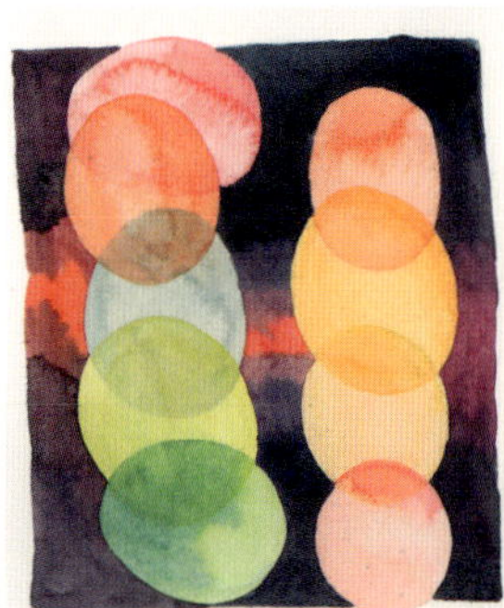

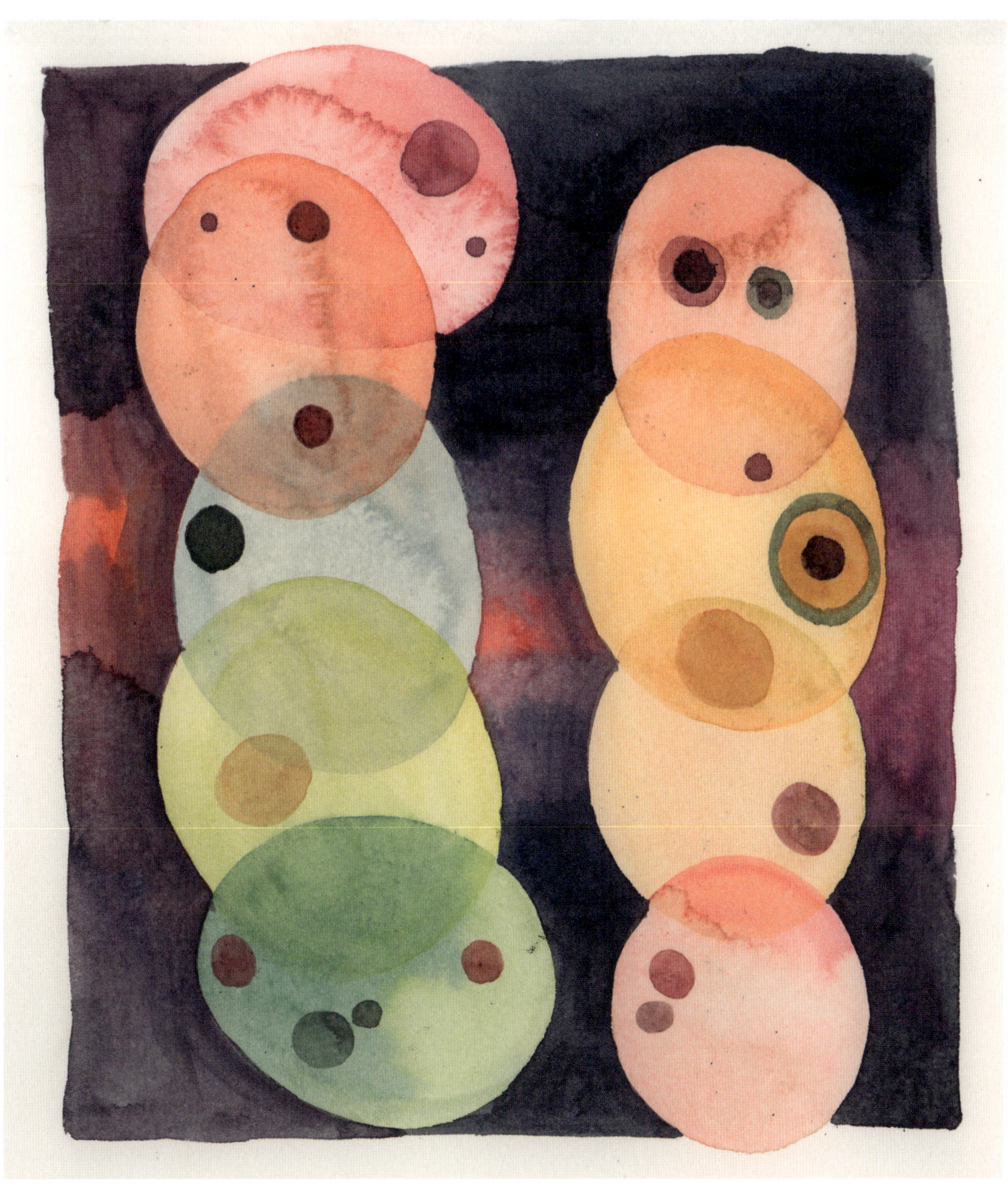

2A

2B

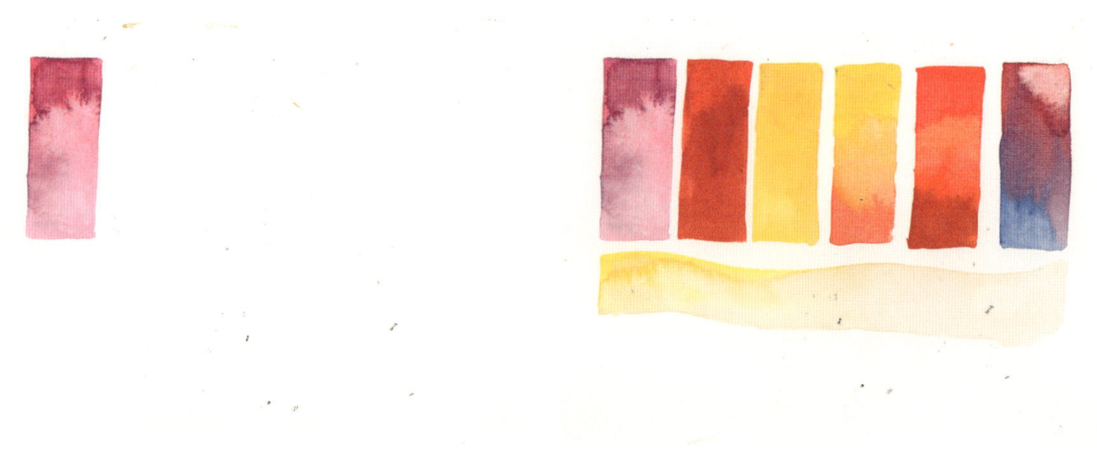

2C

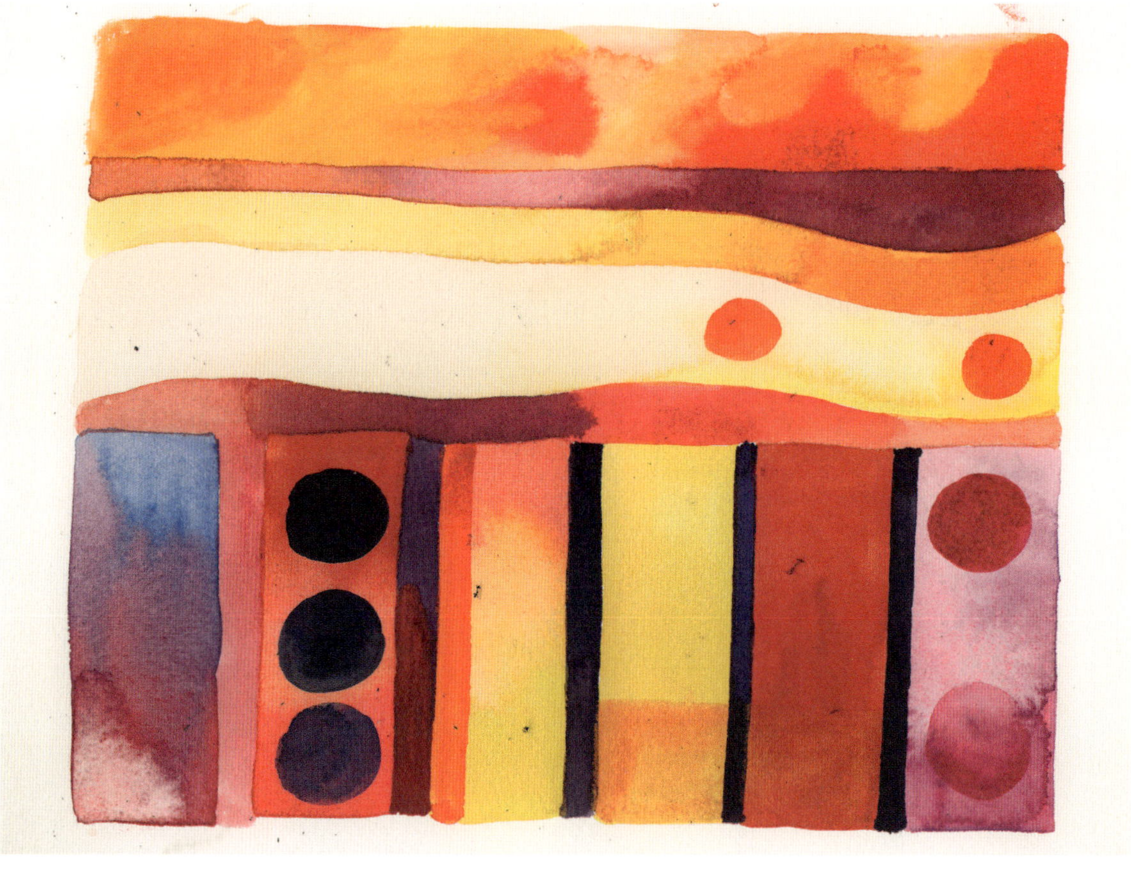

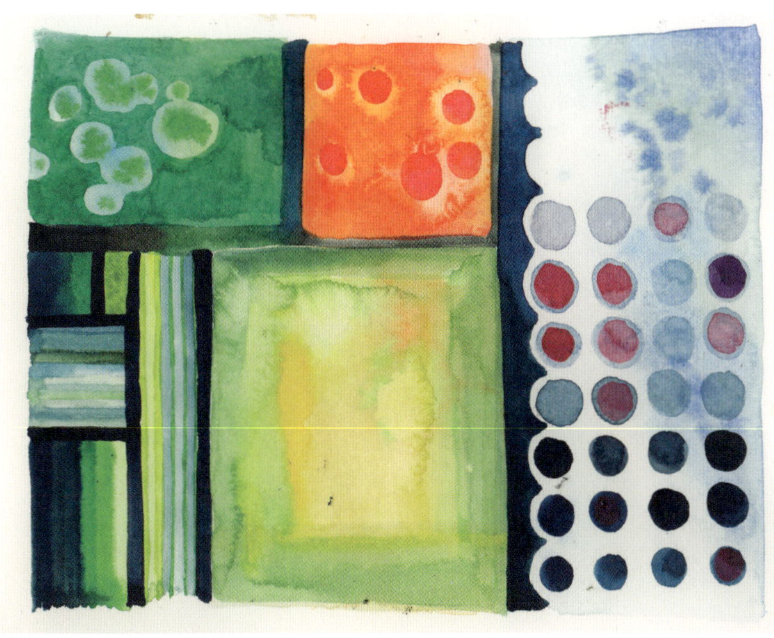

become. Brush control is a proper skill – practice makes perfect – but remember not to try and do work with an old, frayed brush. They become too dry and too frayed, even the artificial fibre ones. You need to keep a fine tip, as this will define the edge of the wash tidily. Keep practising!

Now try laying a new bright wash on top of one of your first blocks. Make sure that the wash below is utterly dry and paint the new one gently. Don't scrub! Again, remember more colour, more water will give you results. The brightness of watercolour is the result of the whole of the paper shining through the translucent paint (in this it differs from chalky gouache, which is opaque and relies entirely on itself and the contrast between colours for its brightness). The better papers will shine through more powerfully.

Different colours have different qualities as paints as well as chromatically. Some are clear and lustrous and become increasingly transparent the more you dilute them. Bright chemicals or minerals do this, while the earth colours (ochres, umbers, etc.) remain earthy or at least chalky at weaker densities. Experiment with your paintbox to discover the different properties of your watercolours. I use that amazing colour, opera rose (see page 56), in so many mixed colours, and its lustrous transparency transfers to yellow and blues as well as to pinks and reds. As we have seen, it is a sort of MSG (or at least a white sugar) of the watercolour spice rack.

# GLOSSARY

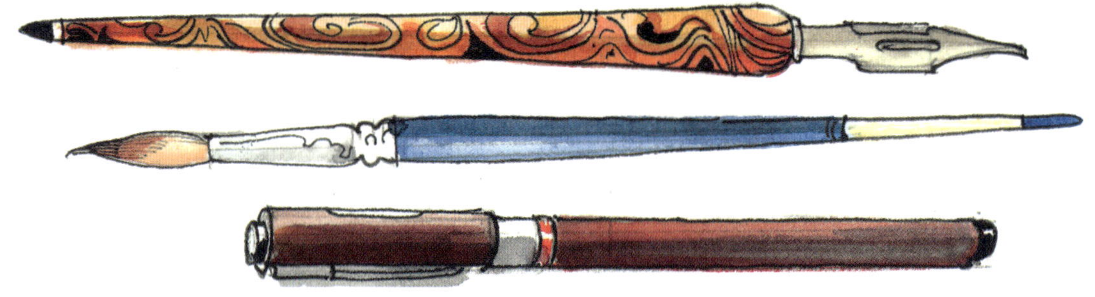

## MY FOUR STAGES OF DRAWING

**1. Plan**
A plan is less than a sketch. It is the roughest stage of drawing and is purely to determine where on the page you will place your image, working out where the extremities of the composition will fit. It is something to be thrown away!

**2. Sketch**
This is a preparatory drawing that allows you to get your thoughts out on paper rather than in your head (which is jolly hard). Sometimes a sketch can be a thing of beauty (why not?), but it is not an end in itself, and it should lead to something better. It allows you to work out proportions and dimensions (often quite hard) on a page that will not be the final drawing.

**3. Drawing**
This is a picture without colour and done with pen or pencil. (I suppose that a monochrome painting might almost count, but really, I feel the use of paint makes it a painting.) It might be pen and ink, pencil, graphite or charcoal. It is an end in itself and not a stage towards a final painting, even if one does in due course ensue. It is a picture you might frame.

**4. Watercolour**
This has a wide and extensive definition. It might be a tinted pencil drawing or be purely paint on paper. Some painters use watercolour sparingly, making pale and subtle colours its character, while others are more muscular and produce pictures as bold as oils.

## OTHER TERMS

**blackground:** A black background to an artwork.

**block:** A stack of watercolour paper joined at all four edges with glue (as opposed to a gummed pad, where the paper is joined at only one edge).

**botanical drawing:** A careful study of a flower or vegetable, often with the whole plant as subject.

**cold-pressed, or not, paper:** Paper with a slightly rougher texture which has been run through a cold press rather than a hot press (hence 'not' rather than 'hot'). The most common kind of paper found in watercolour paper pads or blocks.

**composition:** The disposition of elements in a painting.

**gouache or body colour:** Chalk-based, opaque colour that allows for the late application of white or pale tones at the end of the painting process. It can also be used in washes, but these are not watertight even when dry, so should be used with care.

**hot-pressed paper:** Paper that has been run through a hot press to render it extremely smooth.

**landscape:** A view of a place as subject of a painting. Also, a rectangular image longer than it is tall.

**pen and wash:** A drawing in ink that is then tinted in watercolour.

**pigments:** The minerals and derivatives, or chemical-based imitations, that make up an actual colour in paint.

**portrait:** A rectangular image taller than it is long.

**rough paper:** Paper with a pronounced surface texture.

**still life:** A group of familiar objects arranged to make a pleasing composition. Often a good exercise to improve observational drawing or refine techniques.

**stretching:** The process of soaking a sheet of paper and fixing its edges with brown tape to a wooden board to provide a super-smooth, rigid surface on which to paint.

**wash:** An area of continuous painted surface, tinted without break or articulation, although sometimes with variety of tone or colour.

**watercolour:** Pigments suspended in a water-based medium to produce an effect of translucency and pure colour. The medium might be anything from gum arabic and ox gall to honey and, more frequently, more modern artificial mediums.

**wet on wet:** A technique (one I typically do not use in this book) where colour is mixed directly on the wet page.

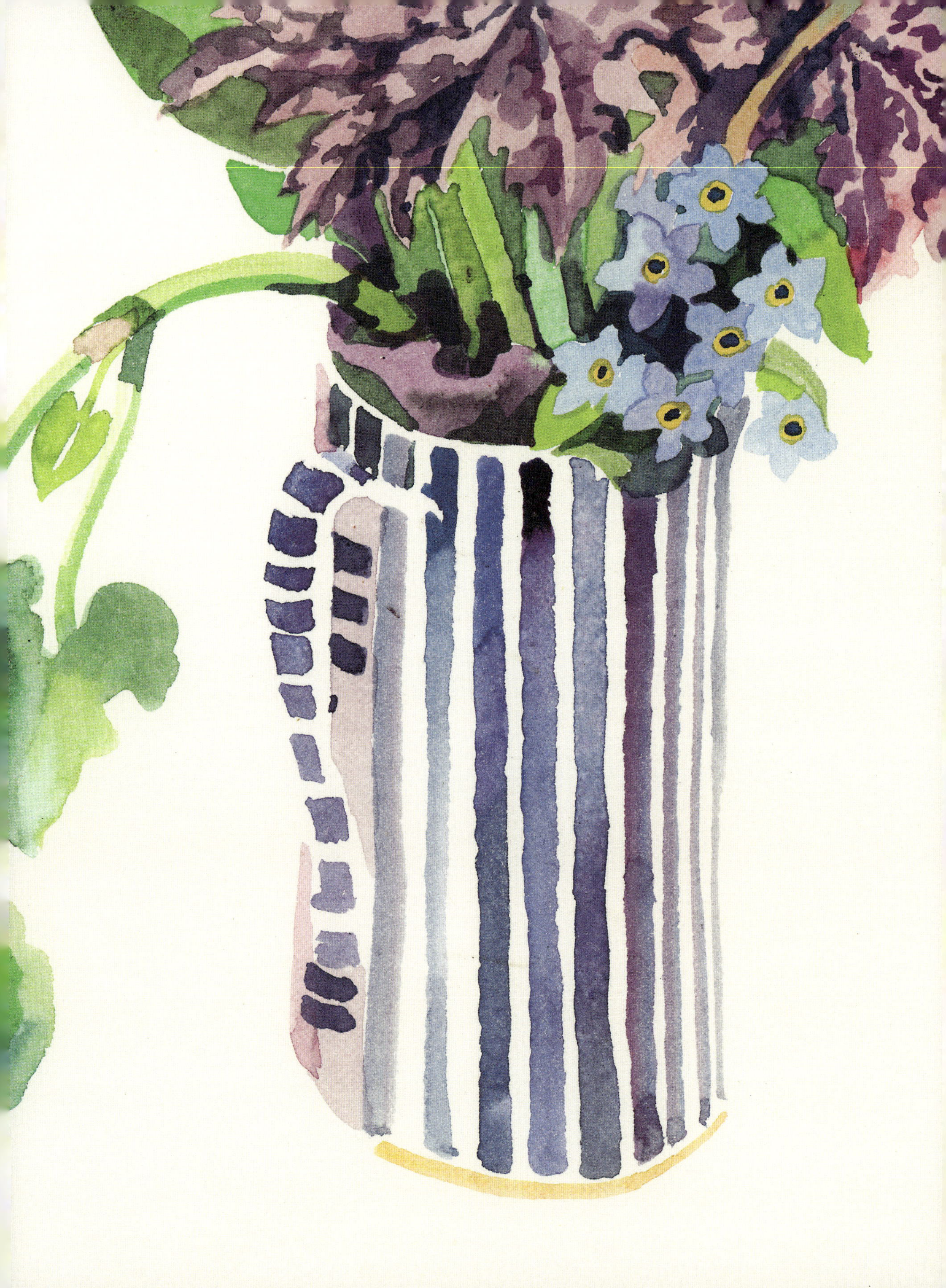

# Exercises

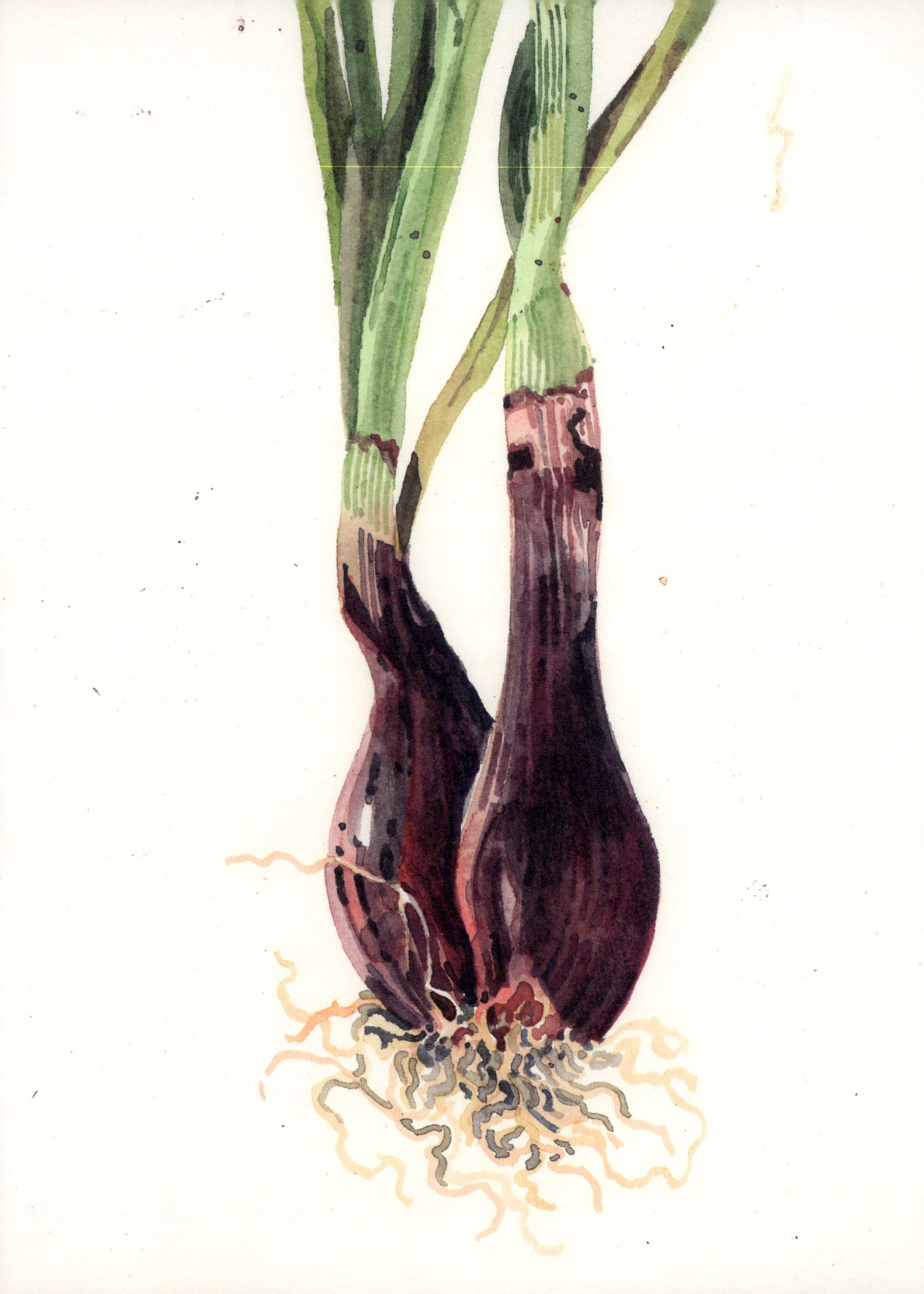

# Exercise 1

## Red onions

For me, the greatest pleasure comes from painting direct onto the white sheet. With the colours isolated on the snowy field, there is a clarity and a decisiveness that comes from doing without pencil or pen, and that also helps you to focus on colour and texture. Watercolour has always been a medium well suited to detail. Think of the drawings of Albrecht Dürer or John Ruskin, who relished imperfections and variants from the norm: drying or dying grasses, peeling, ageing, plaster and lichen-encrusted stone. These surface disfigurements served only to enhance the essential nature of material and subject. This pair of young red onions are a perfect subject. And while you might be lucky enough to have them growing in the garden, there is also a high likelihood of finding just such a bunch in a supermarket or farmers' market. Try to find some with some dryer skin and roots – more detail to get hold of when you paint. I like the red ones, as that ruby colour adds an important element and brings an articulation of colour as well as tone. They are also delicious and can perhaps go into a risotto when you have completed the drawing!

## FIRST LOOK

**Horror or pleasure? The sheet is empty, and the onions are willing and pleasing models. Look long and hard with your brush laid on the table and think about what you find most onion-like about this pair of bulbs. Consider their particular and unique features: the twists and bulges, any yellowing leaves.**

## MATERIALS

I have used a no. 6 sable pointed brush and my watercolour set (see pages 52–5), on Arches hot-press 300lb paper.

## STEP 1

Mix the first wash of your pale-pink onion colour, using a no. 6 pointed brush. Opera rose and cadmium yellow will be the main ingredients, but perhaps also some cobalt blue and violet. Test it out to see if it feels right on a spare piece of paper. Then boldly begin to lay down some simple washes, marking the basic shape of the onions. Take care to leave out the highlight that will survive the painting to find its important role at the end.

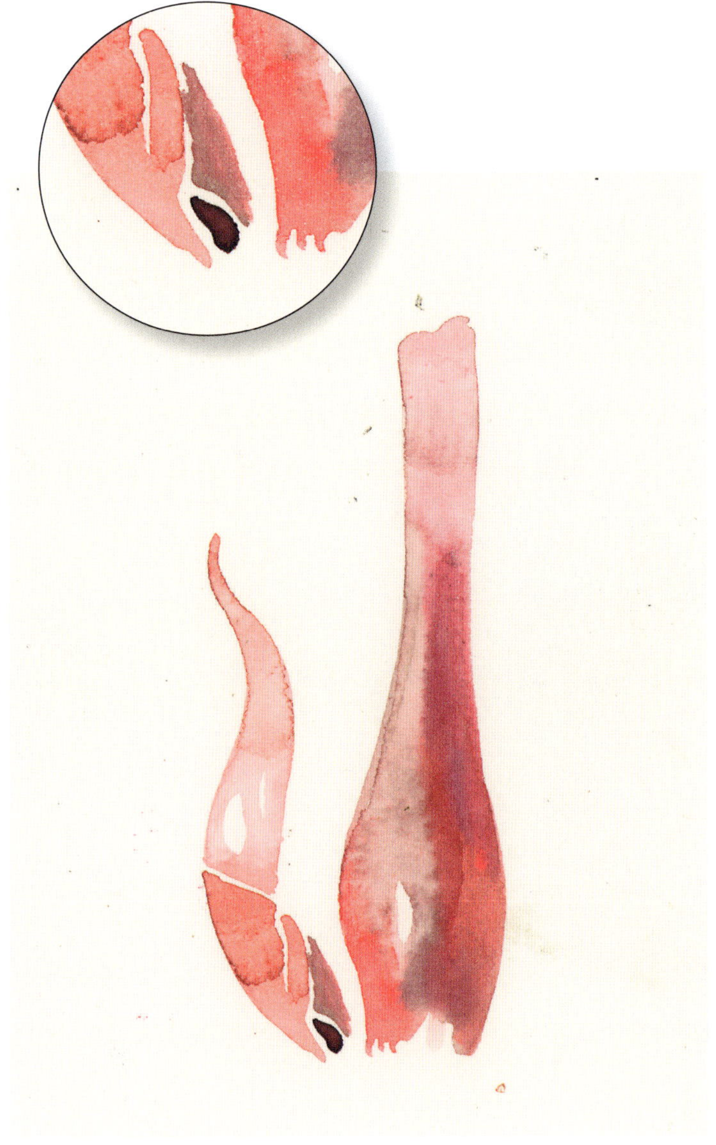

## STEP 2

Add in the first indications of the onion greens, using May and helio greens and some cadmium medium, remembering to let each wash dry before its neighbour is introduced. These colours do not run into each other in real life, so make sure your painted ones stay clear and discrete also. Then add in a second, slightly stronger series of pink washes to complete the drawn onion and to add the first indications of three-dimensional form by indicating an area of shadow. Remember, all the information you need is in those onions, so all the time keep *looking* at the subjects.

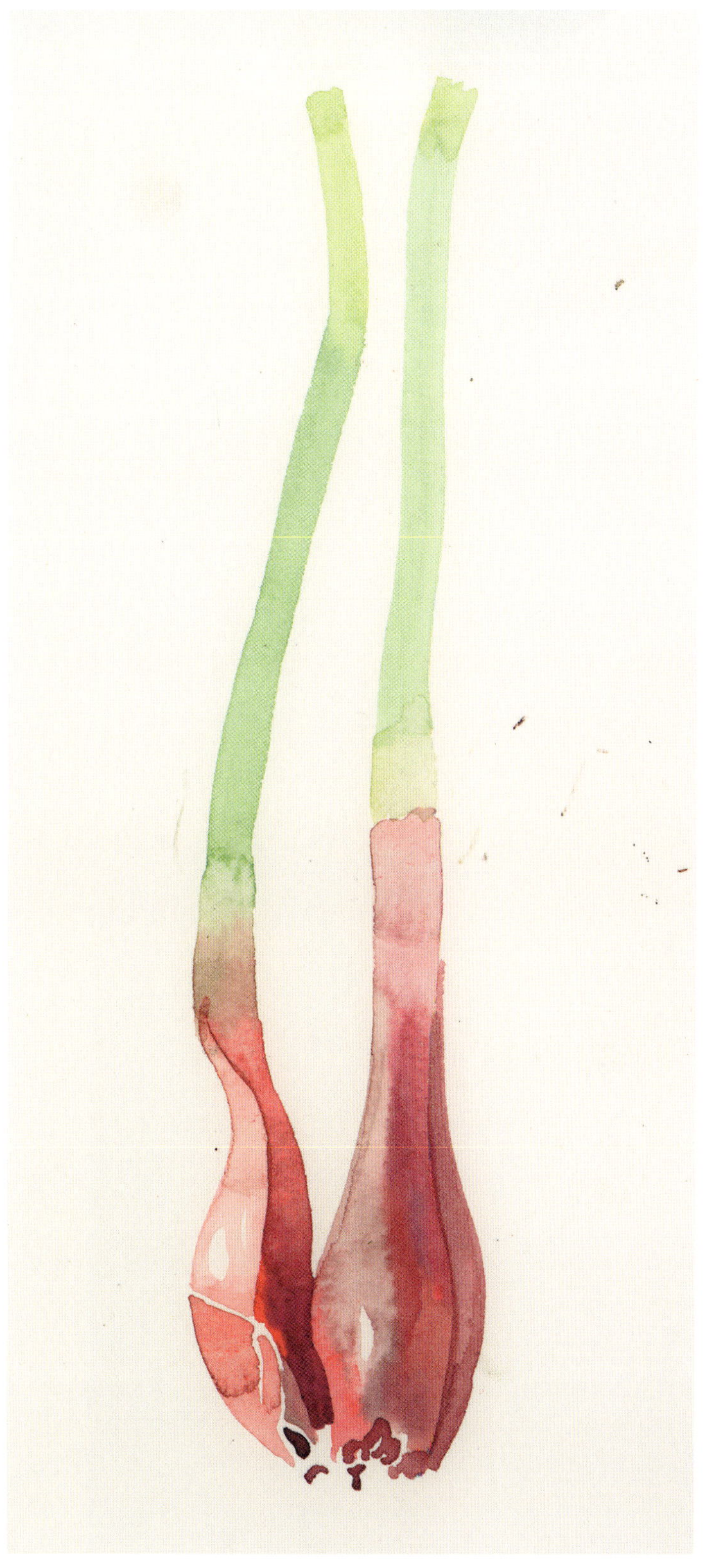

## STEP 3

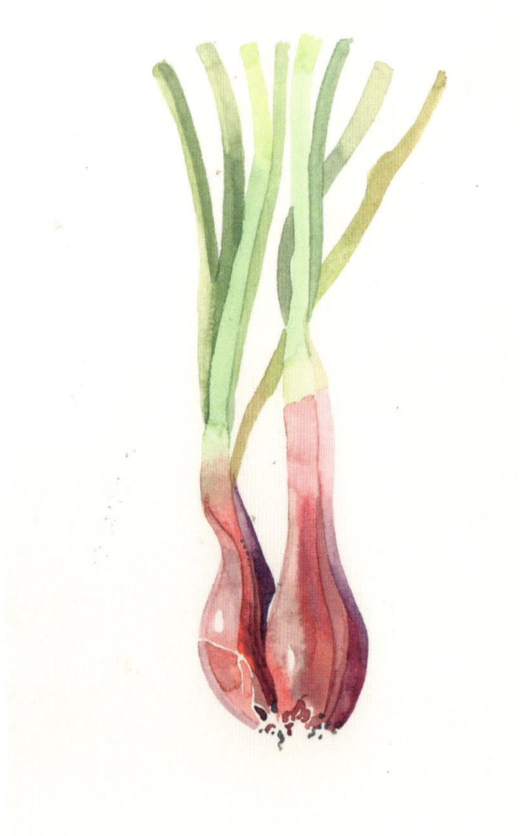

Fill in the rest of the leaves with the green, again being careful not to let one wash run into another. Pause to analyse, and work out which areas are shown to recede, and mark them out in a darker wash. As in all painting, accentuating (without wild, cartoonish exaggeration) the important visual information of this sort will help make the finished picture seem more real. When I painted this, I left the white trail of the lone root unpainted. This will always look better, more intentional and genuinely clearer than a final application of white gouache body colour.

## STEP 4

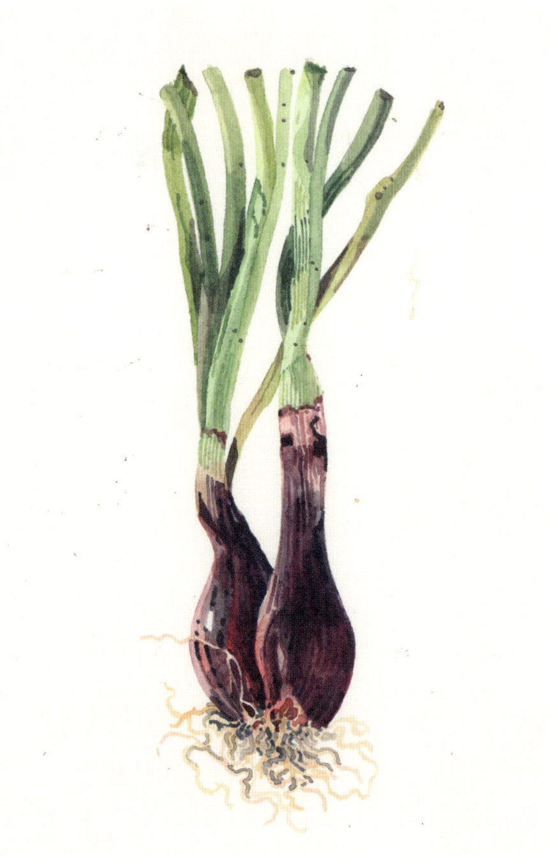

Now you can begin to add a number of darker washes, using Prussian blue and black and some geranium red, to reduce brightness and to illustrate the strong stripes on the onions and leaves. Be careful and don't rush. This is quite a simple picture and needn't take more than an hour, so each brush stroke should be considered. Build more modelling, with increasingly darker greens, to the leaves. Use magenta or dark red to bring in the collar where bulb meets leaves.

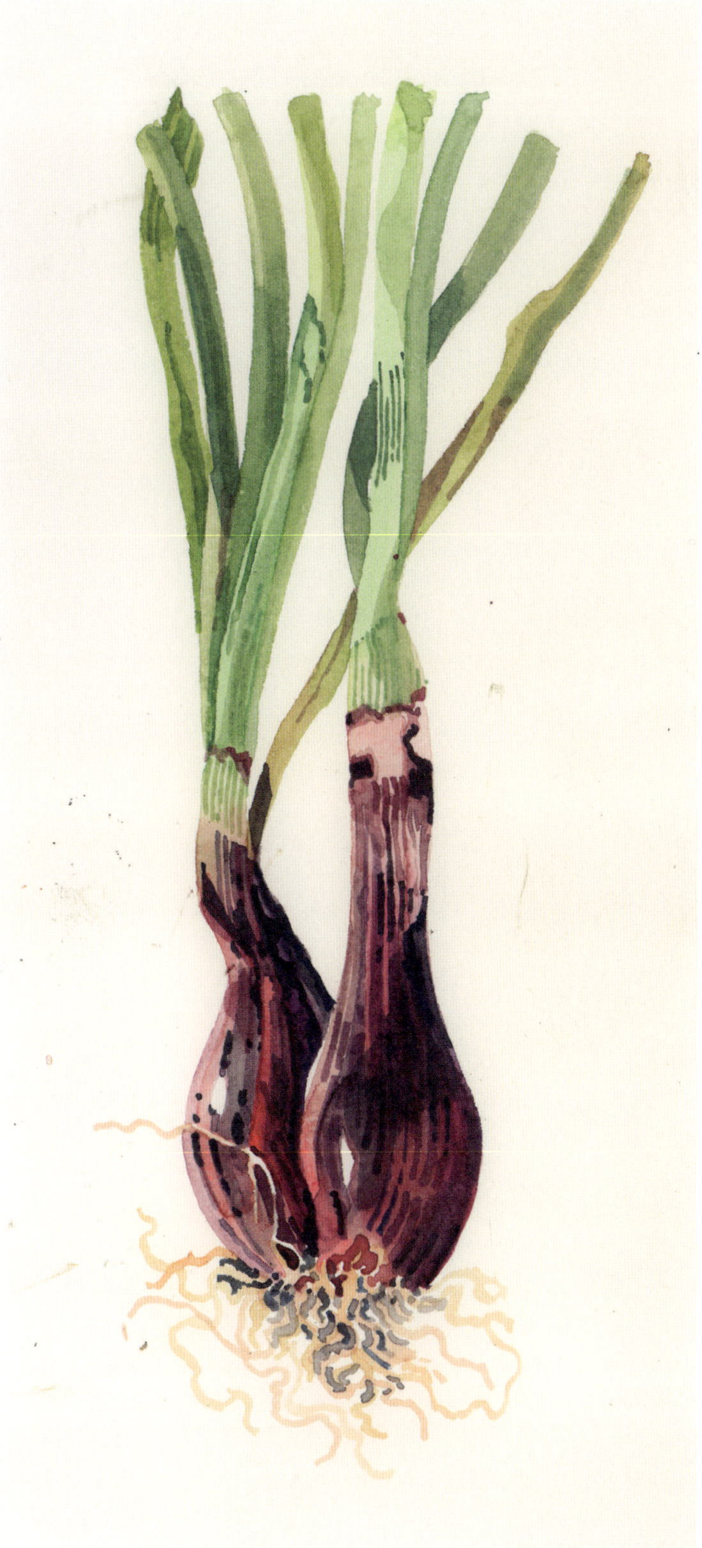

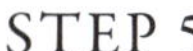

## STEP 5

Final touches involve sharpening up your detail with the tip of your brush. You could use a smaller one – I rarely do but it is quite allowed! If you do, beware the temptation to make spidery lines rather than strong, sinuous brush strokes. The small brush carries very little paint and water, which can incline the line to dry out and become fractured. These final lines, stripes and darkest washes are of their very nature the last part of a watercolour sketch as you work from pale to strong. But they are very important not only as the most visible layer but also as they hold the whole image together.

### REVIEW

This is a study, and while it doesn't really make a painting, it does serve as an achievable exercise in observation and in applying washes. You might do the same with any available vegetable as long as it has either articulation or surface pattern to fasten your gaze.

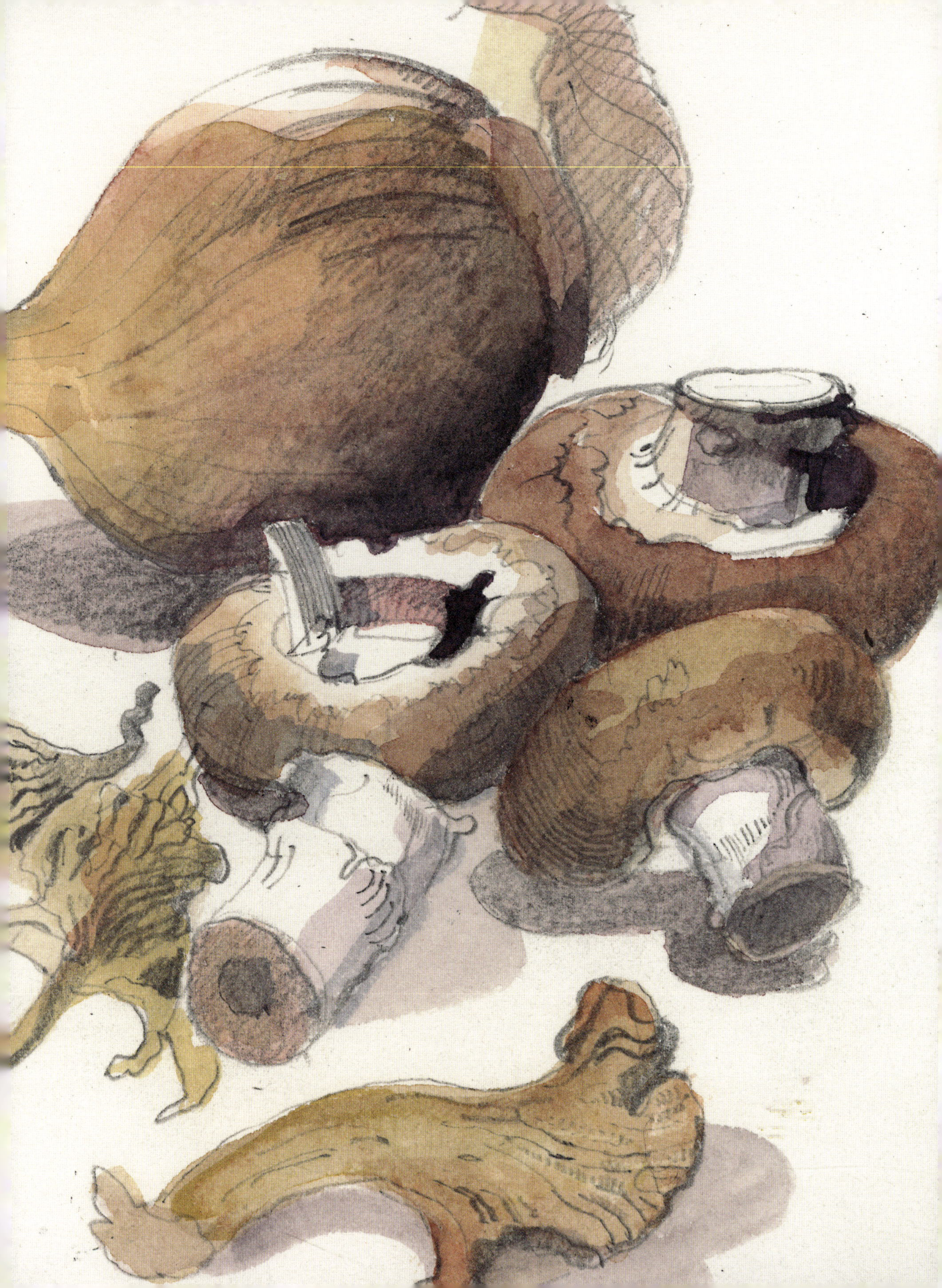

# Exercise 2

## Mushrooms

Whether found among the leaf mould or autumn grass or, more prosaically, bought in a small, brown paper bag for an exorbitant price, chanterelles and girolles are some of the best foods to be found. And they are also worth recording. When I have some, I often bulk them out a bit with delicious Paris brown or portobello mushrooms, and with the onions or shallots and garlic you will cook them with, making a nice and evocative drawing – in this instance, a soft pencil drawing, quite gently tinted in watercolour.

## FIRST LOOK

**What is most interesting about these rare treats? Perhaps the twisted deep gills, the astral-yellow stalks, or the generally otherworldly toadstool associations that all unusual fungi have, with some implied jeopardy? For me, it is the combination of form, colour and texture, recognizable but mysterious. The broken clove of garlic introduces an implied dynamic and adds some helpful pale pink to some rather autumnal browns.**

### MATERIALS

An HB pencil and rubber, our standard watercolour set (see pages 52–5), on heavy cartridge paper.

## STEP 1

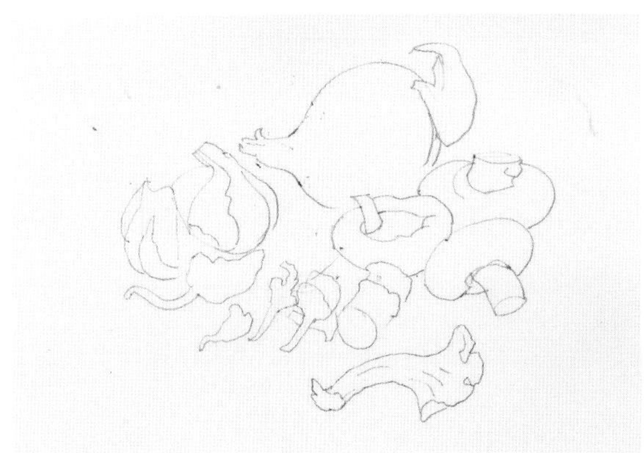

Map out your picture. This is the moment to arrange your group of fungal subjects so that they fill the paper comfortably and some interrelate. In this case, that meant separating one deeply grooved specimen and laying it along the front of the picture. Lightly and roughly sketch out the basic shapes.

## STEP 2

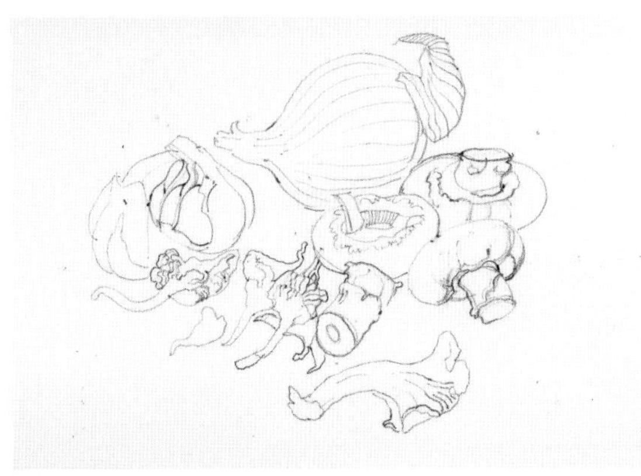

Now it is time to make a careful and sharply observed series of portraits, identifying what is nicest and most characteristic about each shape and then recording: the cup of one mushroom, the stalk of another and the curling peel of the onion.

## STEP 3

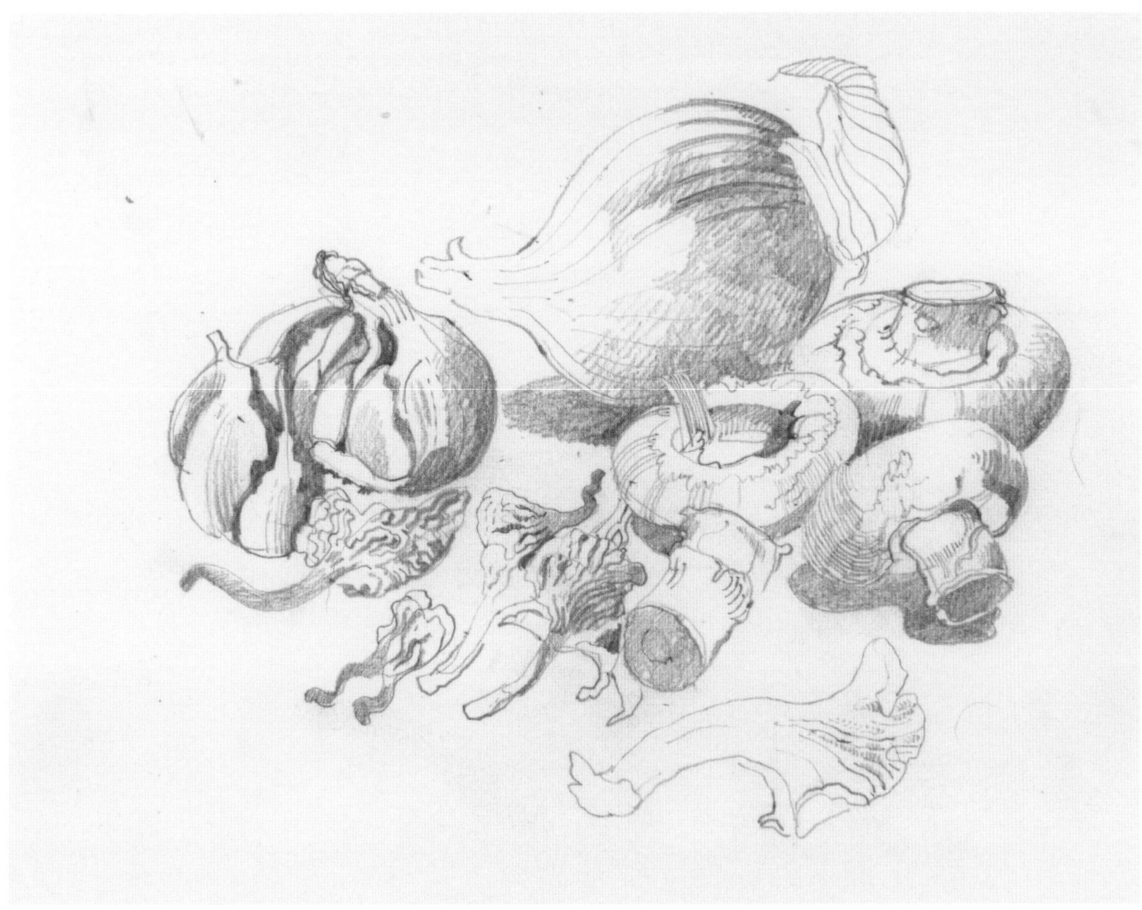

Because the watercolour is only going to be a gentle tint in what is a coloured drawing, not a painting, it is time to use some pencil shading to add form and shadow. Do this slowly with a soft pencil and get down into the dark shadows between the garlic cloves and inside the mushroom caps. Look at the stripes on the onion and the effect of shadow on its form.

## STEP 4

Add the initial washes. Use opera rose, Indian yellow, some violet and also red. Start pale and build up but make sure that the work you did in the pencil drawing remains visible through the golden washes. Beware going for dull browns and keep bright pink and yellow in your mixing even in the subtle dawn pinks and golds.

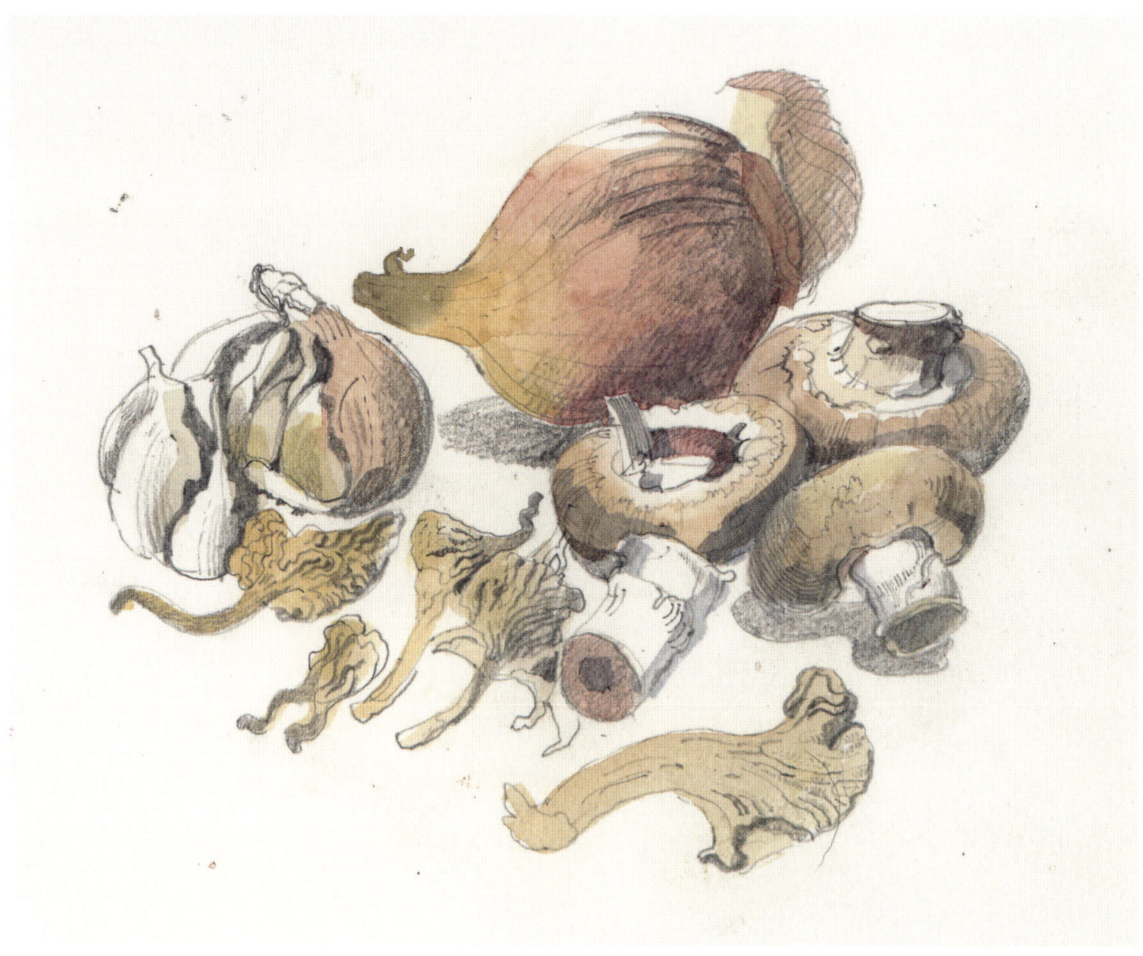

## STEP 5

Deepen and brighten your colours. Use cobalt blue, violet and black to darken your shadows. You might want to add a final phase of slightly sharper, defining pencil drawing.

## REVIEW

This is a gentle study and not a dramatic painting but is a good exercise in looking and recording without a pen.

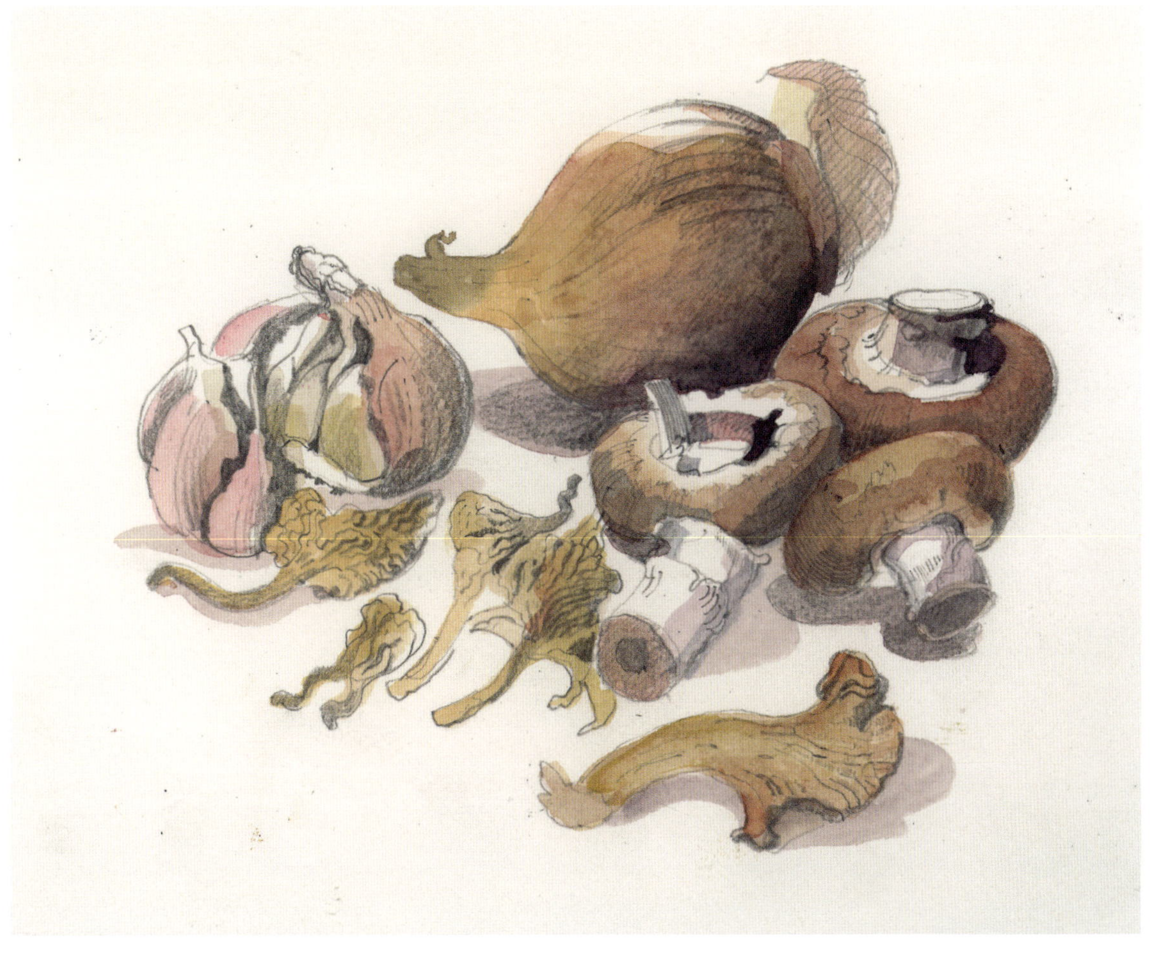

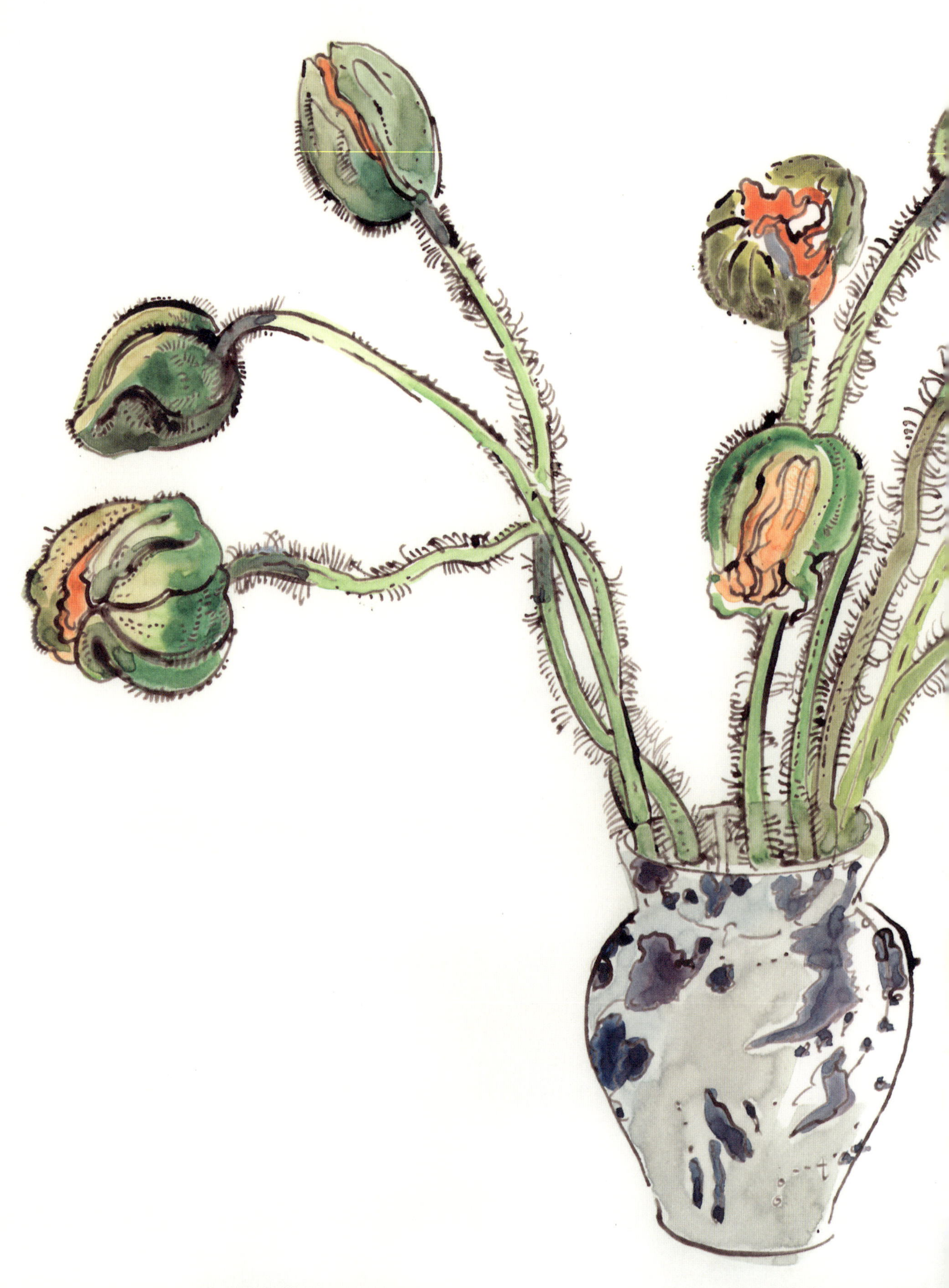

# Exercise 3

## A bunch of poppy buds

This morning, Katie brought me a bunch of unbelievably lush poppy buds. They are just beginning to open, revealing various oranges and paler tangerine petals. Their cursive, almost distorted stems are covered in fine hairs. And the buds themselves are velvety with a fine, dark fuzz of hairs – soft but sticking up, these grow more densely where the stem sticks into each bud, which pales in colour as it reaches the tip. They are in a small, blue-splashed Emma Bridgewater vase (I dug the model up in a Victorian waste heap in Oxford with our son about 15 years ago). That is the subject. The background is irrelevant, as this is just a study on a white sheet.

## FIRST LOOK

**Oriental poppies are the most unlikely flowers, with huge bulging buds supported by deceptively weedy-seeming furry stems. In this bunch, the tissue-paper petals are just revealing themselves, offering contrasting colour and textures in all areas.**

## MATERIALS

I am using a dip pen in some peat-brown drawing ink and working on heavy cartridge paper.

## STEP 1

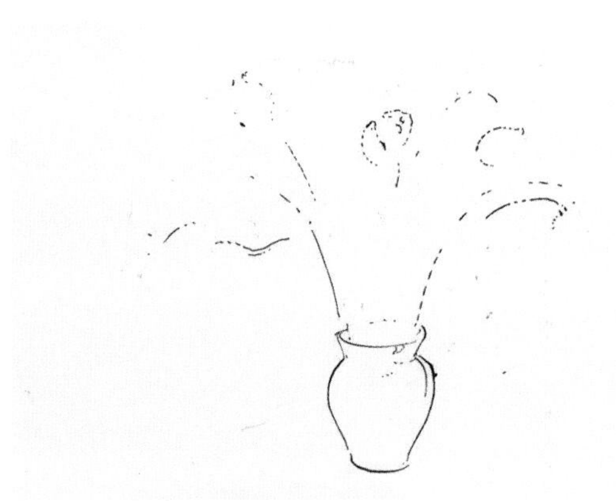

I begin by mapping out the extent of this sinuous bunch, using broken lines and short strokes to map out the shape of the flowers on their stems. I have placed the pot a little more than halfway across the sheet – if it were central, it would be undynamic and dull.

## STEP 2

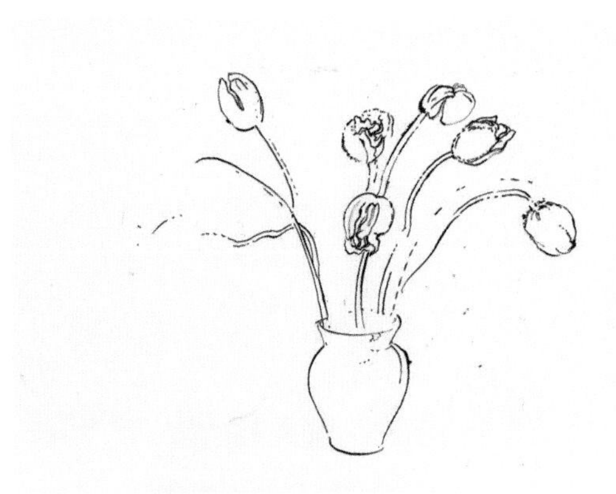

Each flower finds its place, and I am looking at the extent to which some are opening and others remaining tight shut. The lines are more defined but still more indicative. I am mapping this out in pen rather than beginning in pencil, as it is hard to lose pencil lines even with careful erasing, and it can make the lines you use appear less confident.

## STEP 3

Gosh, they are hairy! I can't delay and am now indicating this as well as some of the whorly buds. I am also trying to make sure the stems and flowers match.

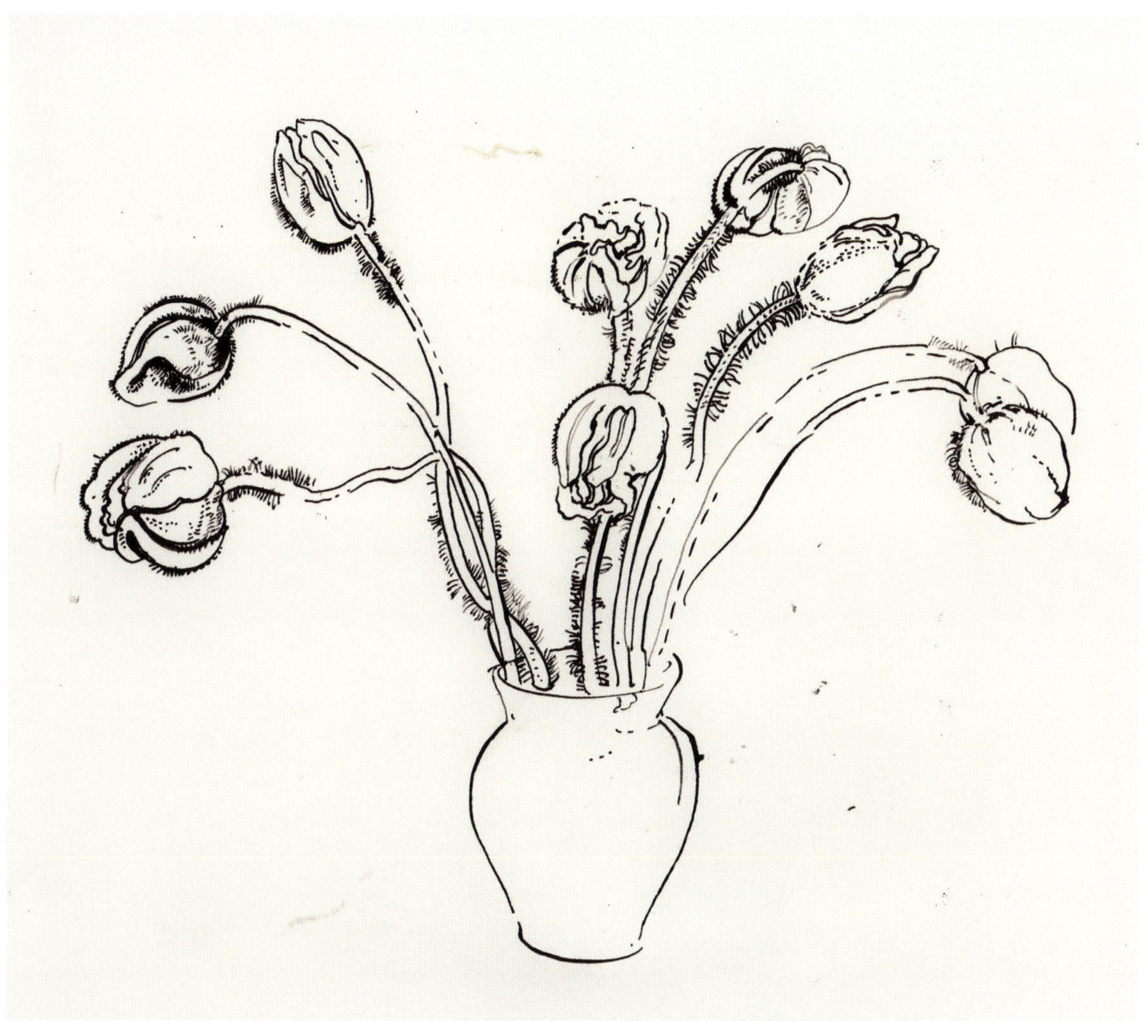

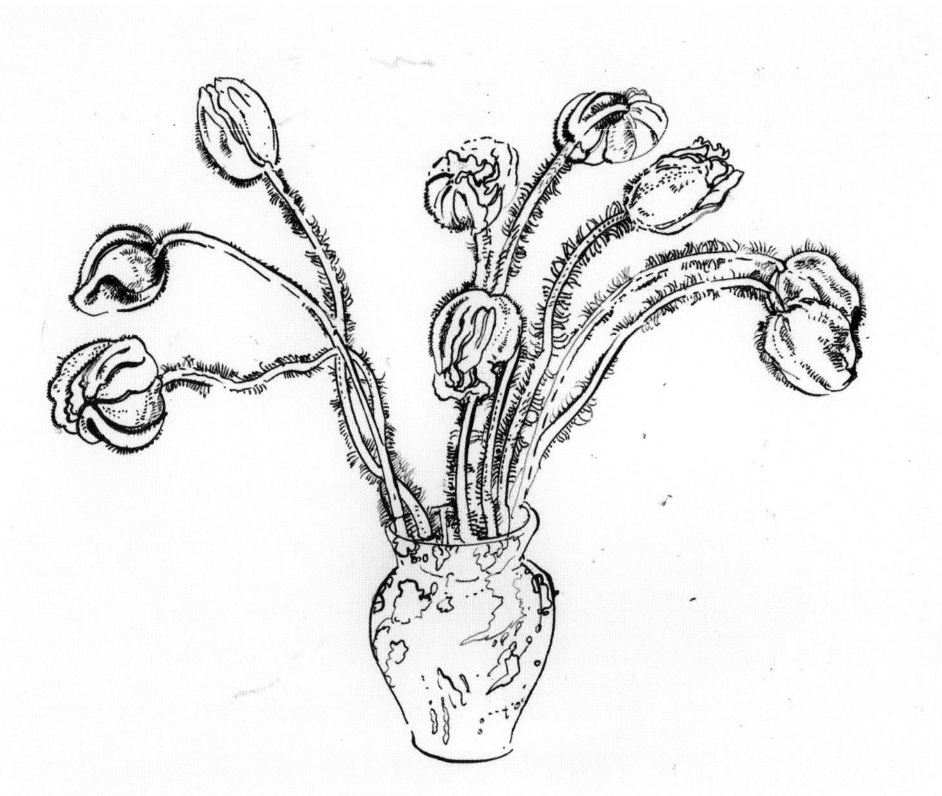

## STEP 4

Now the focus is back on the flower buds. I am adding some hairs, looking carefully at the direction they are growing in. The woolly stems are now complete. Of course, one can't draw every hair, but one can express that bit of character. I have also now picked up on the splatter pattern on the pot. I could have left that for the final stage, and tinted it in watercolour, but this is a drawing not a painting, so I continued with my pen.

## STEP 5

Almost all the information has been communicated in the ink drawing, so the watercolour is only for colouring in. I have used some dark blue, violet, red and black to mix a strong shadow, which gives the buds some three-dimensional form. The pot's fat-bellied shape is emphasized with a graduated wash implying shadow on the left. Make sure you use enough dark tone to emphasize the form of the buds. I have put some shadow where the stem meets the flower to do this as well. Make the orange of the emerging flowers as strong as you can with cadmium medium, pale pink and opera rose, for that is what is exciting about poppies, apart from their extraordinary furry buds.

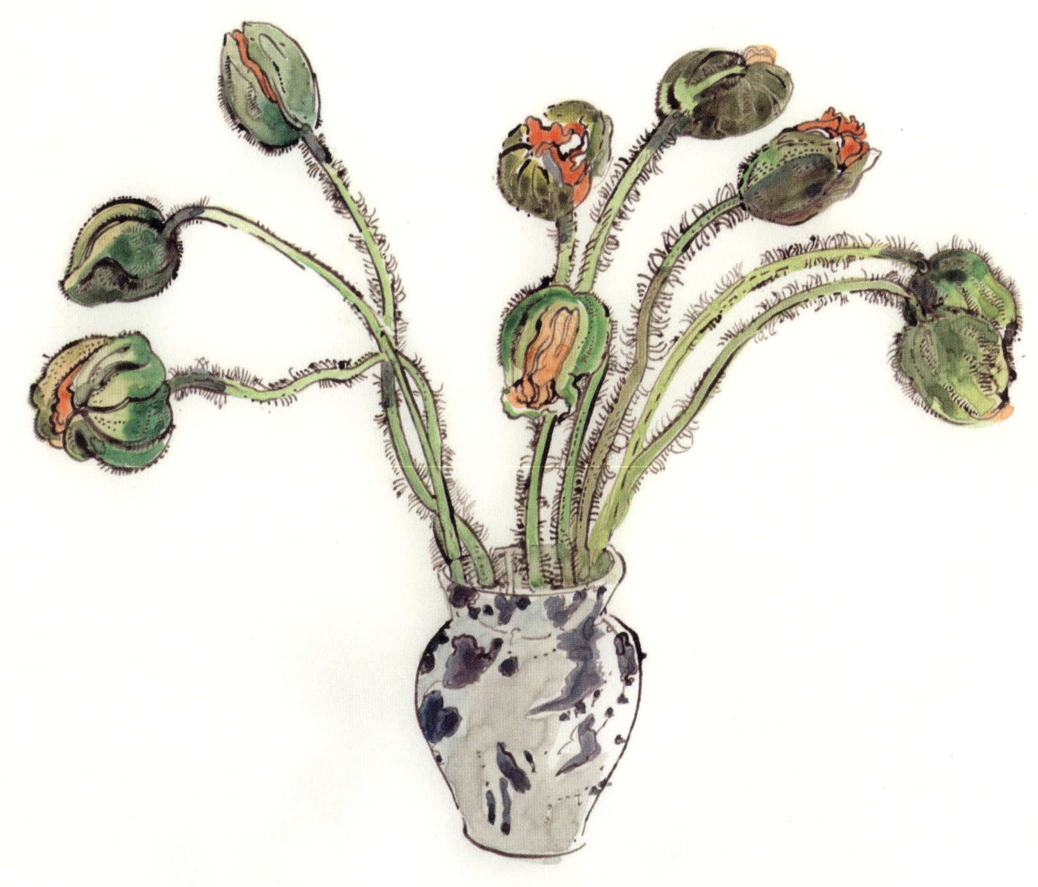

## REVIEW

That was a quick drawing, maybe half an hour's work. I think the initial analysis was important in getting this to feel, as well as look, like itself. While I have tried to be truthful, the actual positioning of the individual stems of the poppy need only be lifelike – to feel as if they are real. There could be one more or one fewer and nobody would know – an advantage of flowers over buildings. You could do this with tulips also, or any nice, flopping flower.

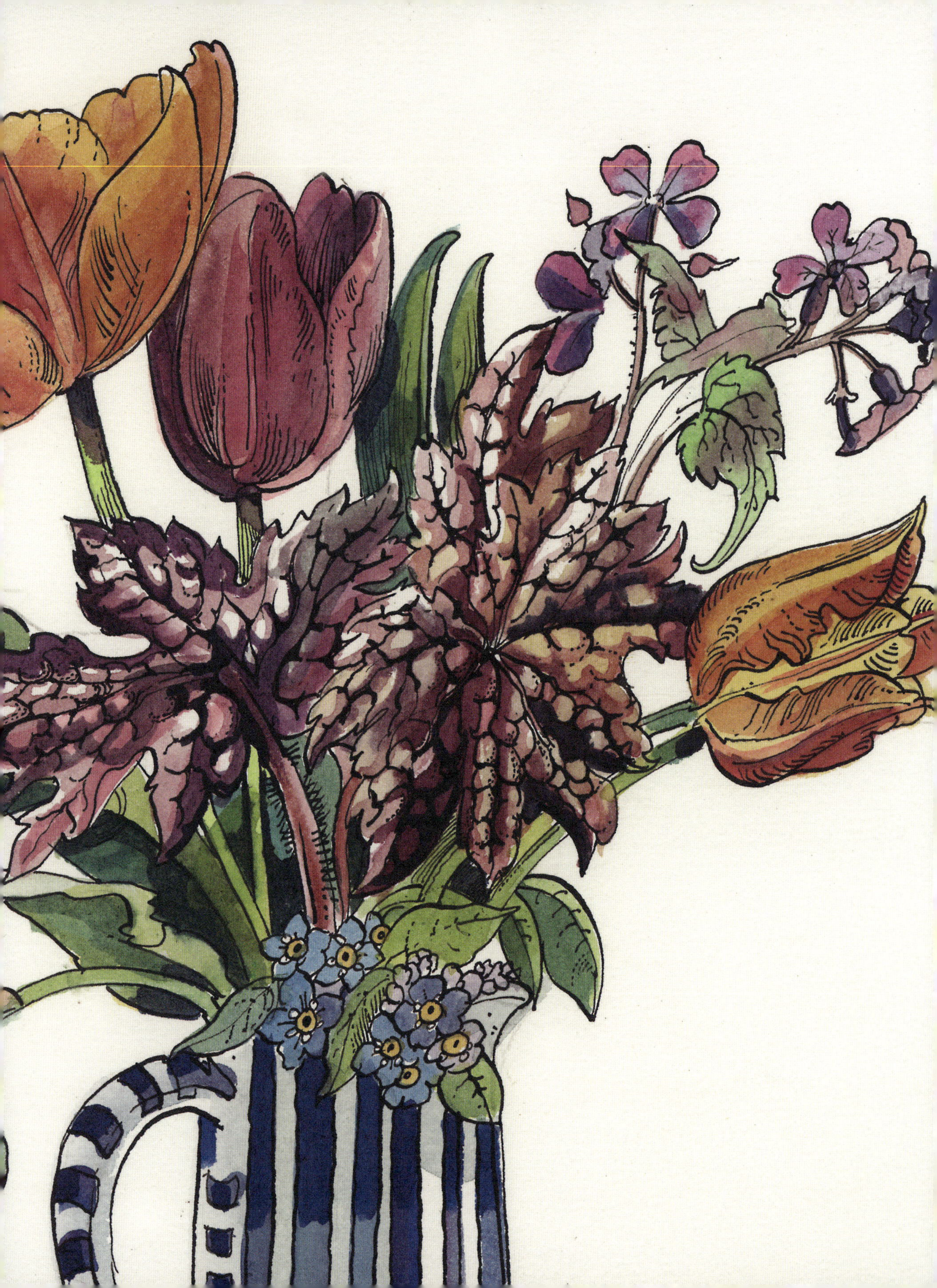

# Exercises 4 & 5

## Stripy jug of flowers

This is really two exercises in one, with one subject (the jug of flowers) but two treatments (plain watercolour, and pen and wash). You are tackling the same subject but using different techniques, both of which in different ways allow you to explore the subject. In some ways, the plain watercolour is the most immediate, unmediated and clear. Conversely, the sharp pen line forces you to make finite decisions about shape and angle which otherwise might have more flexibility.

### FIRST LOOK

**I love this jug, which was my mother's and was often the subject of her own paintings. The stripes are useful to paint, as they are exactly the kind of articulation that is worth looking for in your subjects. The selection of flowers is fairly serendipitous: it is what was in my garden. Tulips and honesty, forget-me-nots and buckler sorrel as well as a deeply serrated purple leaf that I am embarrassed to say I don't recognize, although it must have grown in my garden in May. It's important as, with its almost Savoy cabbage-like surface, it provides a contrast in texture to the silk of the tulip or tiny, jewel-like blue forget-me-nots. It is always worth really thinking what will be interesting to draw as well as what looks pretty, even in a bunch of flowers.**

# WATERCOLOUR-ONLY VERSION

**In this picture, the watercolour washes must do all the work: they must delineate the shapes, express form and record colour. Each of these initial washes uses techniques you have already come across in this book. Remember to mix carefully but also to make sure you have enough of each colour mixed before you paint (e.g. the cobalt blue for the stripes). And look really carefully at the shapes you are making. Also – and most importantly – when planning the picture, make sure you fill as much of the page as possible. Bigger is easier!**

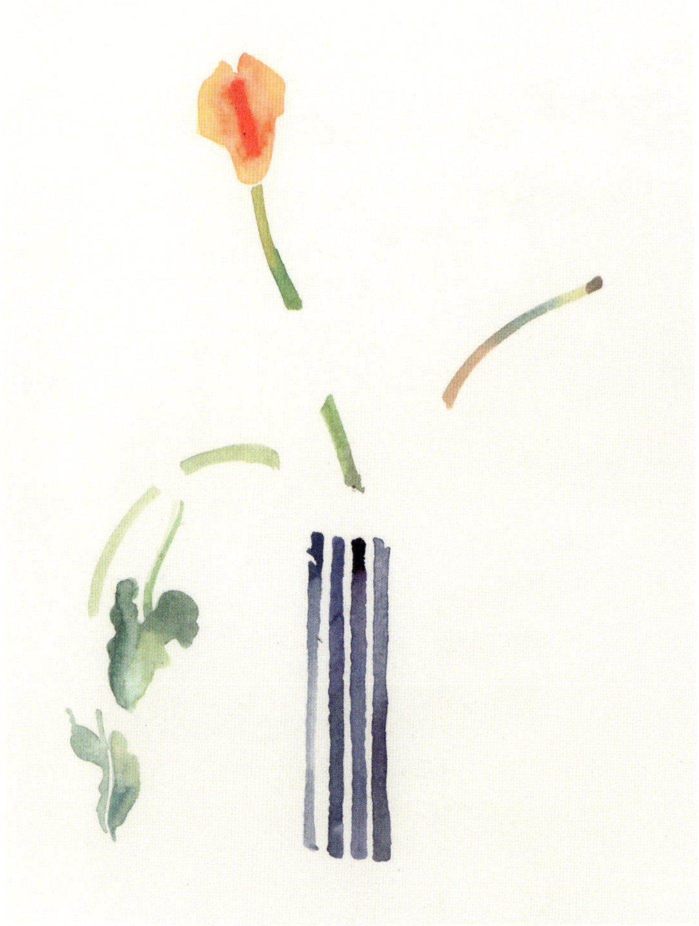

MATERIALS

Arches hot-press watercolour paper, a healthy no. 6 sable pointed brush, and your box of watercolours (see pages 52–5).

## STEP 1

Map in some of the most basic shapes in front of you, keeping your initial washes pale. I have used a mixture of cobalt blue and turquoise, and both the greens with a little yellow. Violet strengthens the stems. It is easy to build up in strength but impossible to go the other way.

## STEP 2

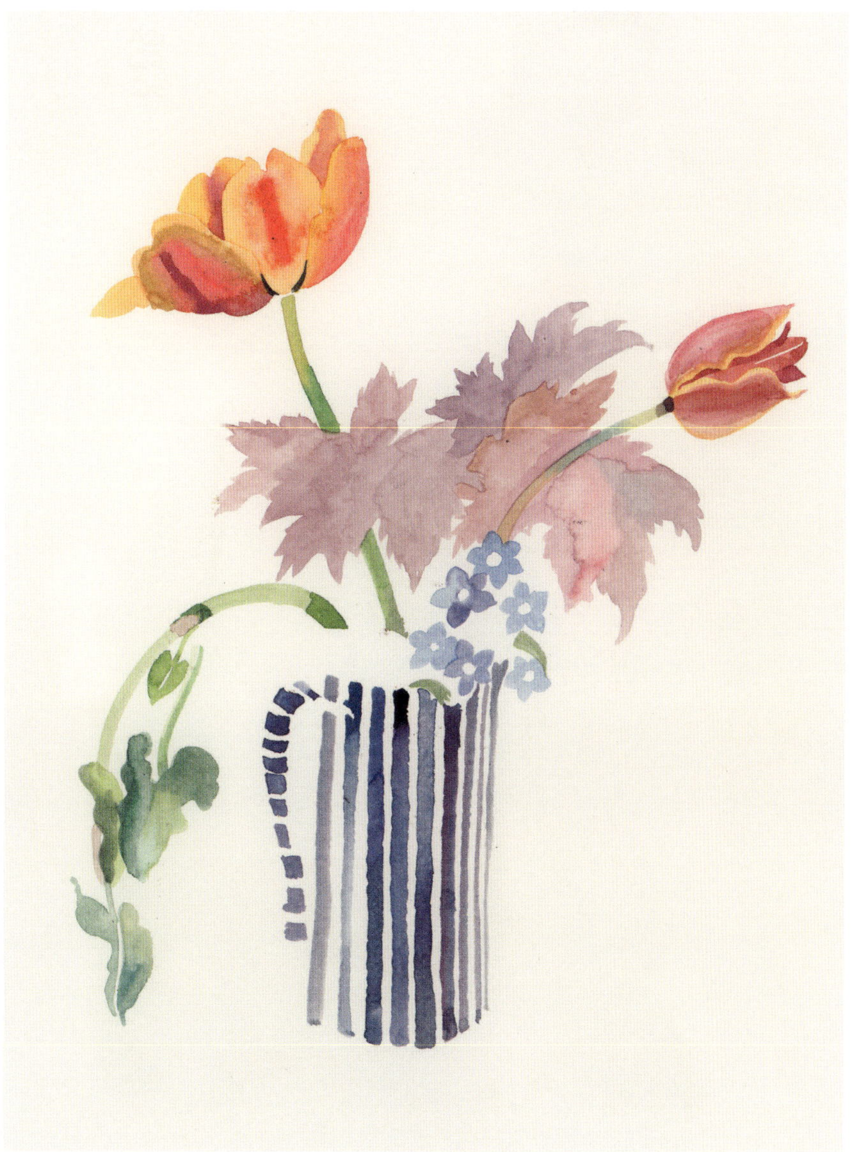

Begin to work on the petals using graduated washes. As ever, try to keep bright, clean colours. Even if they appear too bright initially, they can be dimmed. The tulips are painted with all the yellows and reds, and the forget-me-nots using turquoise and cobalt. Be careful with the white handle of the jug: the stripes are a brilliant way to show the form of the handle without resorting to a line.

## STEP 3

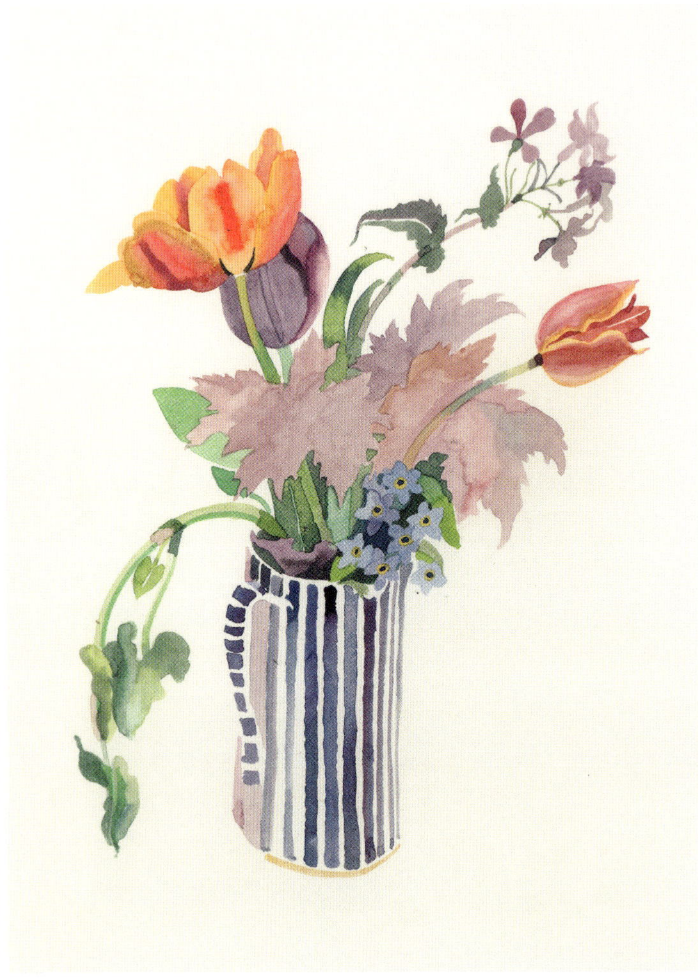

Using pale washes, begin to give some form to the jug itself. Be sure each is dry before a neighbour wash is applied. At this stage, there is *some* paint everywhere and the finished composition is clear – that is, the honesty and the deep-purple tulip have been added. The former adds a more delicate form, while the latter, with its tonal and colour contrast, throws the orange tulip into sharper focus. Begin to use darker tones – for example, a dark green to throw the forget-me-nots forward.

## STEP 4

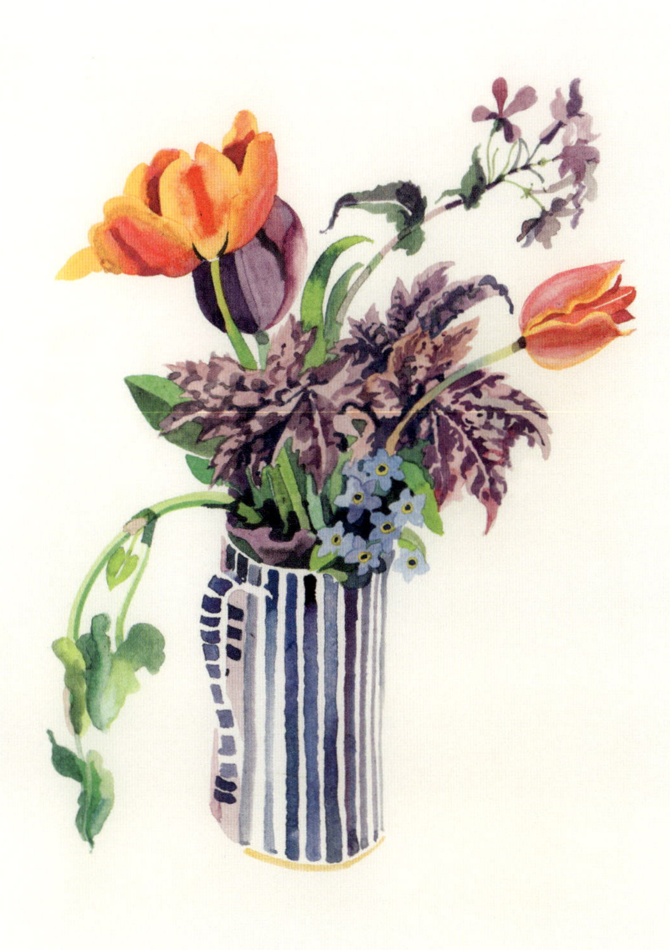

At this stage, you can begin to use stronger washes and to express more detail with your pointed brush. Also (and this does require some sharp observation), start to build up the bobbly surface of the purple leaves and the variation of tone in the honesty. Colour and a feeling of three-dimensional plastic form are established at this stage, and you can really commit to strong shadows that define the brighter areas. Work on detail like the furry stalk of the honesty and draw deeper into the purple leaves. I am a little wary of white body colour (gouache), but I have used it on those leaves and to add the tiny white dots on the forget-me-nots. Shadows are also appearing, thrown by the leaves onto the jug, all of which makes the picture feel more real.

### REVIEW

The hard thing here is not using a pencil. If you are unconfident, try to draw gently and then rub out afterwards. This is not cheating.

# PEN-AND-WASH VERSION

**On this second version of the same bunch of flowers, I am using a pen line and washes to colour in. The official name for this is, in fact, pen and wash.**

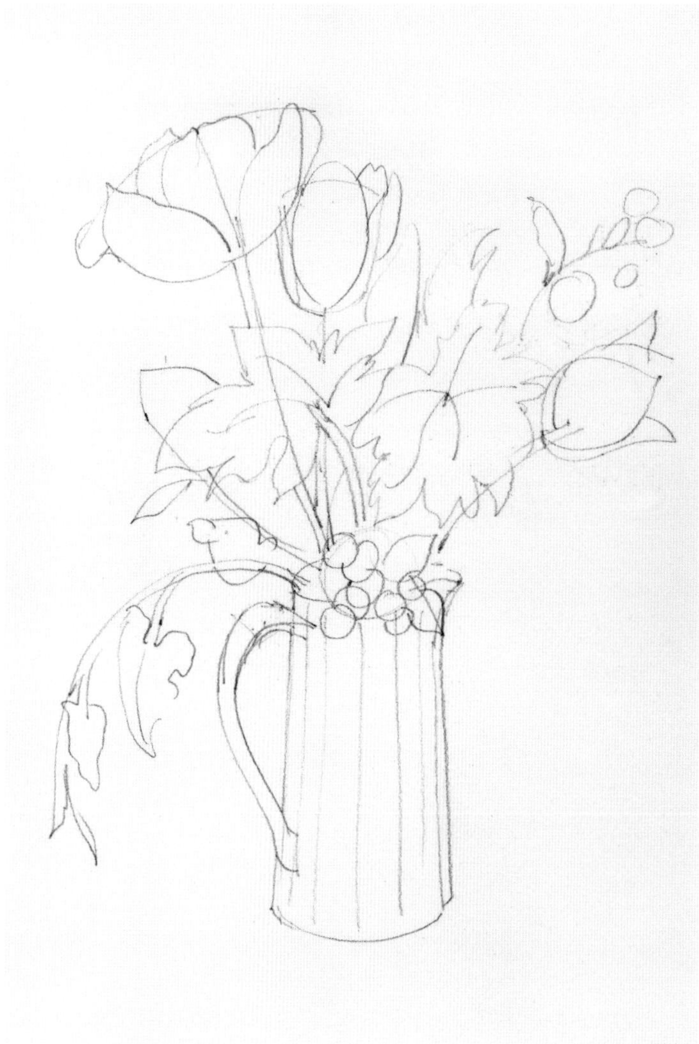

## MATERIALS

You will discover which nibs and ink you most enjoy. I am very keen on Rohrers Antiktusche Bister and a long, brass drawing nib, but the variations are endless. Make sure you use a shellac-based ink that will not run when you overpaint with watercolour.

## STEP 1

I have begun by mapping out the composition in pale pencil. This is not essential (and actually I quite like starting just with ink), but a gentle pencil sketch is quite reassuring. Use it to work out the composition and remember to fill the page.

## STEP 2

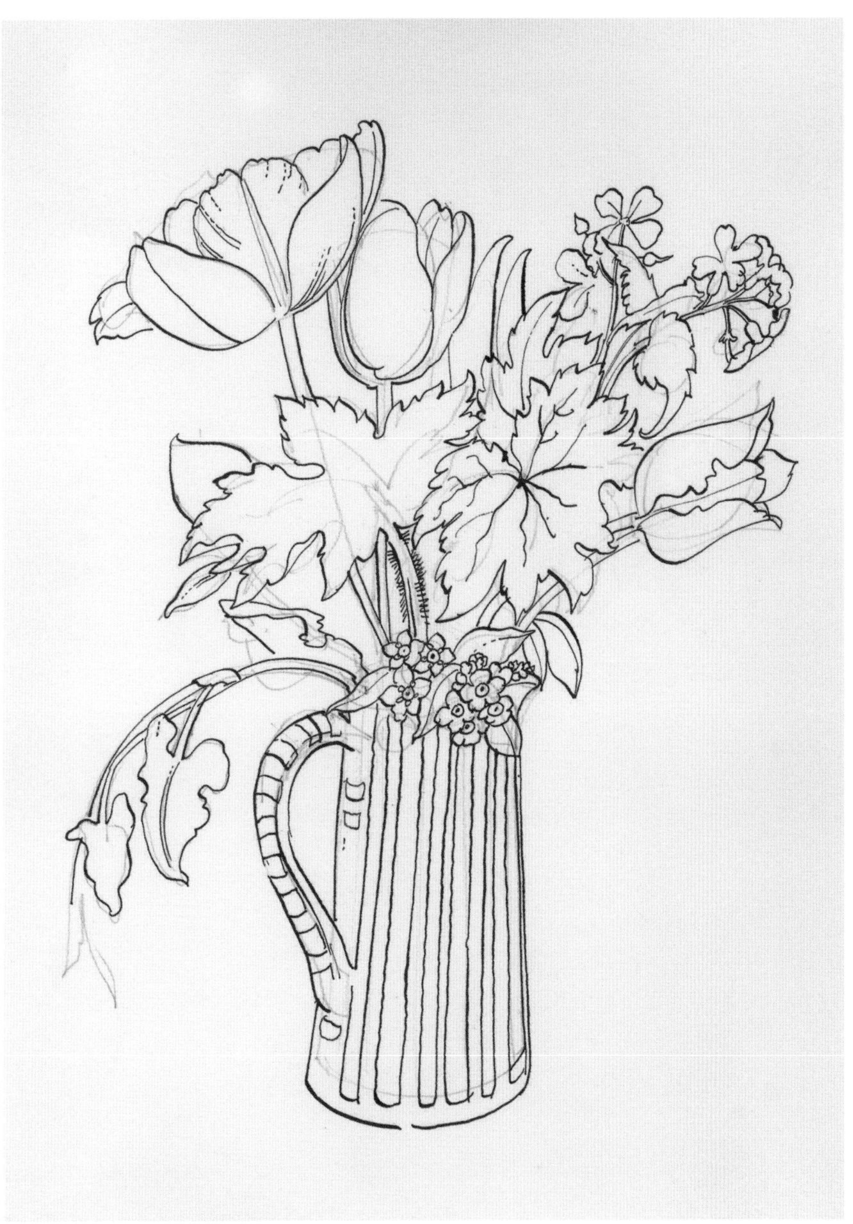

The initial pen line is outline only and is what will define the picture, so be confident but *slow*. Don't worry if you make the odd blot. Rather, just concentrate on drawing nice, cursive lines. And all the time look at the flowers and think what each line is going to tell you. Don't rush and remember not to add detail yet.

## STEP 3

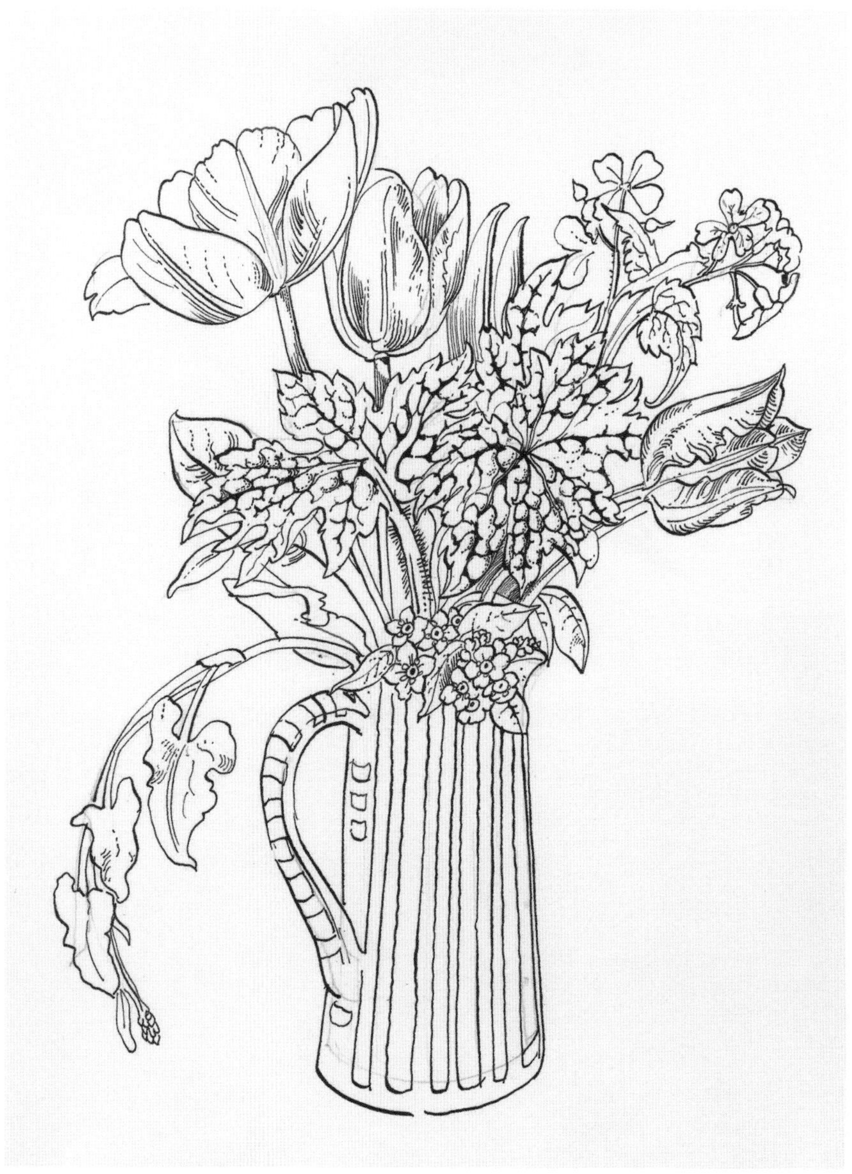

Carefully observing, add some interior detail to your drawing. In my drawing, this is the veins in the tulips and the coruscations on the surface of the leaves. This is the hardest stage in this exercise – as you work out the direction of each line and also try to decide *what to leave out*. Again, take it slowly and keep looking carefully.

## STEP 4

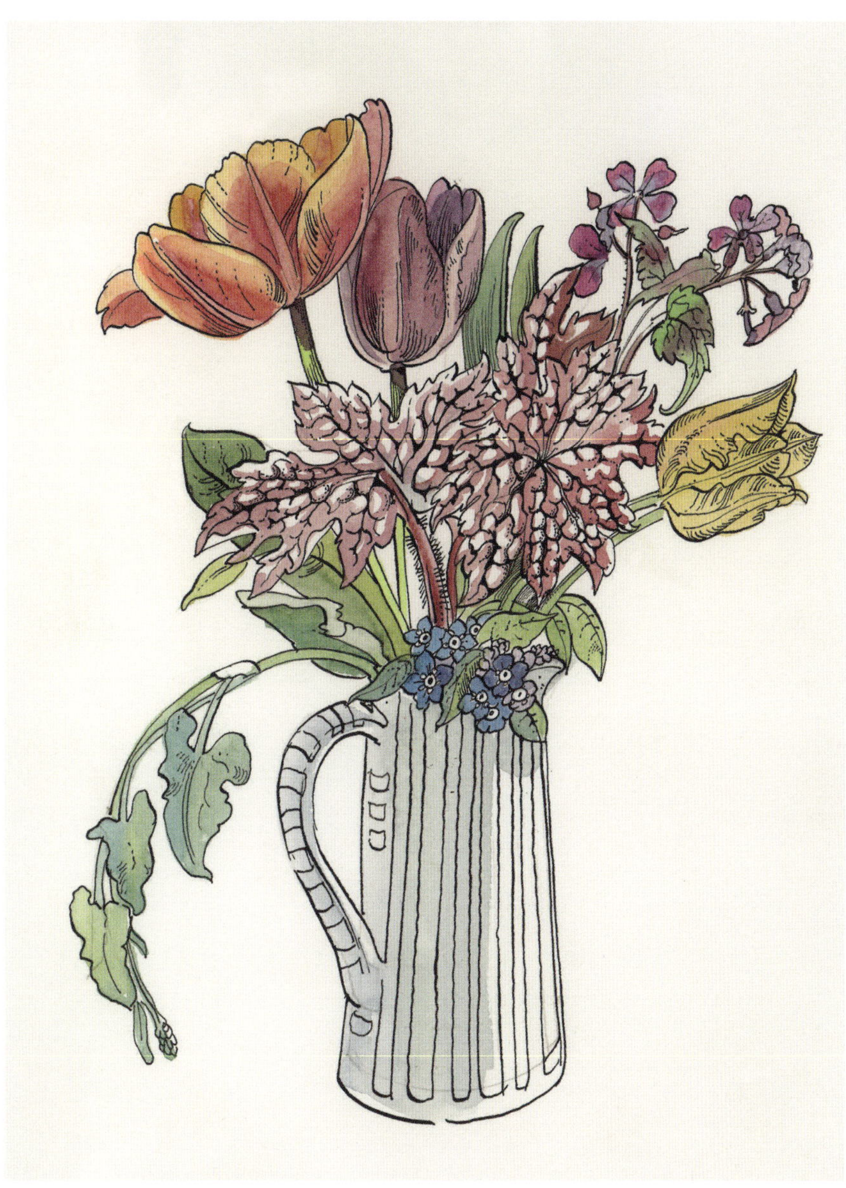

Now, begin to paint. Start with bold, simple washes that show the cylindrical form of the jug and the colour variation of the flowers. You can use the same colours as mentioned in the previous exercise without lines. I have left out the areas of the purple leaves that catch the light. Remember you can always make an area darker, but it is hard to go the other way, so have no fear if this stage feels a little insipid.

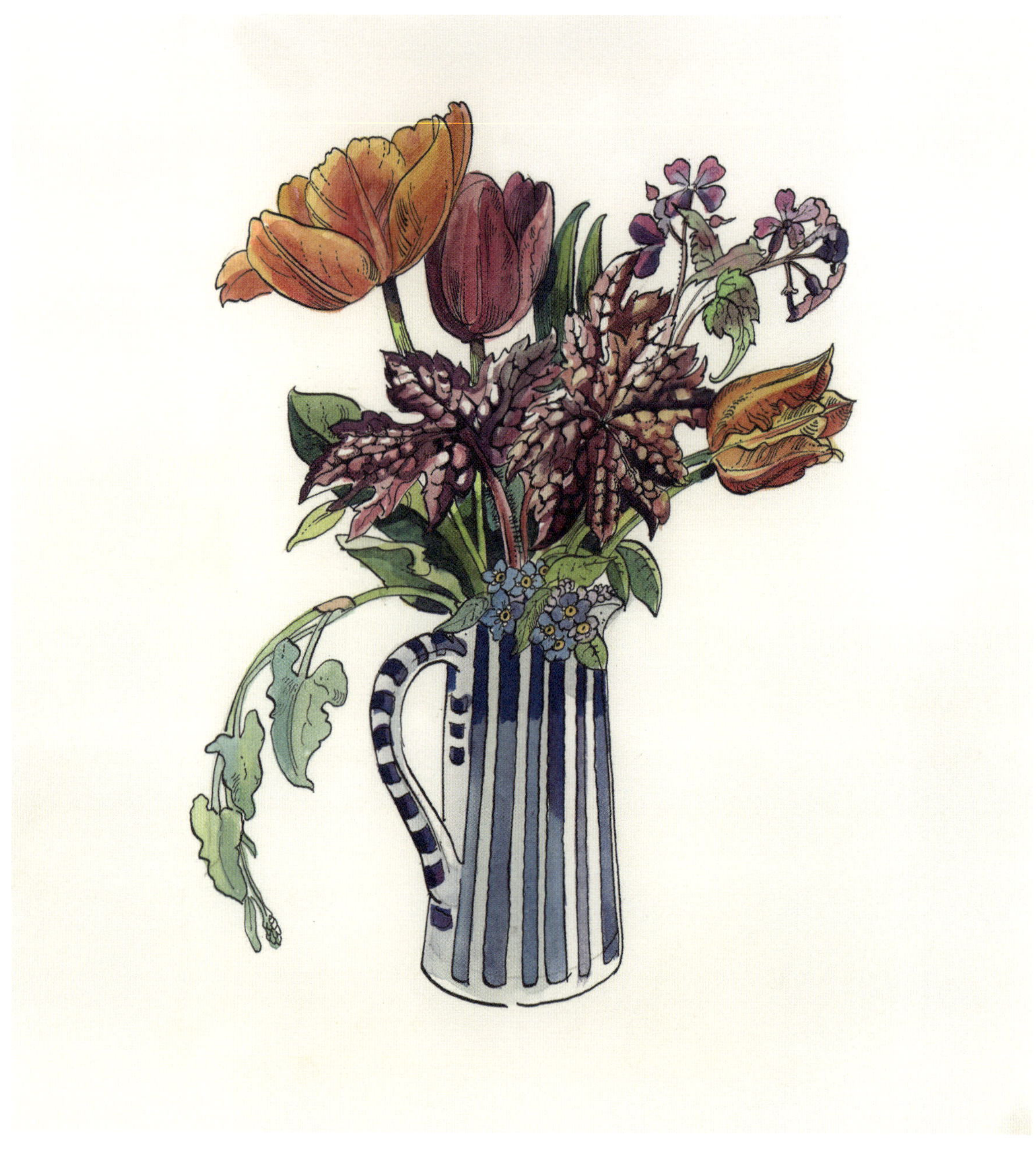

## STEP 5

The secondary painting stage records more detail: the glazed stripes of the jug and the darker tones in the foliage. Use dark green for the leaves in the centre of the bunch to throw forward the paler stalks and to give greater prominence to the bright-eyed forget-me-nots. Further washes of purple and bronze express the form of the tulips and honesty.

## REVIEW

The final painting is bold and bright. While the colour might initially dominate, it is the line that does the heavy work, and the washes are only a way to *tint* the drawing. If you compare this to the previous watercolour-only version, you will see how much less colour is needed when you have the line to fall back on. It is bolder and more illustrative than the watercolour only, but maybe not as elegiac and evocative. They are both good ways to work, and it's interesting to see how differently the same subject might be portrayed.

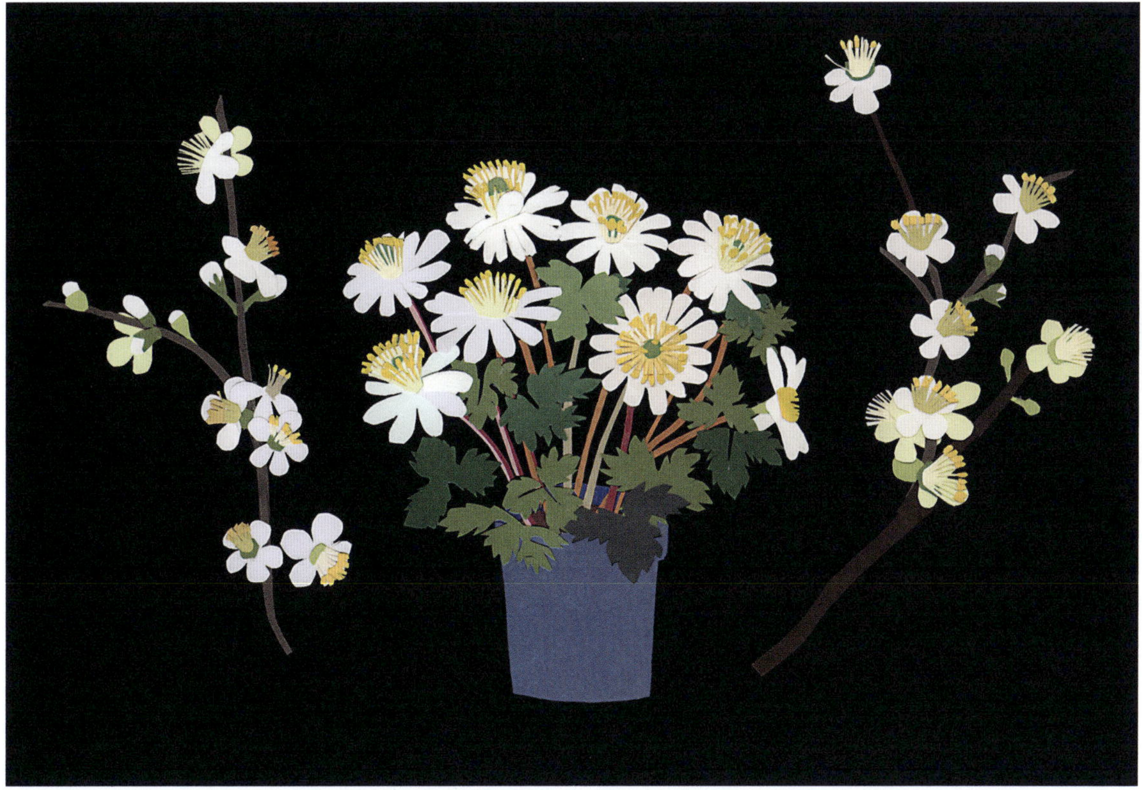

Here is one of my mother's works showing a very similar scene, drawn with neither brush nor pen but with cut paper. She used small nail scissors and paper glue to build up many layers of coloured paper to get surprisingly detailed effects.

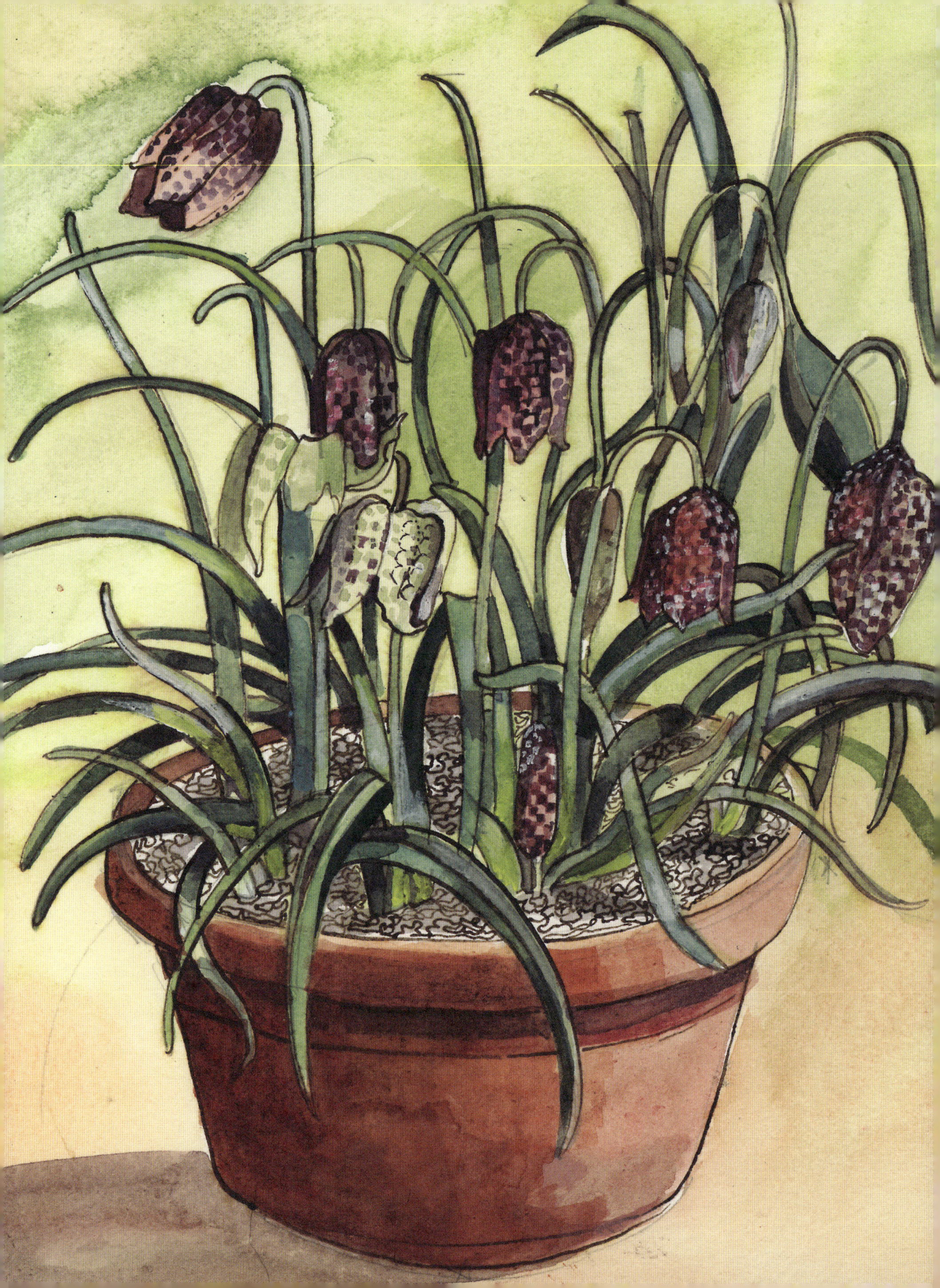

# Exercise 6

## Fritillaries

There are all sorts of definitions of utter luxury. For some, it is a new Aston Martin or a week on a superyacht; for others, the greatest wine or whisky or even a box at the ballet. But, for me, you would need to work very hard to better a low alpine pot stuffed with fritillaries, those *Alice in Wonderland*, flower-fairy lilies that grow wild in a few very well-guarded meadows in the Thames Valley and languish in so many gardens all over. Emerging in early spring through a crisp crust of horticultural grit, they break out into chequered bonnet flowers that are so unlikely they seem artificial. And yet they are real and natural, flowering each year, and here is a pot that I was lucky enough to bring in from the greenhouse to paint. This project is complicated, and I have put in a *lot* of steps, one set for drawing and another for painting, but it is an exercise to be tackled all in one go.

## FIRST LOOK

**There is so much to paint and draw and look at here, but perhaps the greatest challenge is what to leave *out*. The aim is to give a feeling of generosity, a thicket of these perfect flowers, without it seeming a mess.**

## MATERIALS

Arches hot-press watercolour paper, a dip pen and shellac-based ink, and your watercolour box (see pages 52–5).

## STEP 1

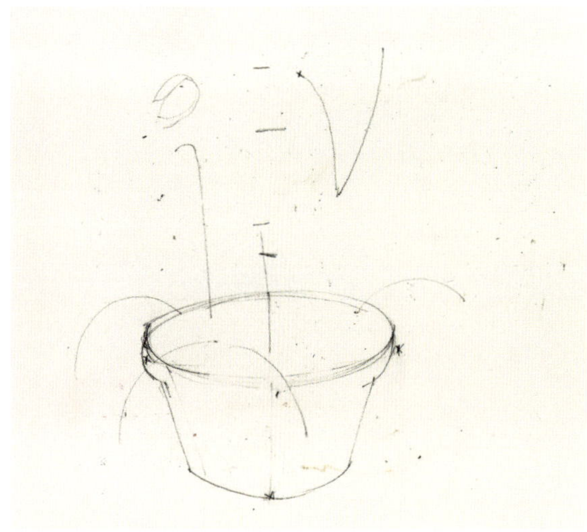

Start with a light pencil drawing and work out the shape of your picture. Be careful with getting the *ellipse* of the pot as correct as possible. You can cheat it with the plants but not the pot! Make sure that you fill the page.

## STEP 2

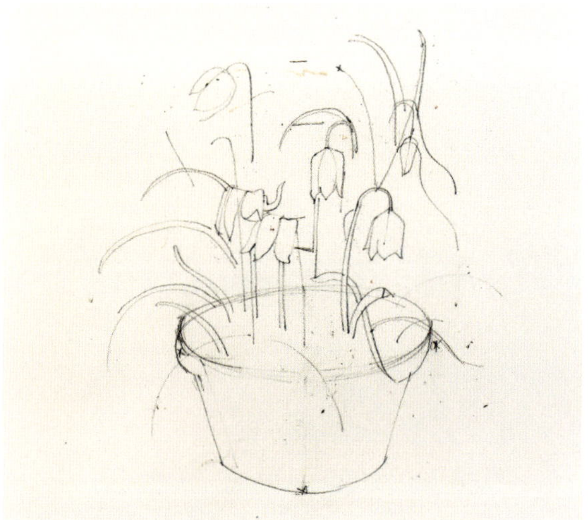

Now map out the individual fritillaries. Again, this is really an exercise in what you must *leave out*, while still keeping the glorious abundance of the subject. Don't draw in the pattern, as it will be better done with watercolour at a later stage.

## STEP 3

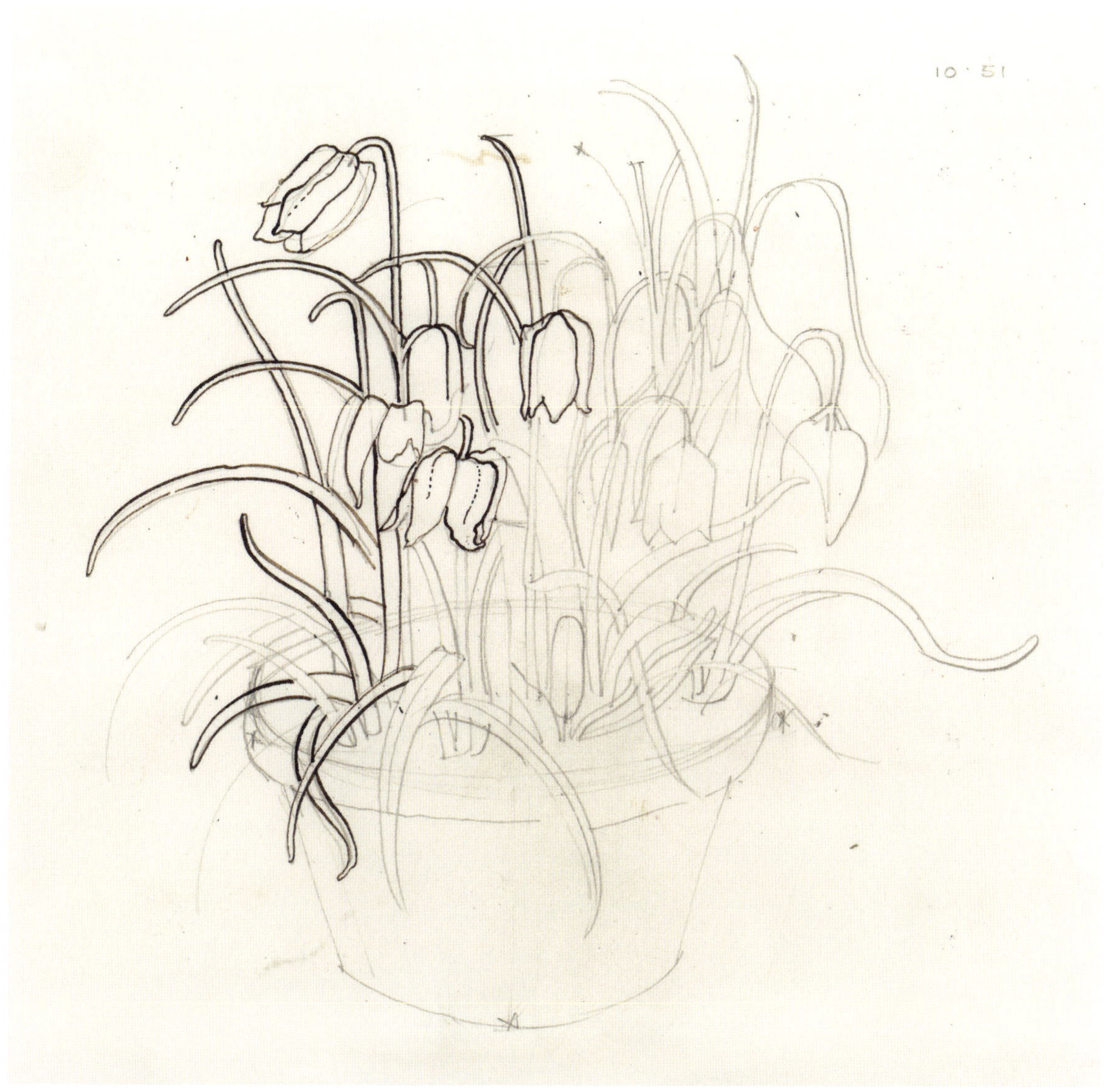


With the rough pencil drawing complete, you can begin the ink drawing. I have done this drawing with a Rotring Tikky fibre-tip pen, which is quite a nice, responsive tool. I do literally start top left and move to bottom right. Look really carefully at all the shapes, each stalk and petal. They are all specific, and each line should be telling and should evoke the particular character of the plant.

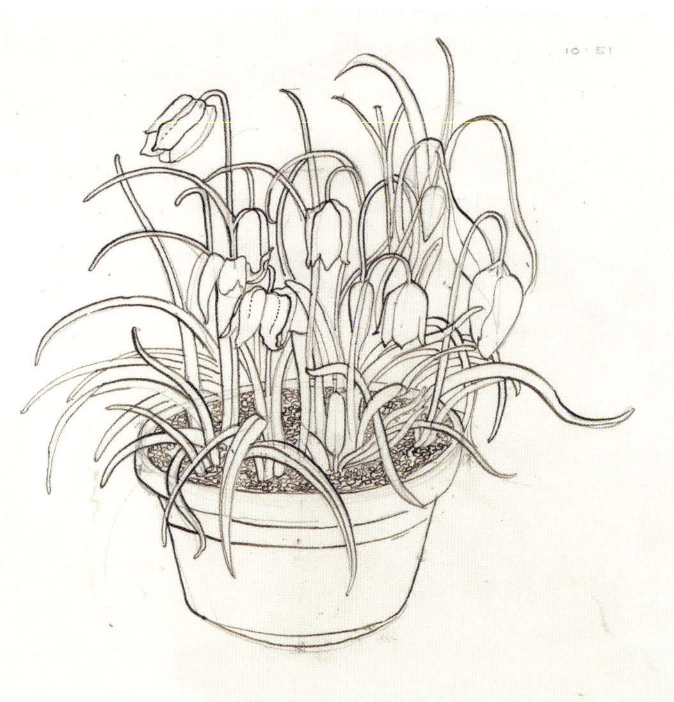

## STEP 4

Keep filling in the drawing, making sure you are leaving the flowers and indeed the leaves blank to take the subsequent painting. Be economical with your drawing and make each line worthwhile and well observed (no scribbling!), so take it slowly. There is no rush.

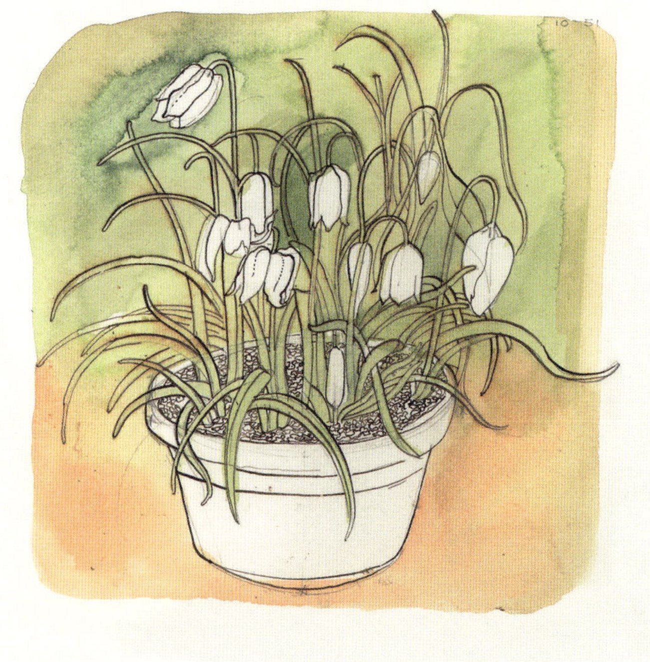

## STEP 5

Next, with a square-ended brush, paint a coloured background using a simple pale wash that grades from green to brown, and perhaps very slightly indicating a table and wall. Paint round the pot and flowers, as this will in due course help keep the focus of the picture on the important things. I have also given the leaves the same light-green initial wash while I'm at it.

## STEP 6

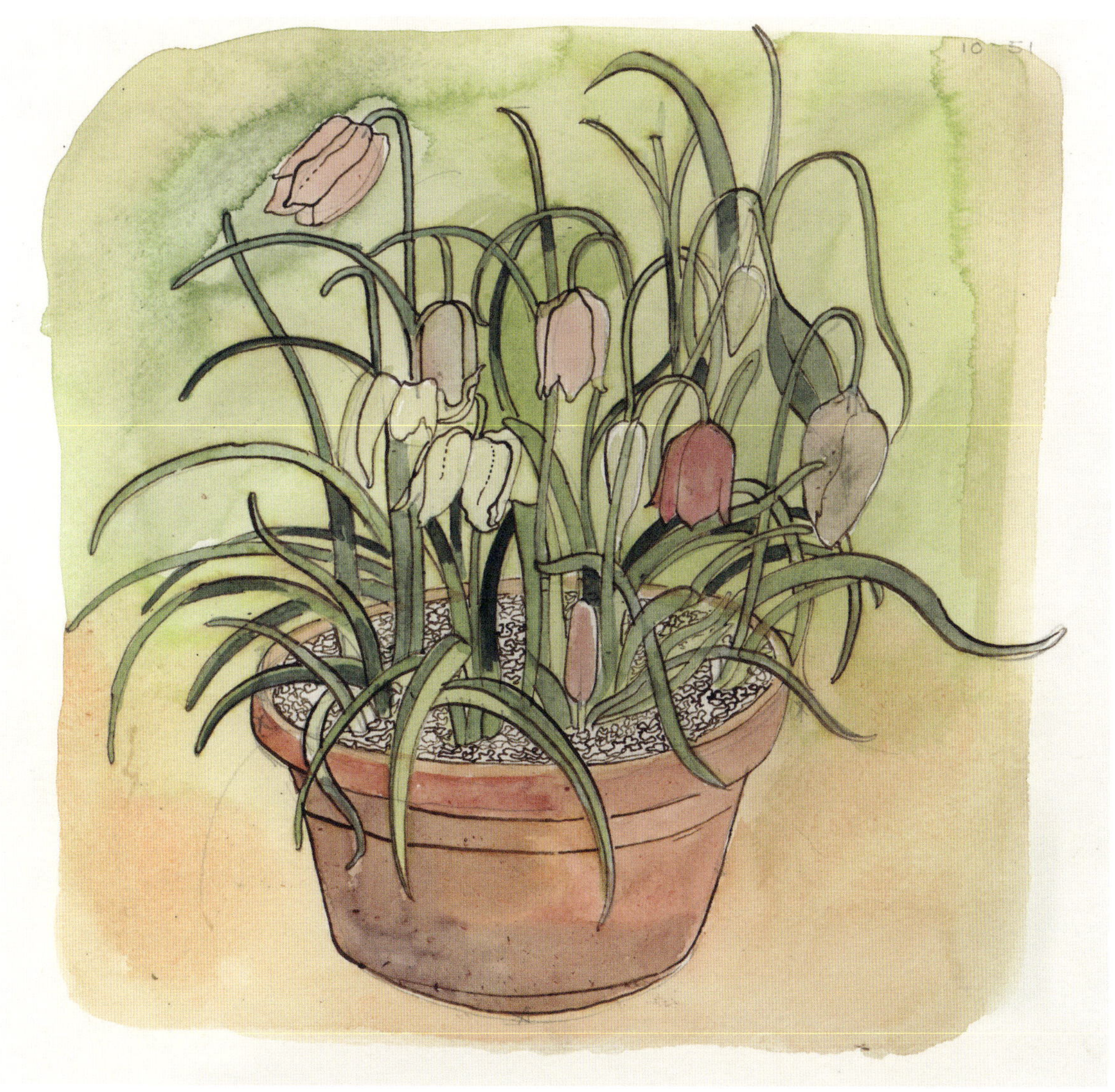

Before embarking on the next step, make sure the wash is super dry. Take a break and make some tea. A cake even! Then, with a pointed no. 6 brush, begin to fill in the drawing. Mix your colours carefully on a separate sheet so that you are sure of what you are painting onto your picture. Look at the variation of tone in the greens (it's all in front of you). Leave off the chequered pattern for a bit longer and concentrate on getting the colours right.

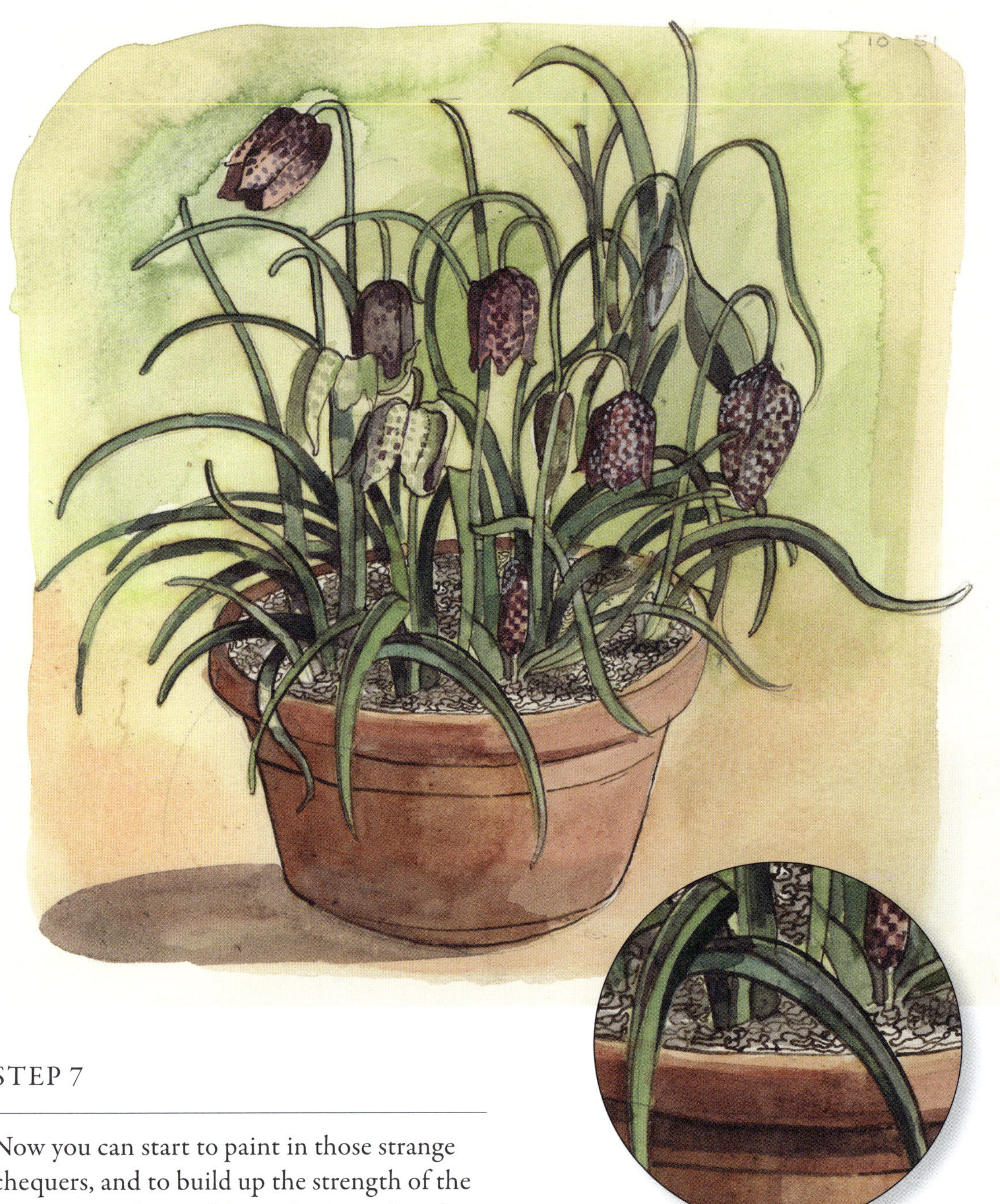

## STEP 7

Now you can start to paint in those strange chequers, and to build up the strength of the greens in the leaves. I have also introduced a strong shadow, which makes the pot sit more solidly on its washy background. It is now more in its own space.

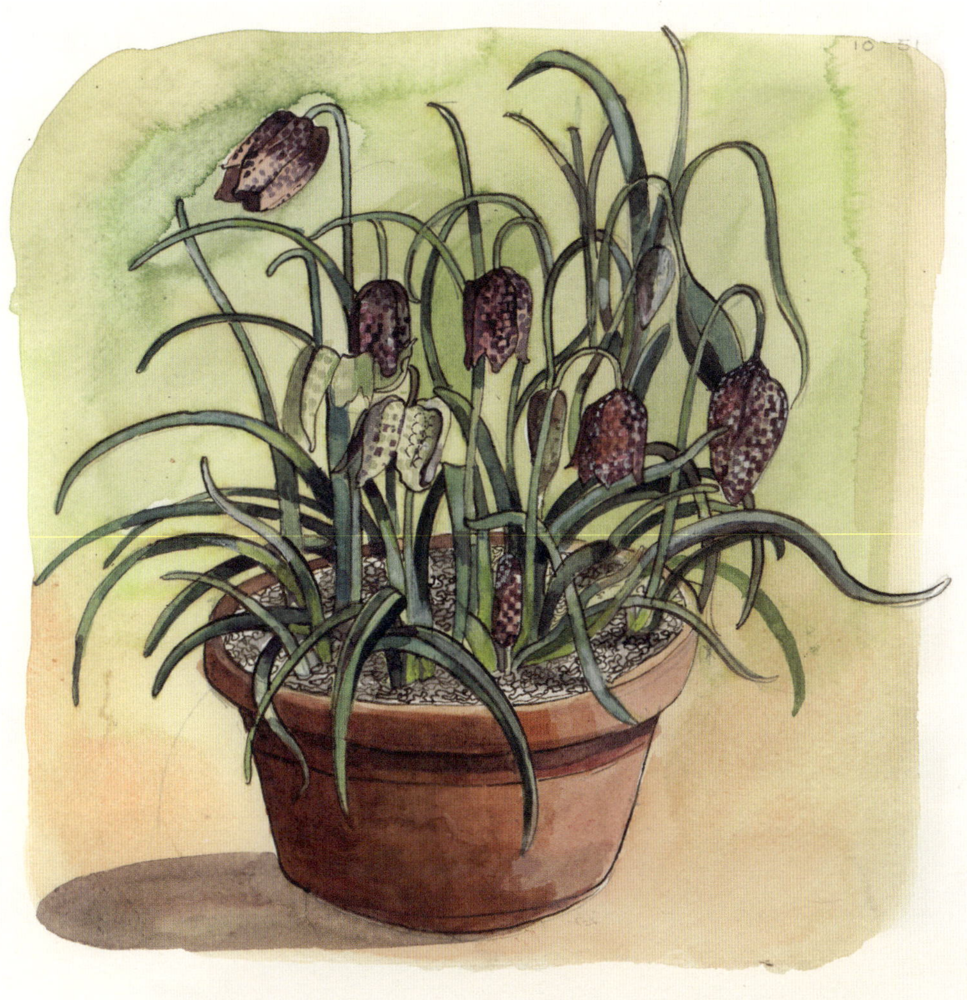

## STEP 8

This final stage has just had some final tightening. The pot itself is now a brighter terracotta, which makes the picture jollier, and some of the darker leaves are stronger, as is the shadow.

## REVIEW

This is a really interesting subject and also (if you look hard) relatively easy to do, especially when using this pen-and-wash technique. It would perhaps have been brighter on a white background, but there is something nice and muted about the colour of it like this.

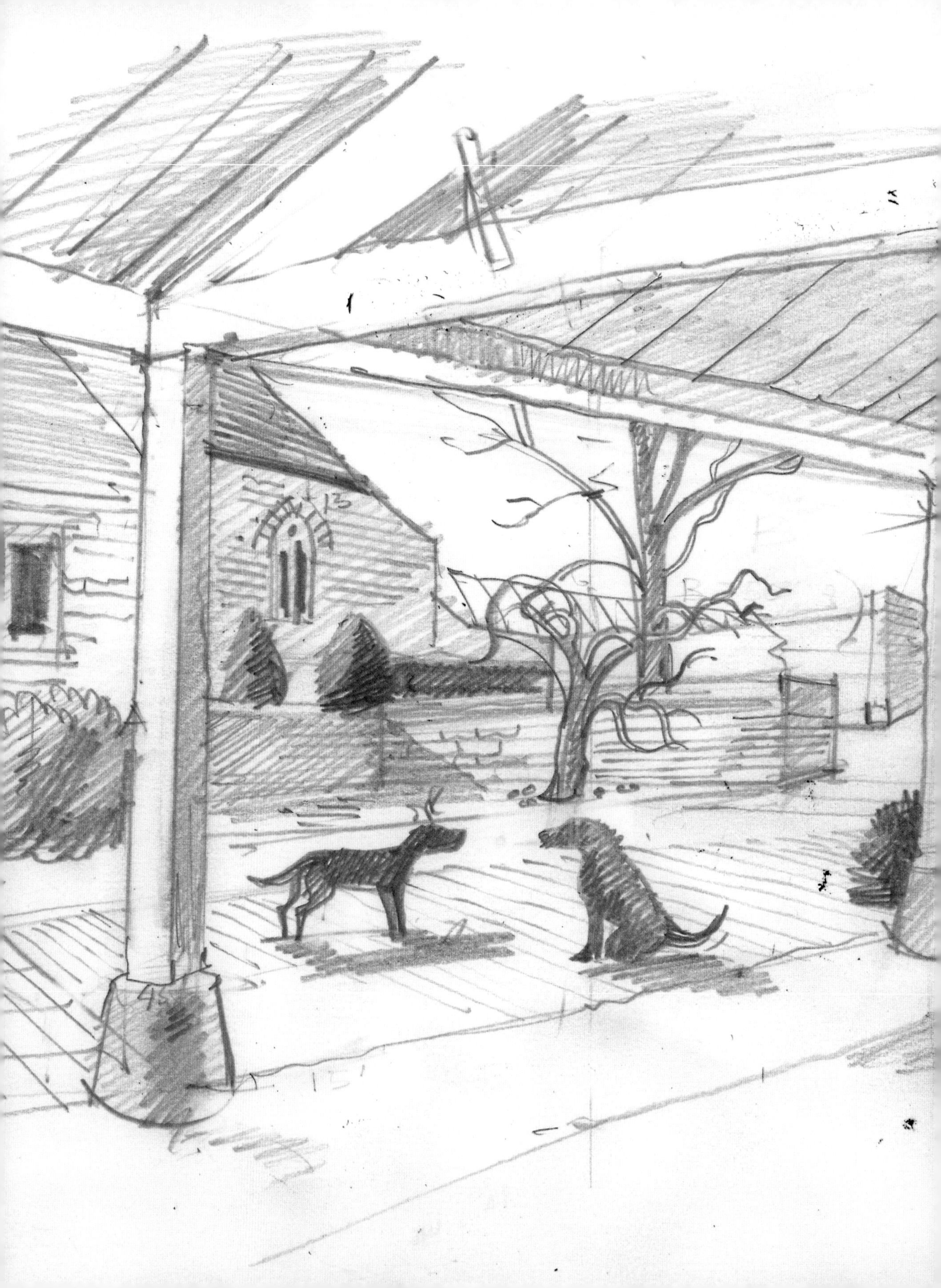

# Exercises 7 & 8

## Measuring & perspective

Measuring is really the very essence of drawing. Analyzing the proportions of your subject is how you will understand it and that will make the drawing lucid and believable. It is what makes a drawing 'grown up' and what makes it seem real.

The easiest way to ascertain both proportion and the angles of lines is to hold up a pencil between thumb and forefinger and use your thumbnail to measure the extent of any line. Keeping your arm at the same distance from your eye, move the pencil to another line and compare it to your calibrated length. In this way, you will work out the relative proportions of your lines and thus your drawing will be correct. A good trick is to imagine you are holding your pencil against a sheet of glass and move it around on that one plane – this will keep your measuring accurate.

# VIEW FROM THE DOOR

**This view from my studio door has lots of straight lines at interesting angles, which is useful for this kind of exercise. You could choose any view that you know very well for this first attempt at introducing measuring and perspective.**

## FIRST LOOK

**Have a good look at your view and work out what you are going to draw. Think about how much you will include: What is interesting? What elements do you think are important? Don't rush this bit!**

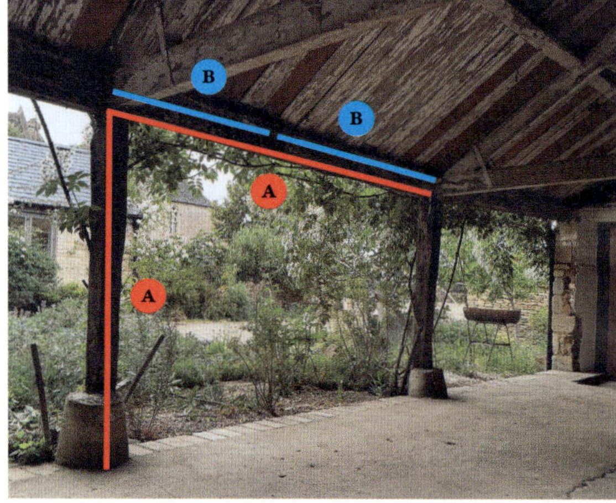


## MATERIALS

A pencil and paper.

## STEP 1

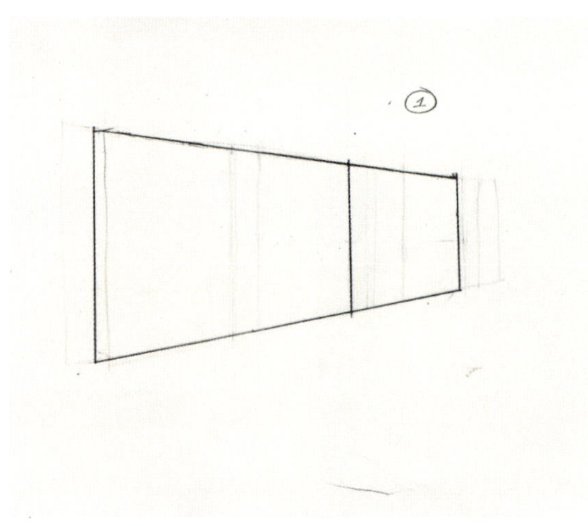


Begin by taking a single component and measuring it. I have used the nearest vertical post. I am labelling its height as *A*. Then, again using my pencil to measure, I have looked for another *significant* measurement that is also *A*. I have found that the gap between the two posts is that. It helps me put that in the right place. Then I have estimated the angle of the beam that connects them in relation to an imagined horizontal.

## STEP 2

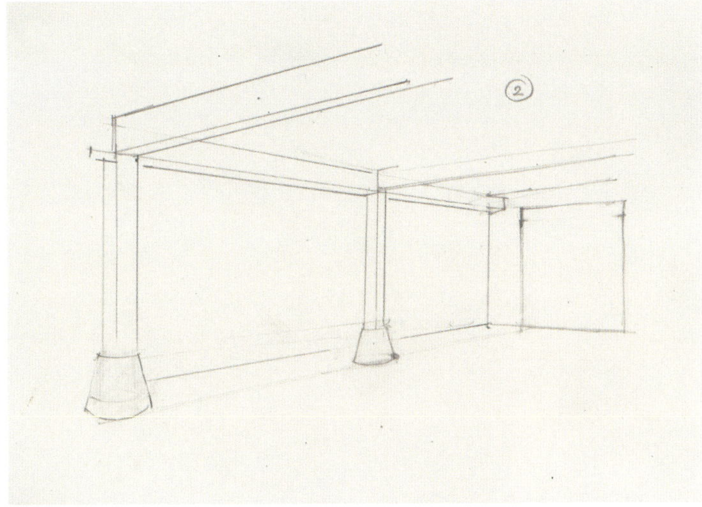

I have now found another measurement (*B*), which is half the length of *A*. This now helps me add in one or two more elements. These are coordinates – fixed points on your sheet of paper that you know to be in the correct relationship to one another. Their correctness makes them good hooks to hang your drawing on.

## STEP 3

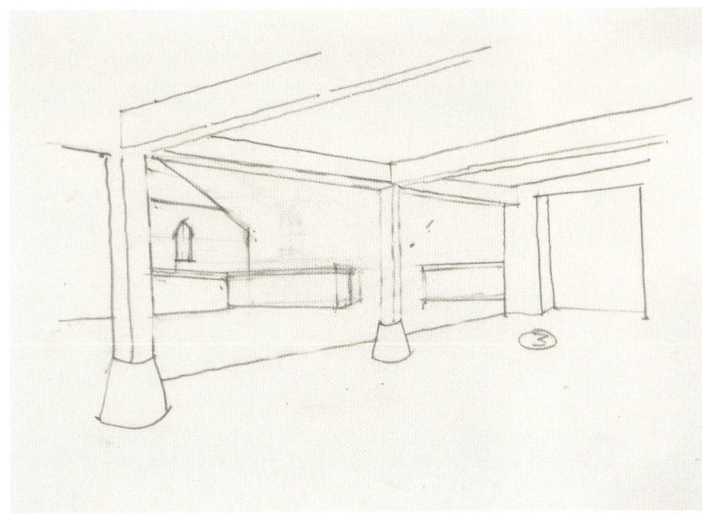

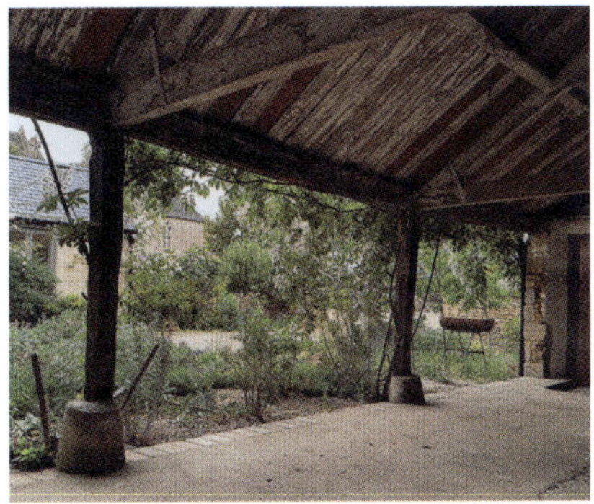

Making use of this framework, I have begun to add in some detail, still measuring as I go but increasingly relying on my eye and always on the known correct coordinates.

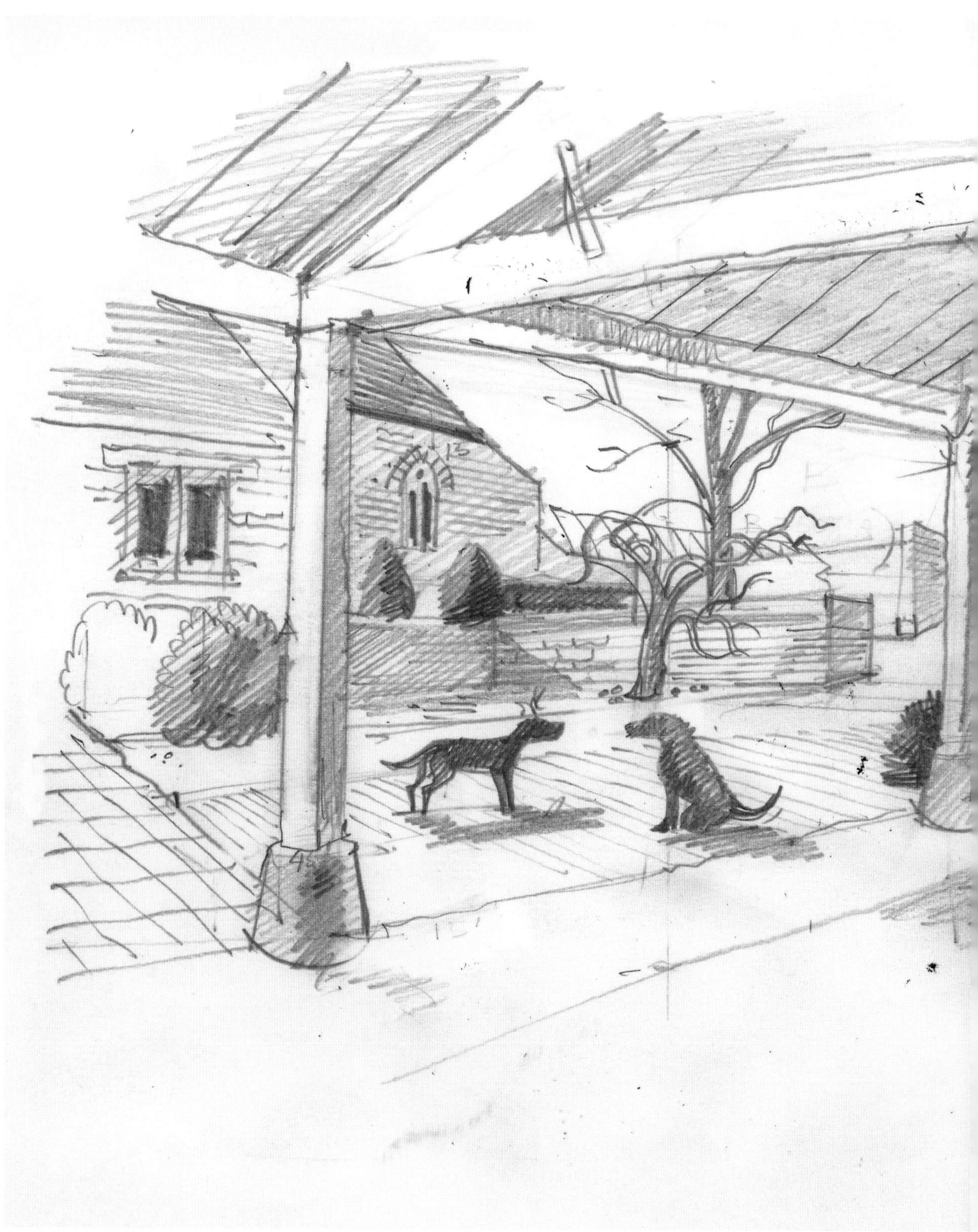

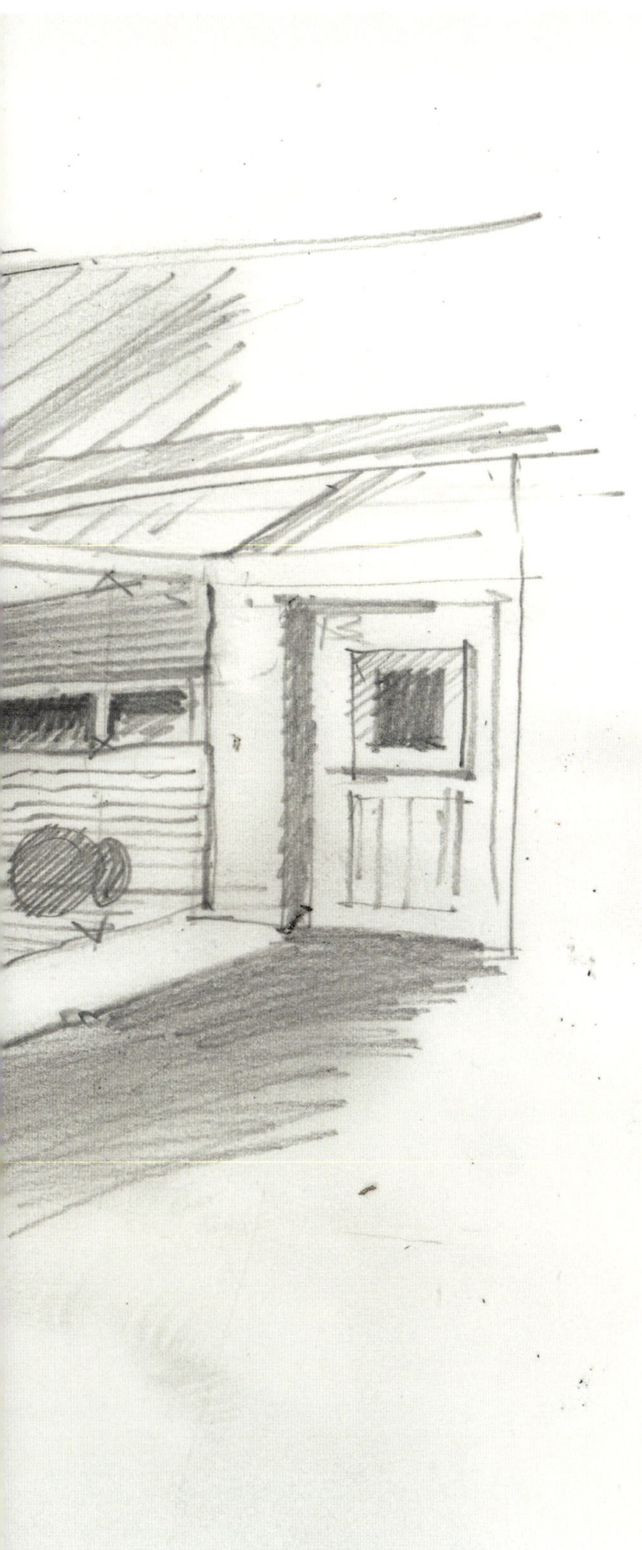

## STEP 4

You are now beginning to act on some of the actual thoughts about the view you started with. Begin to use shadow to create three-dimensional form in your drawing. The sun is coming from outside (in this case, in the west), and it throws a shadow on the opposite side of each component – the posts, the walls and roof. As you fill in these details, you are beginning to make a picture. And, finally, in go the dogs and the odd plant.

### REVIEW

This is a study, so if it isn't *full* of charm, that's why. It is a way of training your mind and eyes. There are a few nicely drawn lines, and they are all considered singly, so if you think it's boring, good!

# MULTIPLE ANGLES

**This is a harder exercise, as the angles of the building are rather unexpectedly complicated. As soon as any angle in real life is not 90 degrees, things invariably do become harder; the various slopes of the roof and facets of the tower in my scene are all set to do exactly this. The yew trees are more forgiving, as they won't ever look 'wrong' and they also give a welcome contrast in tone. Sometimes a familiar scene is actually harder to draw well, as one is inclined to imagine that one already knows it back to front. Just keep looking.**

## FIRST LOOK

**This should be a testing project – you will need your wits about you! The key is to measure very carefully, especially the angles. Notice where any shady areas are darker and perhaps practise a few of the more complicated lines before you get started (e.g. the tricky main Gothic arch in my scene).**

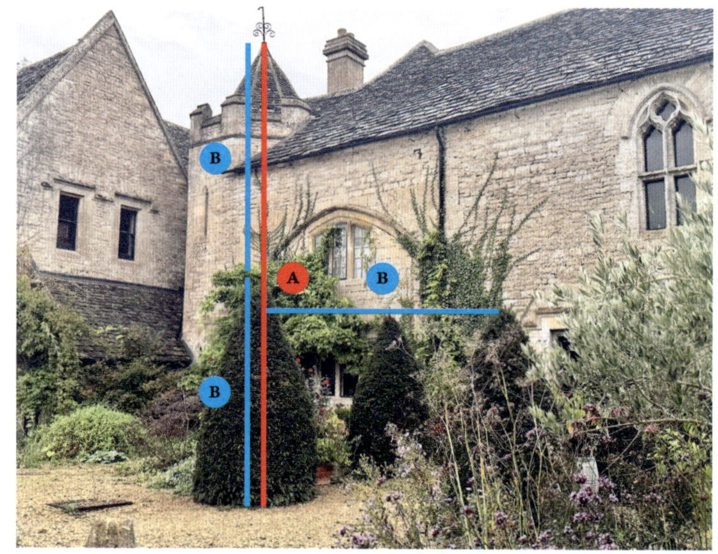


### MATERIALS

A pencil, paper and plenty of patience.

## STEP 1

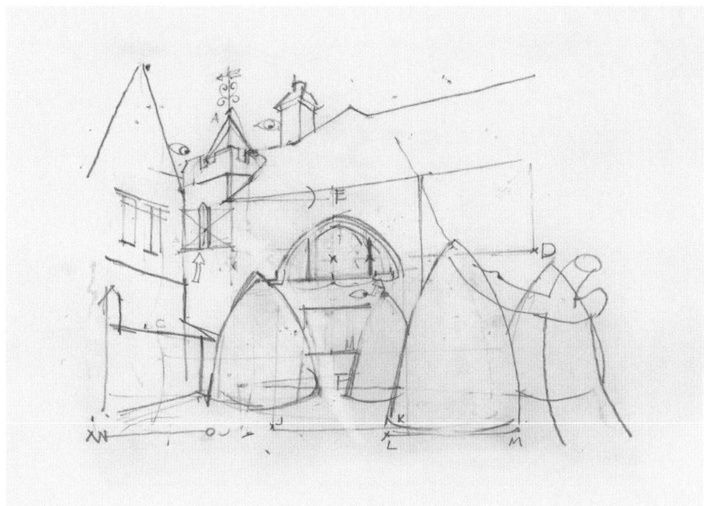


Pause and really look at the view, working out what you wish to include and to emphasize, and, conversely, what you want to eliminate. Begin your mapping out, measuring and comparing all the time. This step is the hard bit *and* the important one.

## STEP 2

With the framework established, look at the subject in terms of light and dark, of texture and detail, and build up some form. Try to define your areas as light, medium and dark in tone.

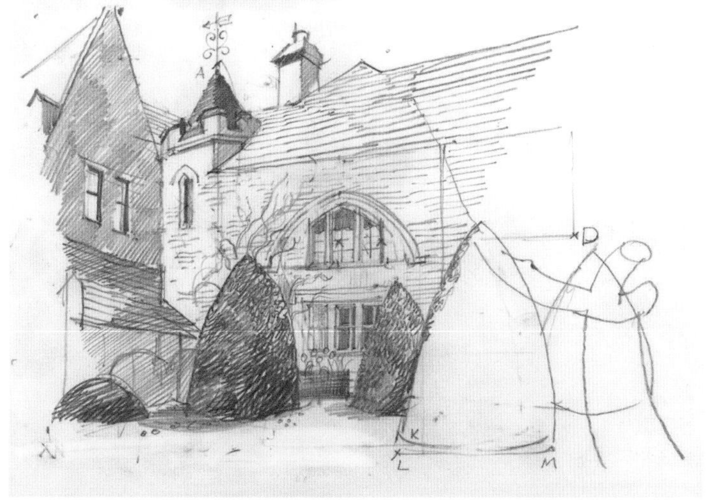

## STEP 3

Finally, build up the finer details and enhance the contrast. This step makes the drawing more interesting and emphasizes the shape and form. Remember you are relying on this, as there is no colour being used.

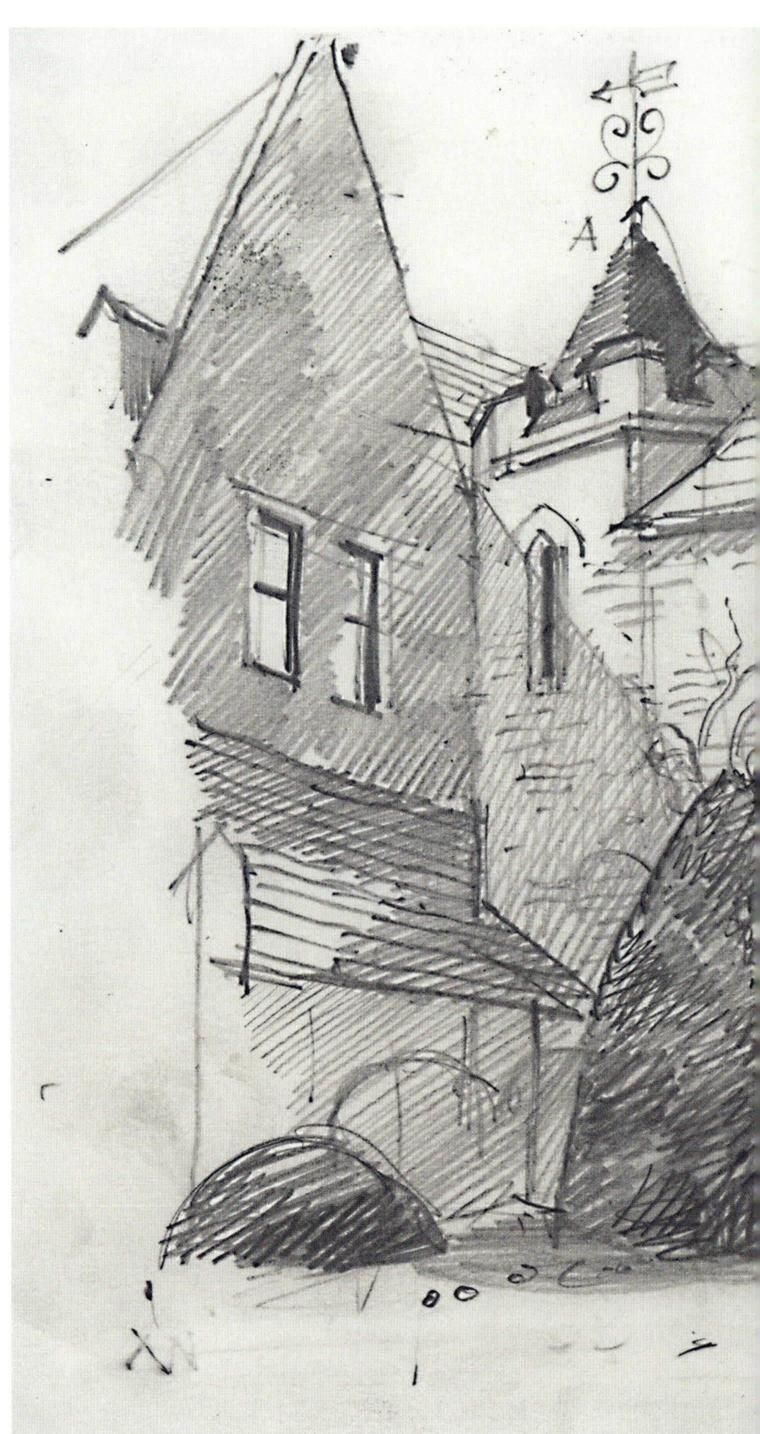

### REVIEW

These are difficult calculations to make, and eventually you will just use your eye. But until then, a system by which you compare dimensions, one to the other, is a way of checking you are on the right track. So, if this feels impossibly complicated, persevere, because you will find it a useful lesson in the end.

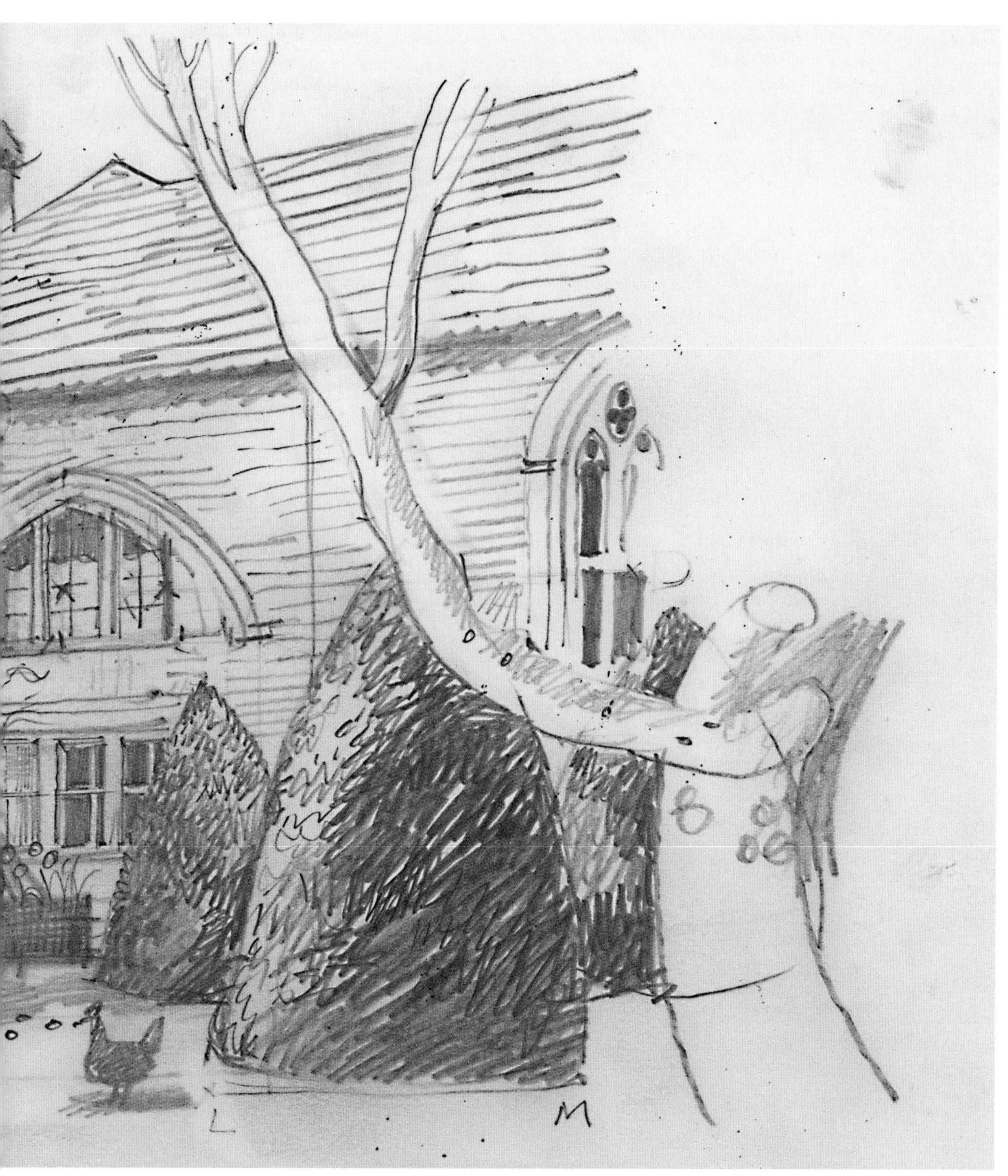
L
M

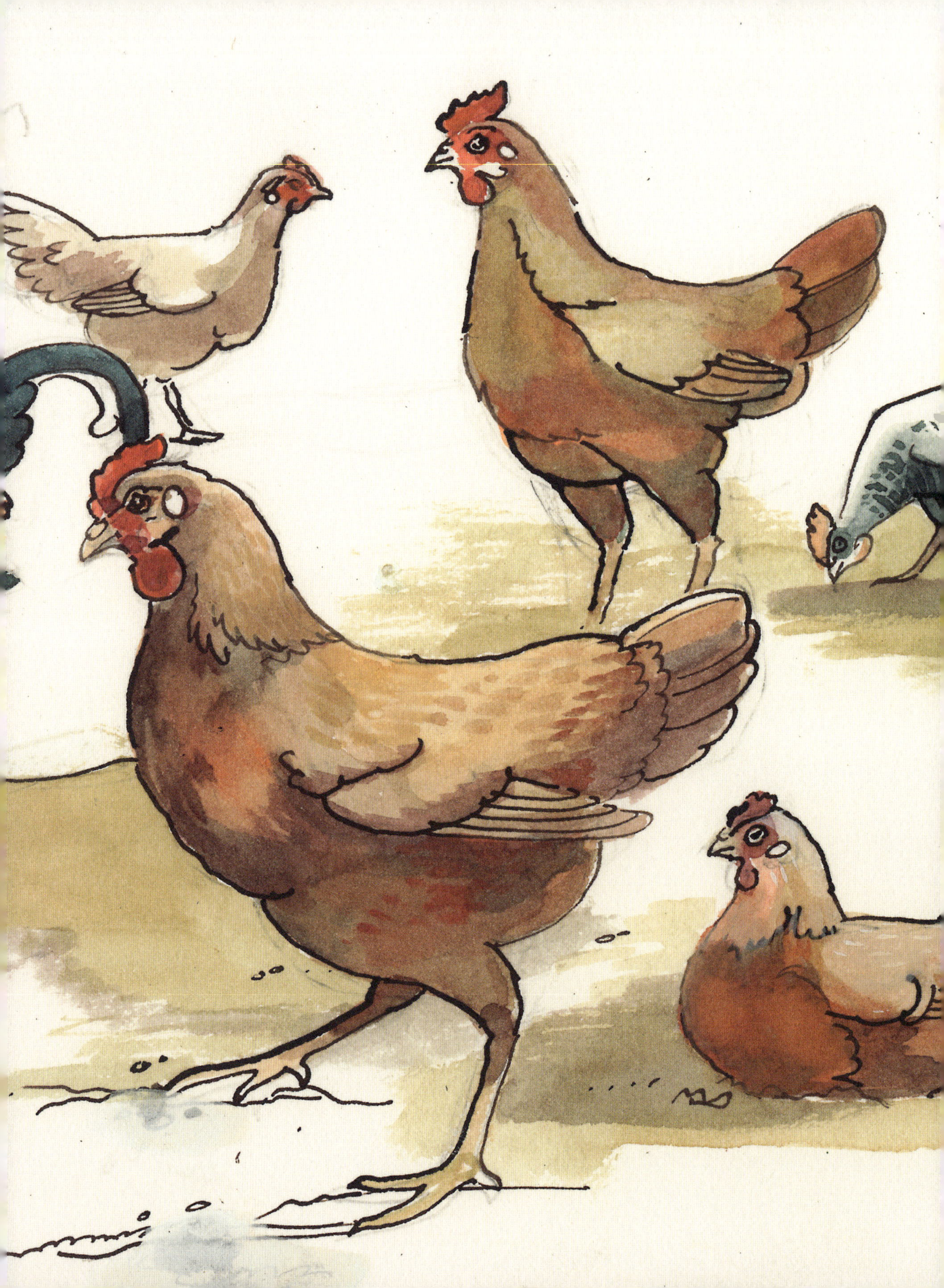

# Exercise 9

# Chickens

Drawing animals is tricky unless they are stuffed. And if they are, they are dull to draw. But their very liveliness is their main challenge, and they provide, as they scratch, peck, stretch or prowl, an alarmingly moving target. A yard full of hens is quite a good place to start, whether at home or at a friend's, or perhaps at an urban farm. Chickens are joyful to draw and familiar enough for one to know if the drawing is off target. But, most importantly, they are usually in a flock and so offer what is essential: a selection of simultaneous poses. While one lies in the gravel, another walks and pecks, thereby giving the drawer a series of drawings to circulate around from feathery model to model.

For this exercise, you could really choose any animal you want that is likely to give you the same variety of poses. This could be your cat, a pigeon outside the window, or a flock of your own chickens (my preferred target).

## FIRST LOOK

**Before you put pencil to paper, watch the animal(s) for a few minutes to get a feeling of their habits and mood. Your initial plan for the drawing should identify some of the more common poses they provide: for my chickens, that means some facing in each direction, one seated, one walking, and all making very different shapes.**

## MATERIALS

Heavy cartridge paper, an HB pencil, a drawing pen, a no. 6 sable pointed brush, your watercolour set (see pages 52–5), a rubber and a tube of white gouache.

## STEP 1

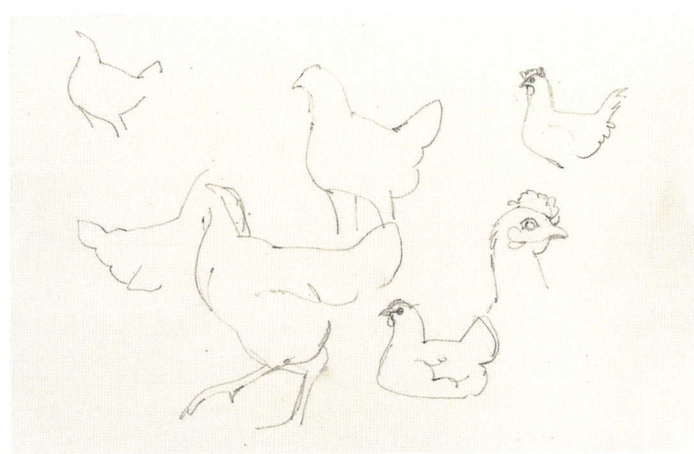

Thinking only of shape and form, of the way each area of feathers forms a block that is almost like a muscle, I begin to draw the outline of each bird. As soon as one moves, I swap to another. Don't worry if you make a mistake: you have plenty of time and a rubber. Keep looking at your subject rather than at your drawing. It will keep the lines meaningful and telling.

## STEP 2

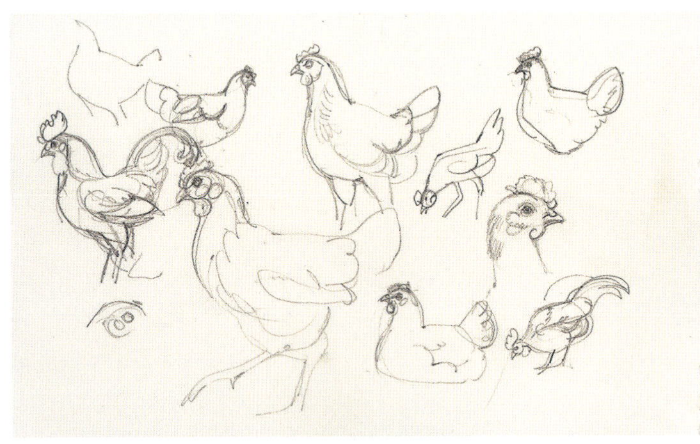

I'm now looking at the rounded forms of the chickens and trying to express their three-dimensional form. Focus a bit on how the animal's feathers or fur lies, and indeed even how any patterns are fitted to the sections of their anatomies. This is the most important phase, as it is the foundation for what will come next.

## STEP 3

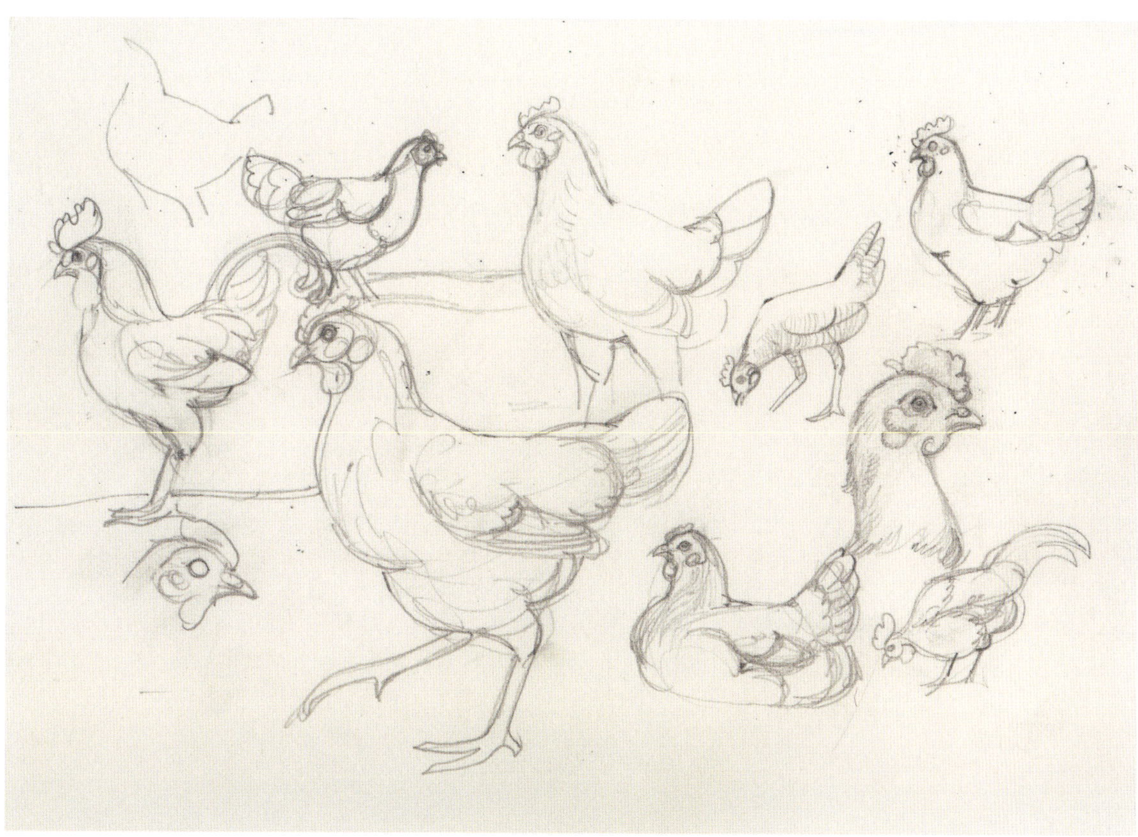

Oh no! Rather counter-intuitively, you now have to rub out most of what you have done, as the real line work will follow in pen and you want those lines, those marks, to be the ones that count and that resonate. But the work you have done is not wasted: it has allowed you to understand your subjects while, in wraith-like form, providing the guide for your own drawing.

## STEP 4

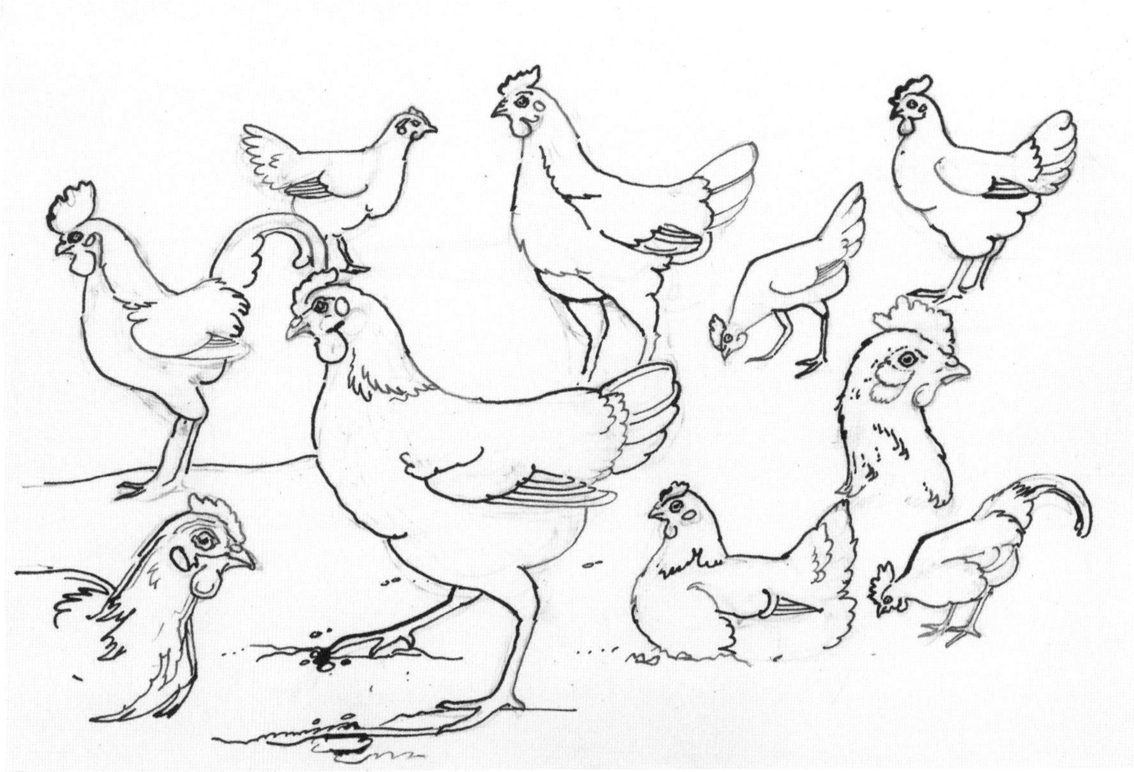

Now with felt pen or preferably (for me anyway) a dip pen and ink, begin to draw the sharply defined outlines of the animals. Be careful and make each line as beautiful and as controlled as you feel you can. One great advantage of this is to make you choose a single line rather than a fuzz of possible ones. It forces you to refine your drawing, to be economical. Here, it is forcing me to work out what information I need to put down to describe the birds' form, as I am cutting out much of what I originally drew.

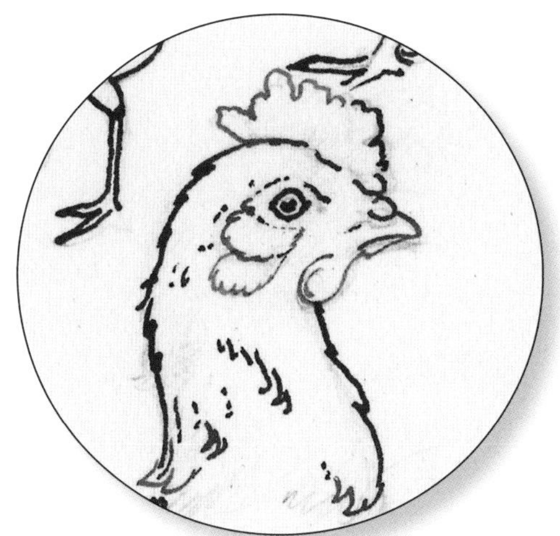

## STEP 5

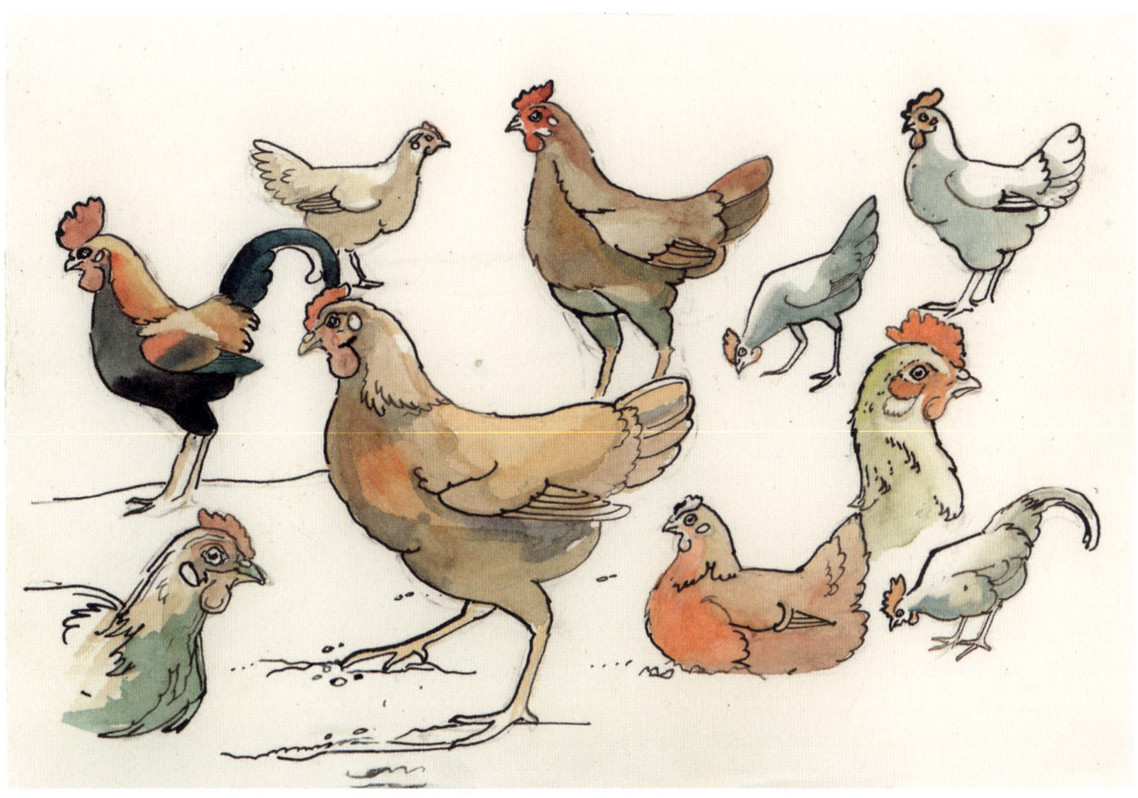

Make sure that the ink is *truly* dry before moving on to the next step (make a cup of tea while it dries to make sure). Then start to tint the drawing with some plain washes. I have used a square-ended brush for speed and ease. Remember that you can always *build up* washes, but it is far harder to reduce their intensity. Next, add some more intense colour to give your animals form, and think a bit about the divisions of colour. Some of my chickens are very plain and brown, but others, like the little bantam cock, have clearly delineated areas of plumage (the iridescent black breast and nether parts, golden capes and rusty-orange hackles).

## STEP 6

Now with a pointed no. 6 brush, add detail, building up the darker tones. I am recording again the barred plumage on some, and the darker neck feathers on the head-and-shoulders detail of others. After building up the bright red of the comb and wattles (called the headgear), I have then used a sandy colour on the ground – both to express the colour of the rather grubby wood shavings they are on and also to more clearly define the white plumage of some of the birds. Lastly, I have added a very little white gouache to their body colour. This has just slightly enhanced the whiteness and accentuated the form. This should be done only at the very last stage since, once applied, you cannot paint over it.

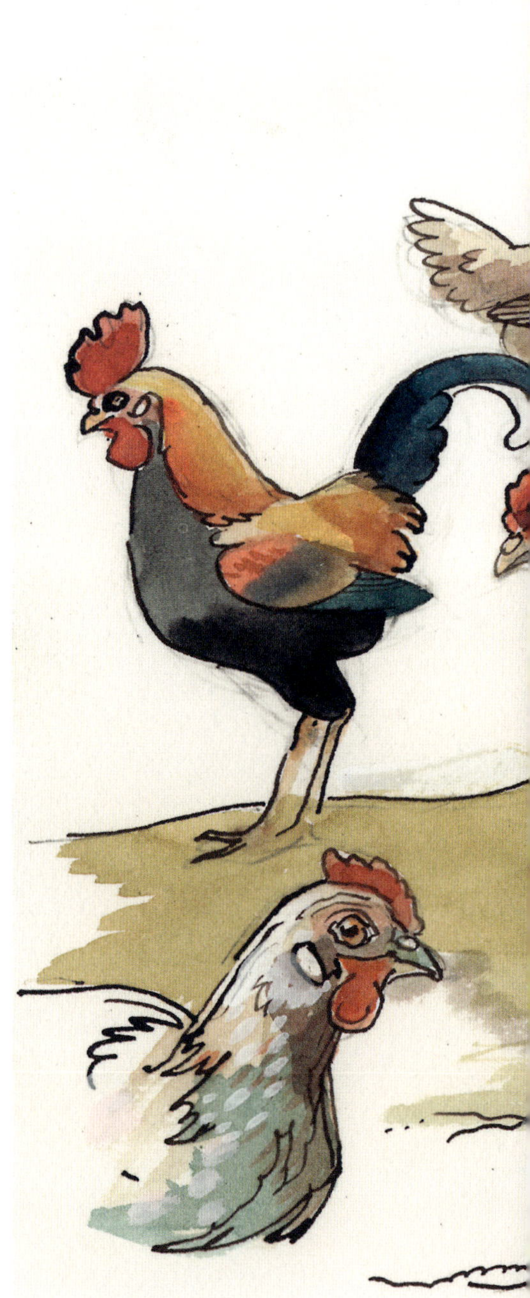

### REVIEW

It is inevitable that some of your chicken portraits will be better than others. They are not well-behaved models. That is why one should have several poses running at the same time. Don't worry about the bad ones.

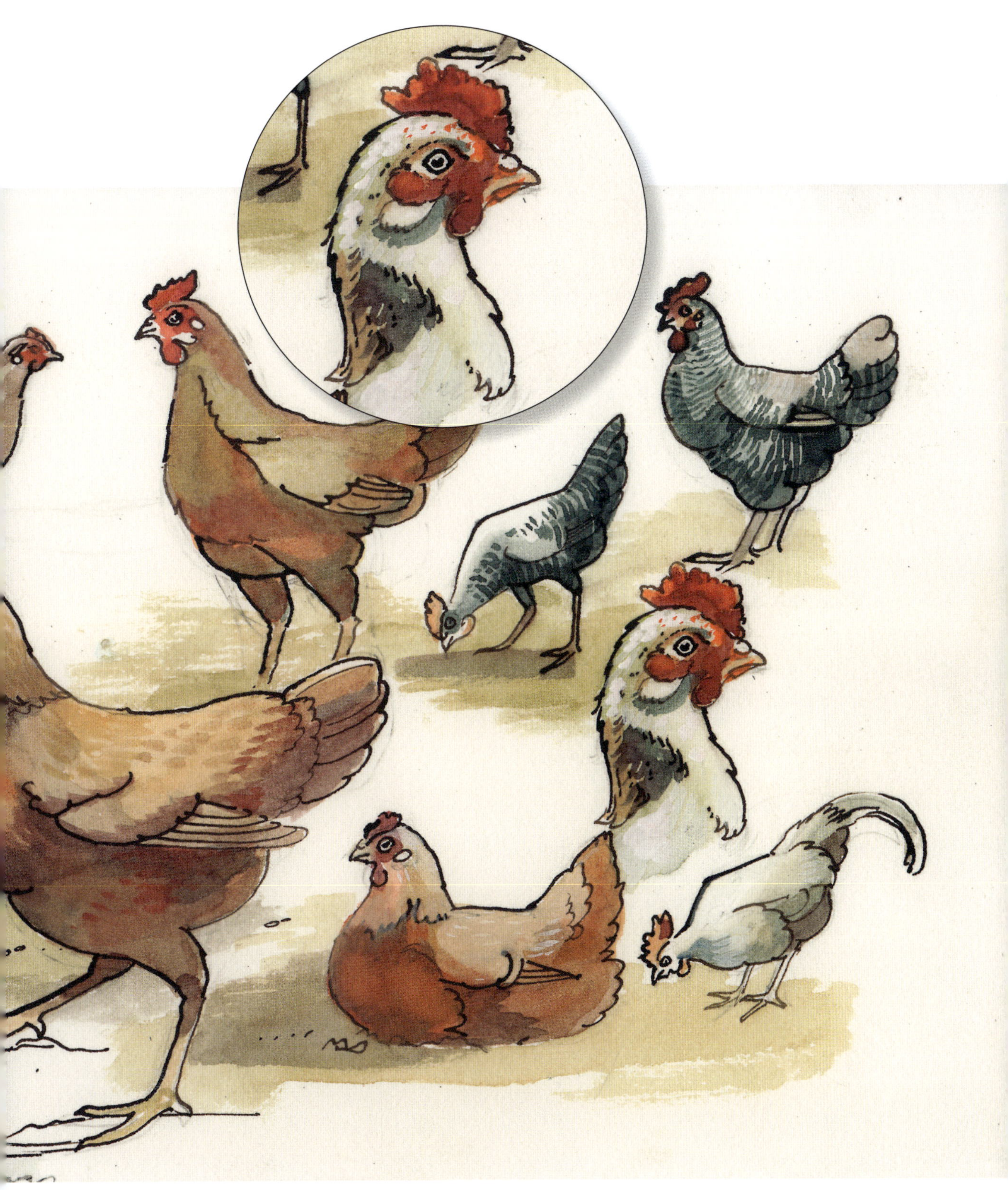

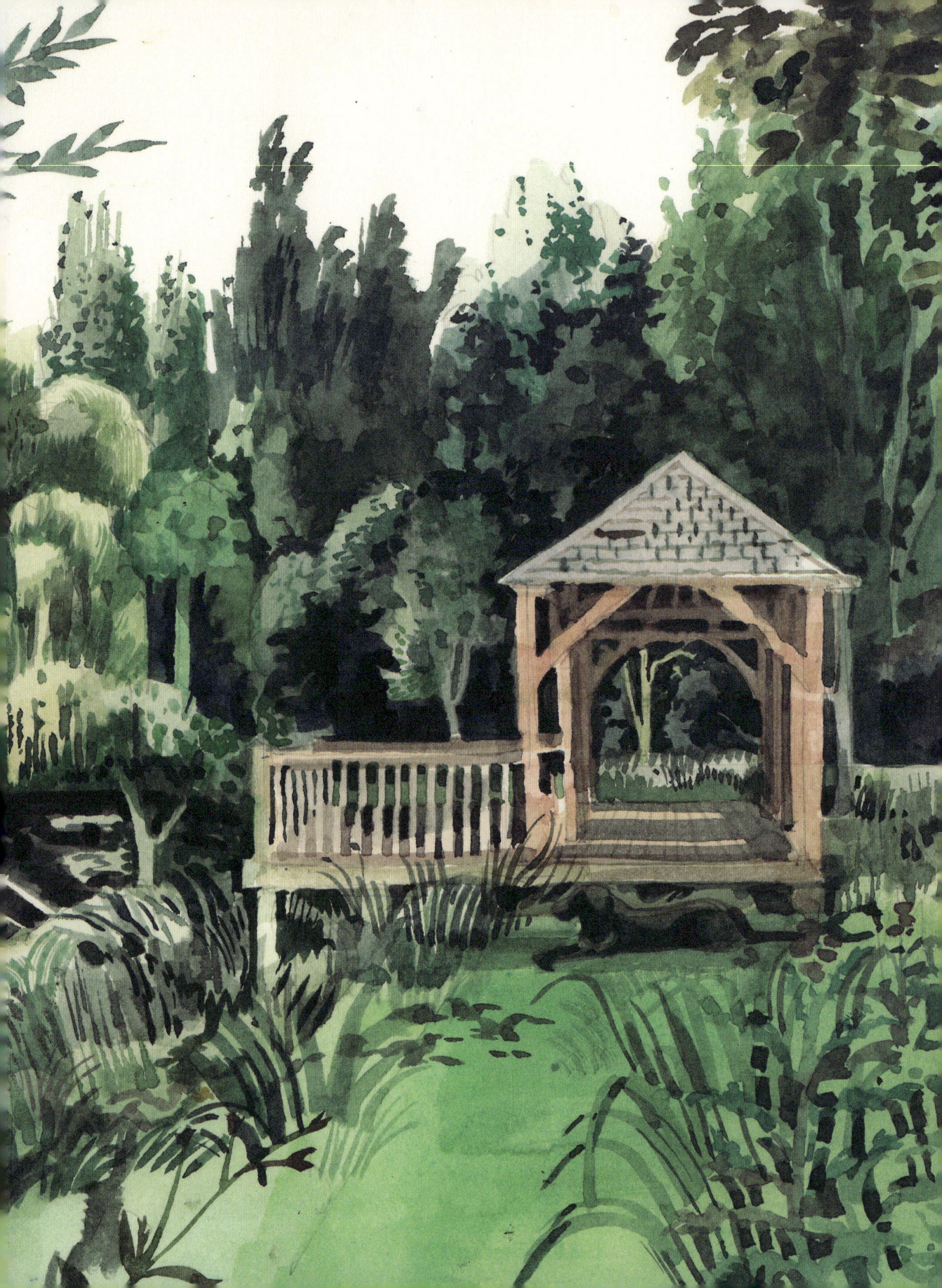

## Exercise 10

# A view of a garden

Painting a landscape is a serious business. And while it might seem counterintuitive to introduce a more challenging drawing component, the inclusion of some kind of building or construction gives something to focus on as well as providing scale to its surroundings. It's important, too, to *like* the view – to want to walk into it and to *own* the image – as you will spend a couple of hours looking at it. During the course of the day, the light will change, so if you can do this exercise in one session, it will be easier and also allow you to be really absorbed in your view. You might pick a picture of your house or of a church or castle, maybe seen from your chair while on holiday. Try to combine the man-made and the natural world.

## FIRST LOOK

**I picked a view with foreground, middle ground and (modest) distance, and with trees of varying form and colour. It is going to be a fairly green picture. The building is simple but with robust straight lines: in contrast to the natural form of the foliage, its new timber frame is bright and in a contrasting colour. I have used a rectangle of watercolour paper because, while it will begin as a pencil sketch, this will serve only as a guide for the later watercolour painting, and you don't want to do it twice. If you are uncertain what your composition will be like, you could do a couple of rough sketches in your drawing book first just to help you decide. It might also help to quickly study the building to get the drawing right because, while the trees are forgiving, the hut will need to be right.**

## MATERIALS

Arches hot-press 600gsm watercolour paper, your watercolour set (see pages 52–5), a pointed no. 6 sable brush and a no. 12 square-ended sable brush.

## STEP 1

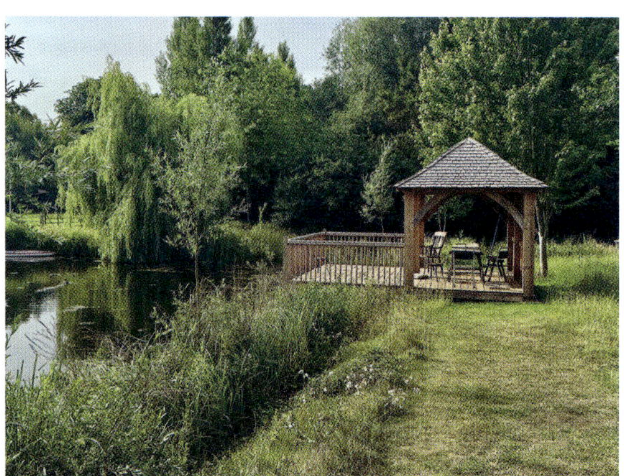

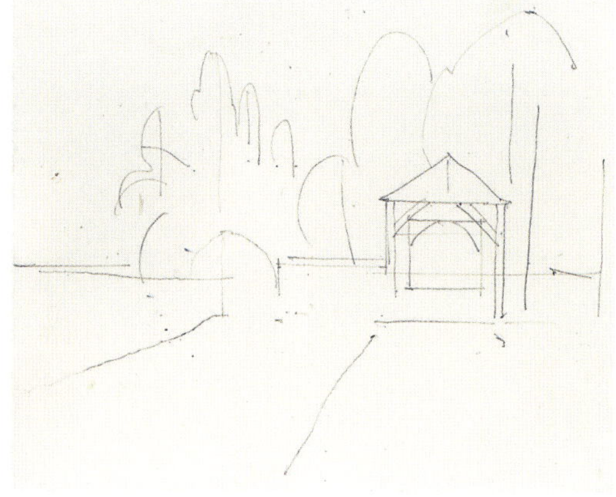

On your paper, very lightly map out the view. Work out the design of your painting and decide on the hierarchy of the elements: building, water, trees and field. Look at the angles, measure and get them right, and look out for useful verticals (in this case, tree trunks) and horizontals (the fence and field in the middle distance). Assess whether you might need to improve on what is there a bit. You might want to emphasize some sections over others. This is what I mean by the hierarchies of the picture. So, in this view, I have chosen to make less of the dull-looking grass in the foreground and more of the varying tree shapes behind the hut. You will not be arrested for cheating a bit! And you may later find that you take details from elsewhere in your view to use for this purpose.

## STEP 2

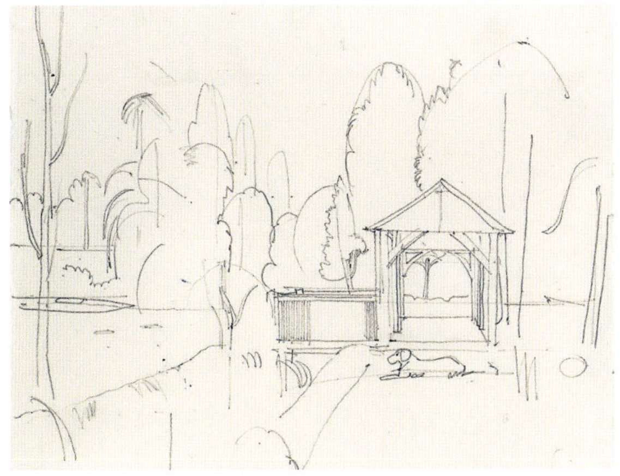

The dog has usefully plonked herself in the view. This feels like an advantage, so she has gone in. The second stage of this drawing sees greater resolution and deeper observation of the scene. While the map of the picture is becoming clearer, I am anxious not to make a scratchy, heavy drawing, as it will in due course disappear beneath the finished watercolour. It is just a guide.

## STEP 3

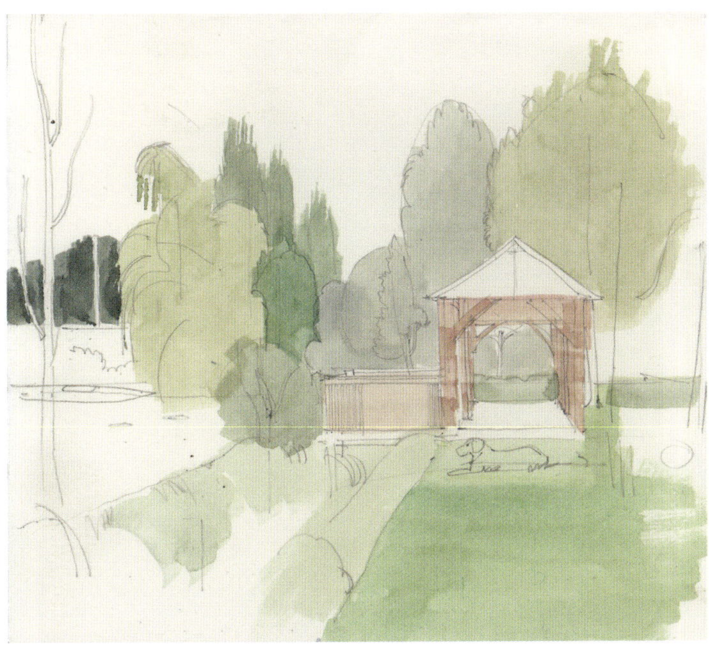

For the first washes, I have used a square-ended brush, mainly because it is a quicker way to get the initial colour applied. Use the two greens and a darker blue to get the heavier colours. None of these washes will be clearly seen in the eventual picture, but they matter, as they are the underpinning of the piece. There is far less contrast than in real life, but it is easier to build up intensity than to reduce it.

## STEP 4

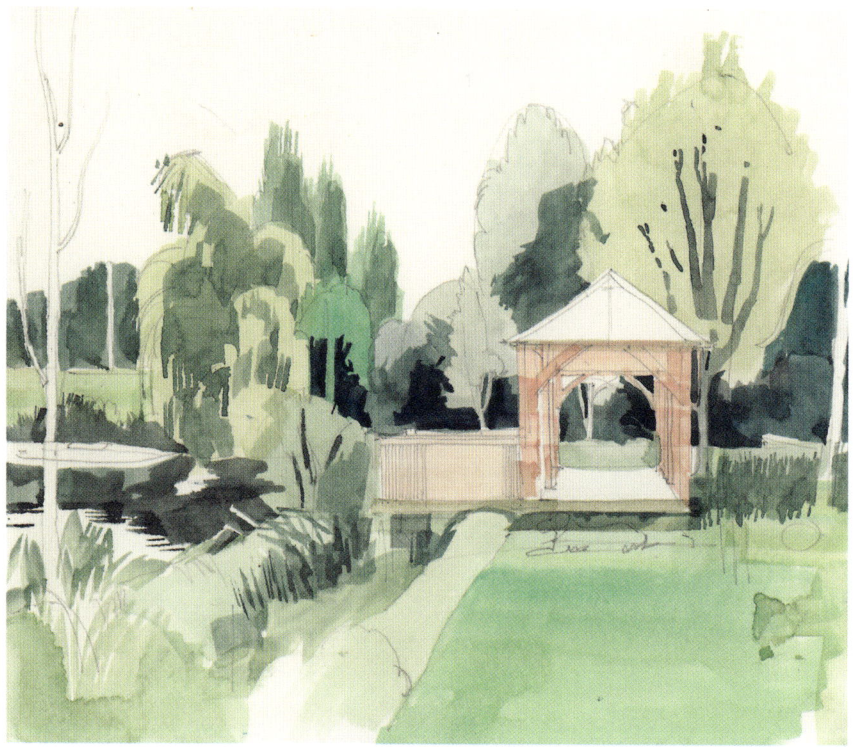

In working out the tones of green and greyish browns (using my green paints, along with the red, pink and Indian yellow), I am resolving the darkest and palest tones (the distant shadow and roof, respectively) and then breaking up the mid-tones in between. I am also experimenting with the rushes alongside the water. All this stage is still done with the square-ended brush, using the side of its end to get accurate lines. It proves quite a good tool to draw the rushes easily and quickly.

## STEP 5

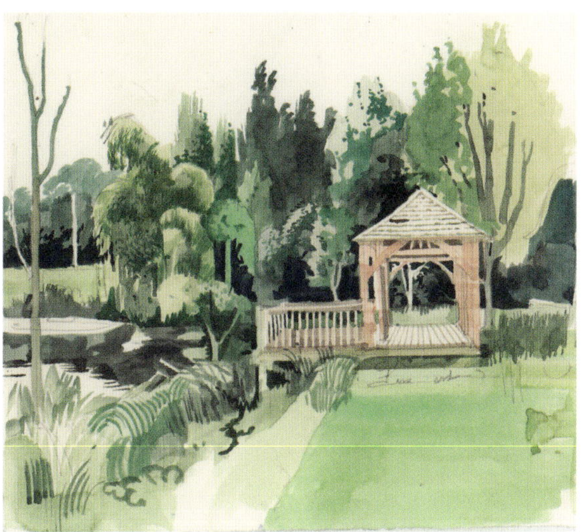

Moving on to a normal-pointed brush (no. 6), I have begun to actually paint. I am looking at the different foliage patterns and exploring the way that shadow can give form to the young trees. The trunks are really painted by drawing the shadows behind them and so as negative shapes. The original pencil drawing has basically disappeared now, and as I work on the foliage in the foreground, I can see that the new grass is making rather a dull front to the picture. Hmm. Something to think about as I paint (or as *you* paint).

## STEP 6

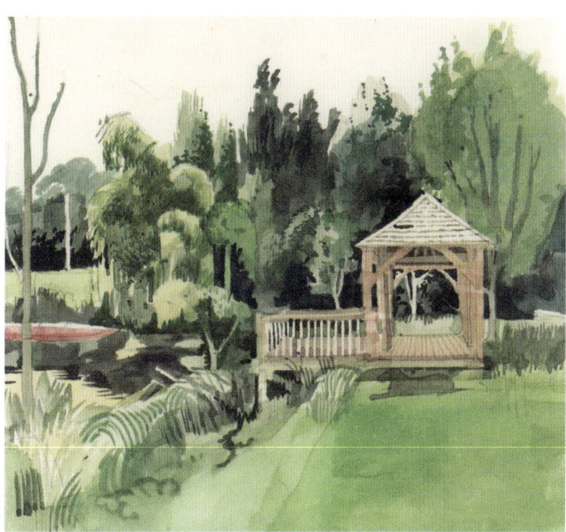

This is an undramatic intermediate stage where I am enriching the painting with transparent washes that build up the strength of all the colours, being careful to always go slowly, as the darkest tones of all are to come at the very end. I am working a bit more in the detail and colour of the hut. This building is the focus of the picture, and the care taken to look at the building's lines earlier will now pay off (if the drawing is *wonky* now, it's a bit late to correct!). I am now certain that the dog is not enough to make the foreground interesting, so she disappears.

## STEP 7

Quite a lot has happened in the final stage. By borrowing plant forms that I can see around me, I have reduced the bland lawn to a path that leads to the hut. They are *real* and *observed* plants but moved to this more useful position. Careful painting is needed for the willow leaves in the trees to create elegant and pointed cursive lines. You might practise a few in your sketchbook if you are unsure before adding to the actual painting. I have also now made some final touches to the hut, defining the shingles in the roof and some of the contrasts created by the components of the timber frame. I have left the sky white. In a complex composition like this, there is no need for dramatic clouds or indeed hard-to-achieve clear blues. Our minds can fill in those elements. And always *beware* missing the right time to stop – before the picture becomes overworked.

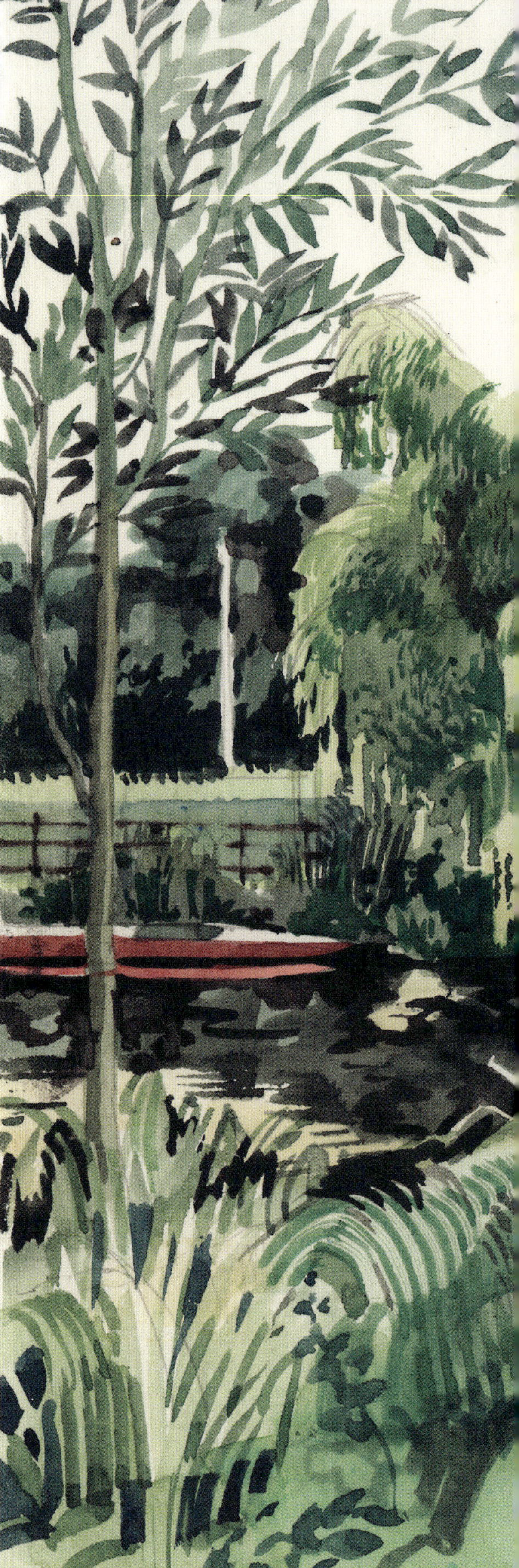

### REVIEW

This may be a romantic scene, but there's an awful lot of green in it. It is only by using a lot of dark tones to throw the others into contrast that you will keep it interesting. All the greens serve to make the hut the focus of the drawing.

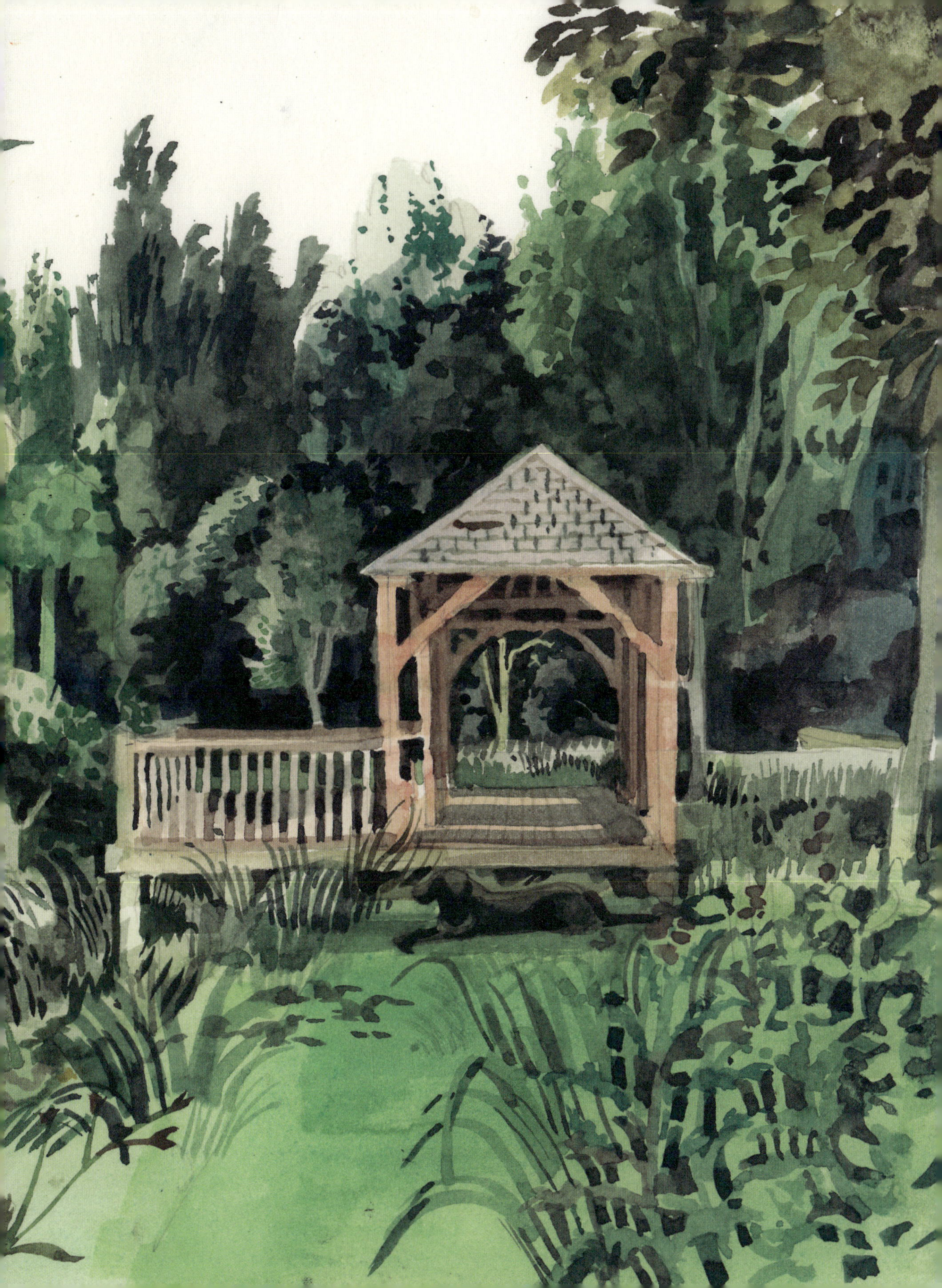

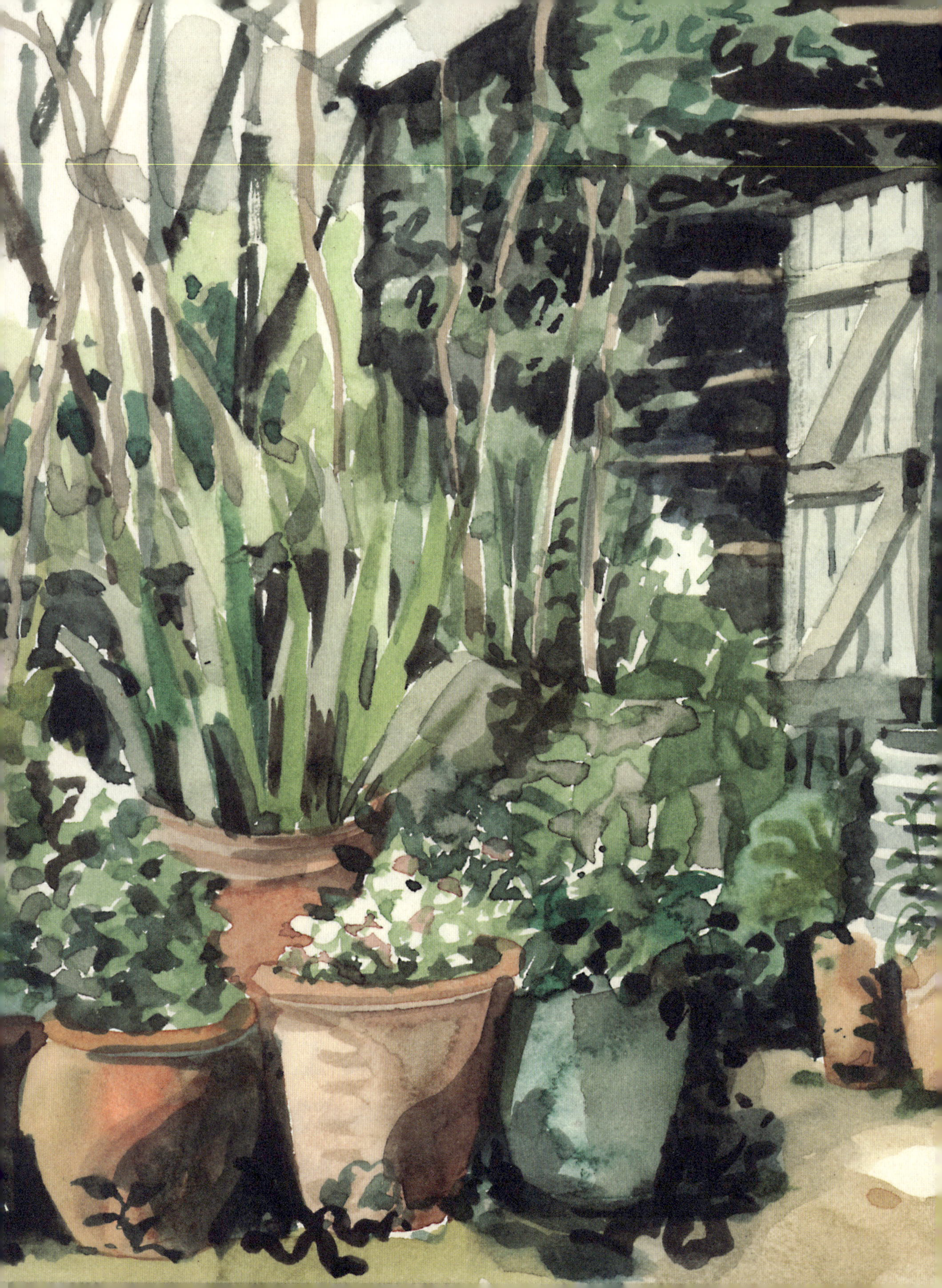

# What next?

# GETTING OVER THE HARD BITS

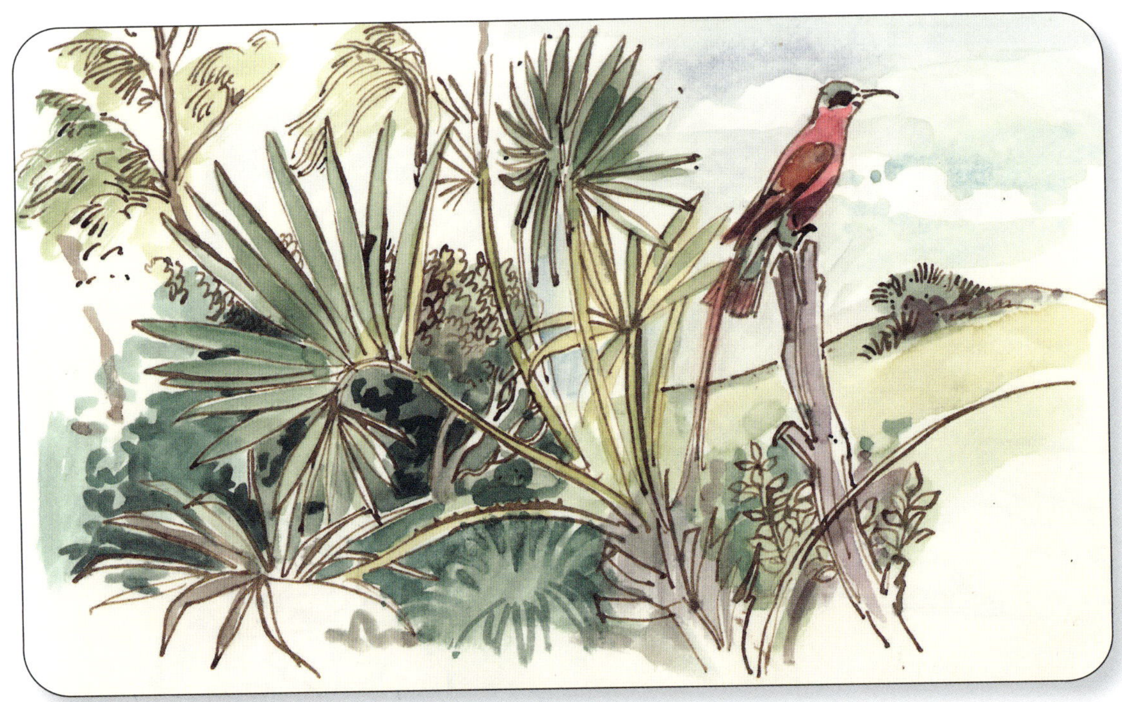

*Always have a piece of the same paper you are working on by your paintbox to try out the colours. Mix on there and in your paintbox palette, and not on the painting.*

There is no way round the fact that, while drawing is joyful, enriching, engaging and satisfying, it is jolly difficult. To make the translation from three dimensions to two and to carry out the relevant analysis, calculation and editing required is challenging. You can learn tricks; perspective drawing can become more or less automatic as one subconsciously makes the reductions in information needed to create a convincing rendering of a building or room; or you can build up your own visual language, a vocabulary of shorthand expression and battery of techniques that allow your drawing to appear confident and not distract the viewer (usually oneself) with obvious ineptitudes. But however assured your line or confident your brushstroke, creating a composition and drawing in such a way that it doesn't look as if a Labrador has done it is *hard*.

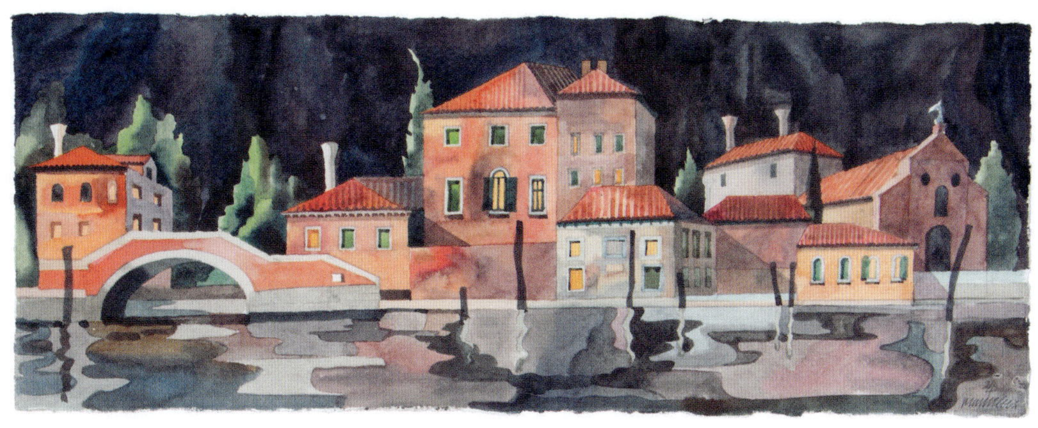

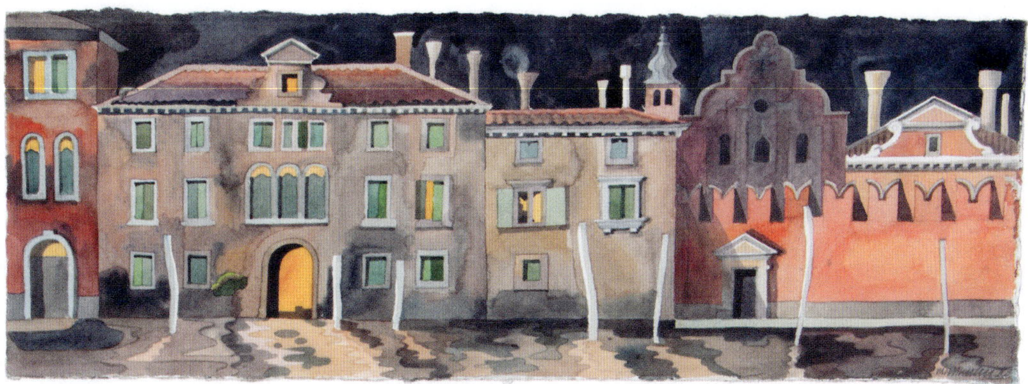

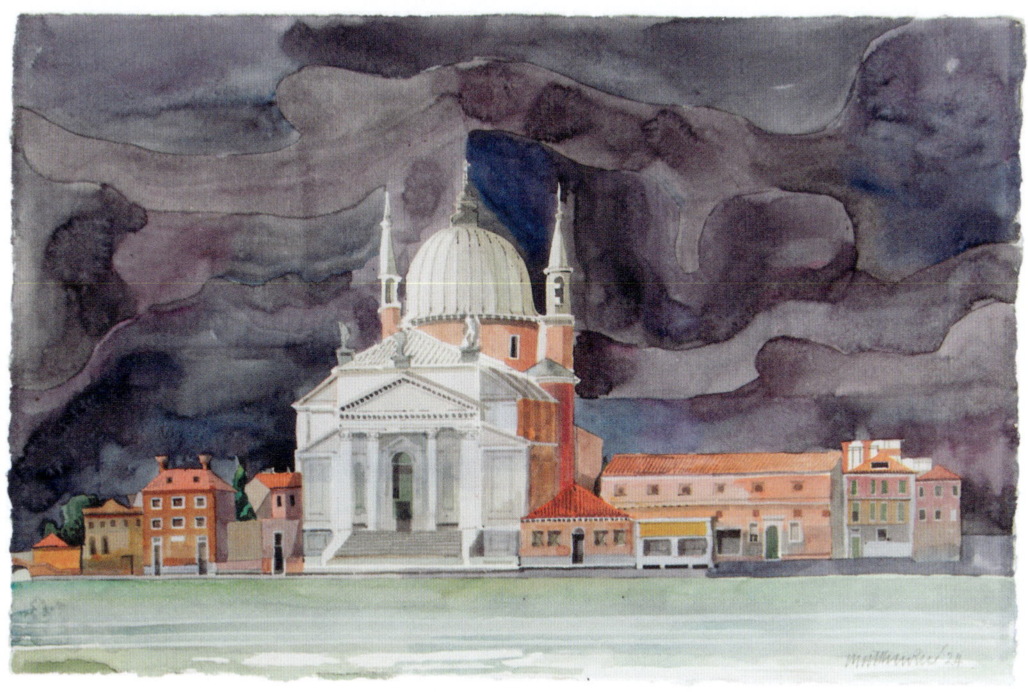

# WHEN THINGS GO WRONG

*Drawing is a pleasure, and in most cases, it makes one happy. The process of looking, understanding what we see, and then translating that into marks on your paper seems to be one that is deeply satisfying, if frequently quite challenging. While practice helps improve one's ability, there is no avoiding the fact that things do sometimes go wrong.*

When they do, we can immediately spot the 'wrongness', even if the reason behind the uneasiness about the work is initially hidden. When this happens, the happiness can be compromised, if not wiped away altogether.

For most of the drawings you are likely to tackle, the worst problems stem from errors at the very beginning of the process. Inaccuracies early on are hard to hide, and some subjects, like buildings, are particularly unforgiving. For this reason, in this book, I have emphasized the business of waiting and *looking* a lot before starting. The old carpenter's adage – 'Measure twice, cut once' – is worth remembering. The early lines and measurements are what will make the later developments convincing.

Here are five examples of things going off the rails, with explanations and some suggestions for avoidance or even treatment.

Of course, there are many other potential pitfalls, but these ones do seem to turn up again and again. They do happen to everybody, and it is worth remembering that it is never a disgrace to start a picture again. Almost all my paintings have a failed attempt on the back of the paper!

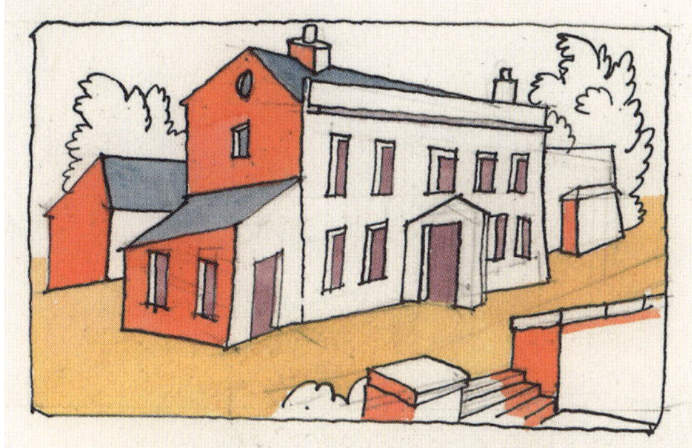

A

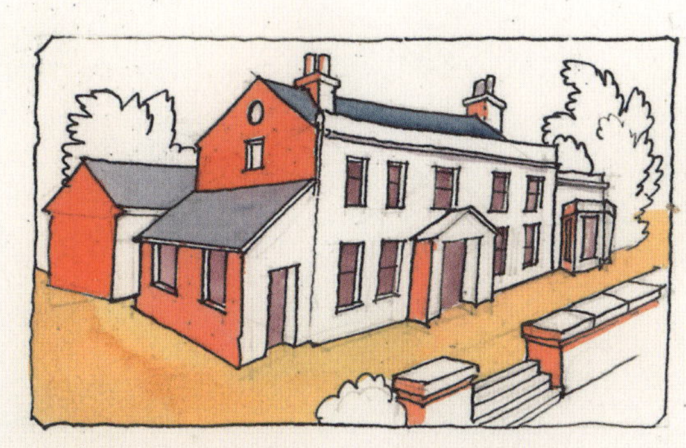

B

These two drawings show the house in question at the same size and position on the sheet of paper. But while superficially similar, artwork *A* quickly starts to show problems. Many of the important lines are measured inaccurately, in some cases literally going in the opposite direction to the correct one (see artwork *B*). The result is to make the whole picture look childish and wrong, and despite the correct use of shading, careful painting and nice washes, it is easy to see that those initial calculations were wrong. In this matter, unless striking out into a new drawing language, ther*e is* a right and a wrong, thus the uneasy feeling that artwork *A* induces.

**What to do and how to avoid**

When embarking on a drawing that needs correct perspective, be especially careful and methodical about measuring. Use the pencil method (see page 105), and, where possible, double-check those decisions by relating one point to another in the building. The initial drawing is the skeleton – the armature on which the drawing will be built – so go slow and check carefully to give your final drawing a better chance.

## 2. BAD PLACEMENT ON PAGE

This church and its round tower are the subject of a simple picture. In artwork *A*, the building is placed too high on the page and too far to the right, meaning that it must be squeezed into the cramped space provided. This also means that the tower must become squat. As a result, the whole building is contracted.

**What to do and how to avoid**
No surprises here. Stop and think before you draw. Perhaps make a thumbnail plan of your picture to help you decide where and how to place it on the page, and how to design the picture. Work out the proportions of the building to make sure you can fit it in, and also which features you think are especially important. Begin your drawing with a clear idea of where everything should be on the page. That way, you are more likely to produce artwork *B*, where the building sits comfortably in the centre of the picture, allowing plenty of space for all its features to be clearly expressed.

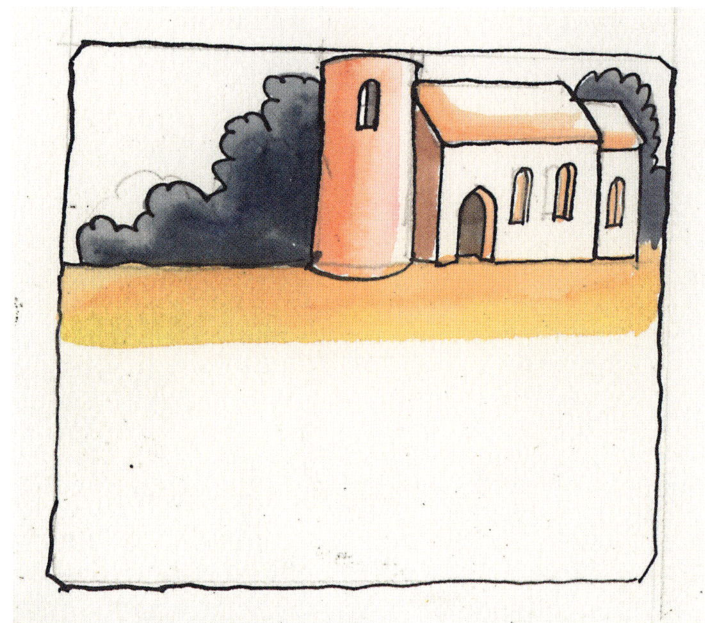

**A**

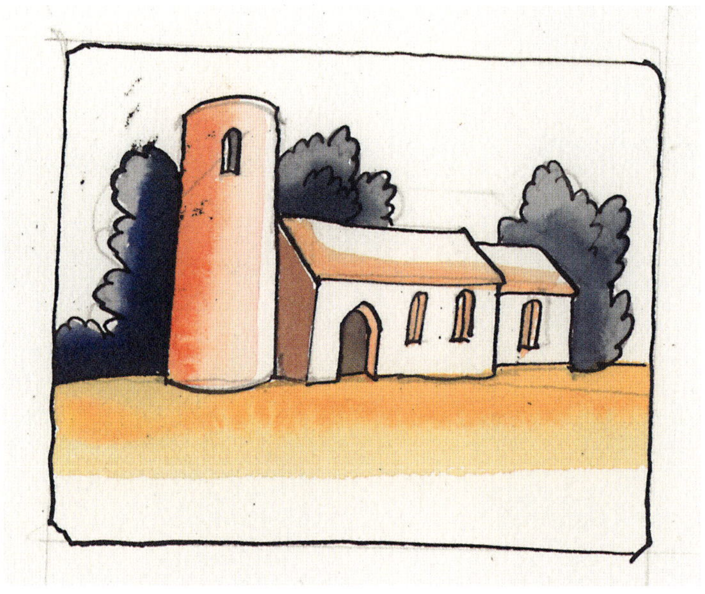

**B**

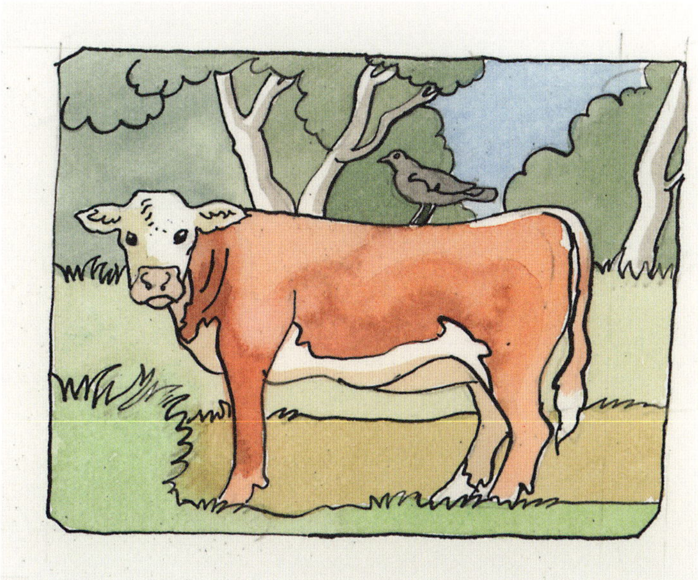

A

Tonal variation, the disposition of dark and light areas, is hugely important in making a painting well articulated and interesting – and thus legible to viewers. The cow in artwork *A* is so similar in tone to her leafy background that she does not stand out well. The friendly jackdaw, similarly, barely registers, and there is no feeling of foreground or background, as everything is rendered in the same pastel tones.

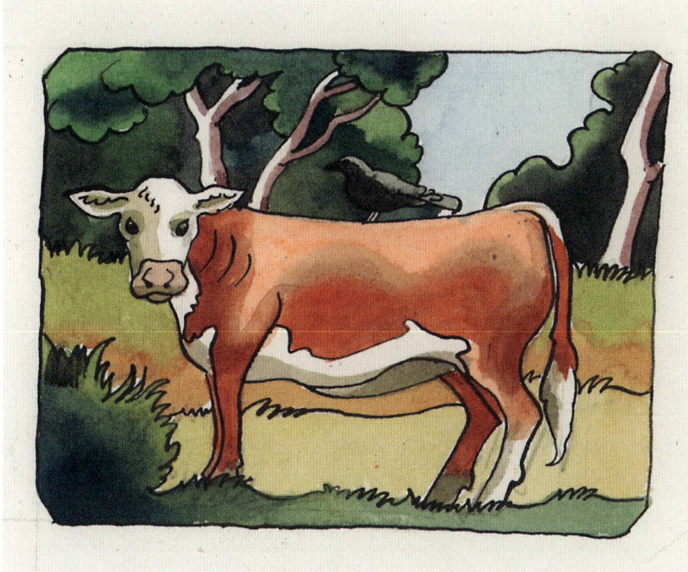

B

**What to do and how to avoid**
When embarking on your painting, work out where the light and dark areas of the view are by half shutting your eyes and looking carefully at your scene. Finding the dark and light tones should become much easier. Try to use darker areas to throw the subject of your artwork into focus and work some secondary washes into the subject itself to emphasize its form. The stronger foreground helps indicate an actual place: sunny in some areas and shadier in others.

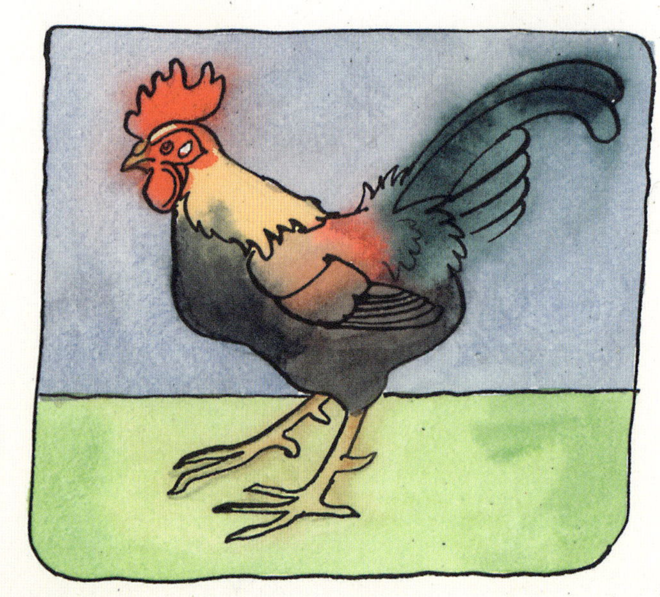

**A**

These two bantam cockerels are identical in drawing, and more or less identical in colour, but chicken *A* suffers from washy, smudgy colour, with colours flowing wetly into each other. Not only does this make detail indistinct, but as the colours blend, they also tell a new story that does not represent the fact.

**What to do and how to avoid**
Luckily, this is easy to avoid, although actually rather hard to put right once it has happened. The key is to slow down (as always) and to let each wash in each separate section of the subject dry properly before applying its neighbour. Tackling non-adjacent areas at the same time is an easier way to track this.

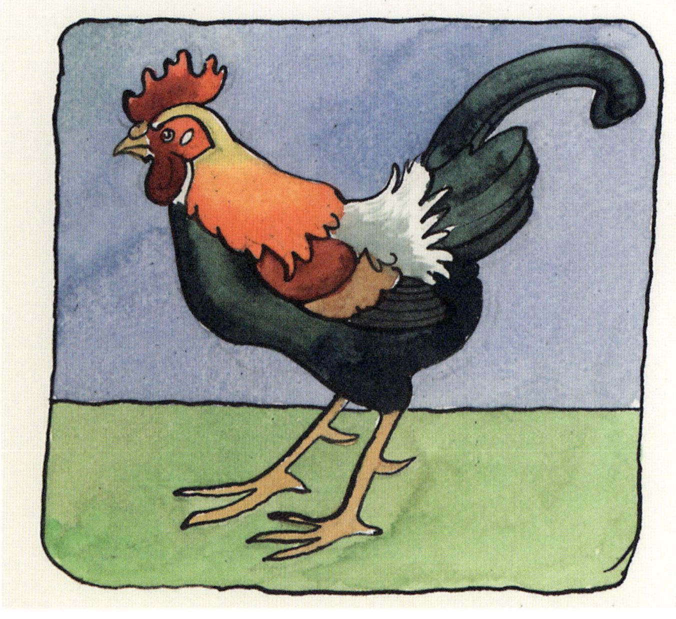

**B**

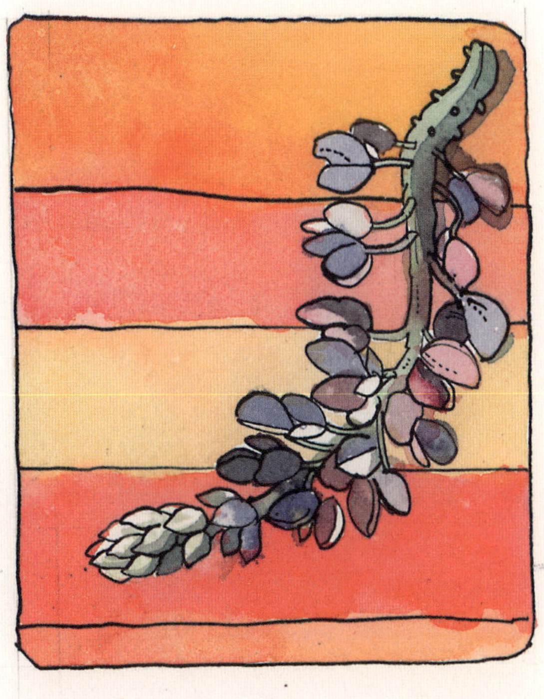

**A**

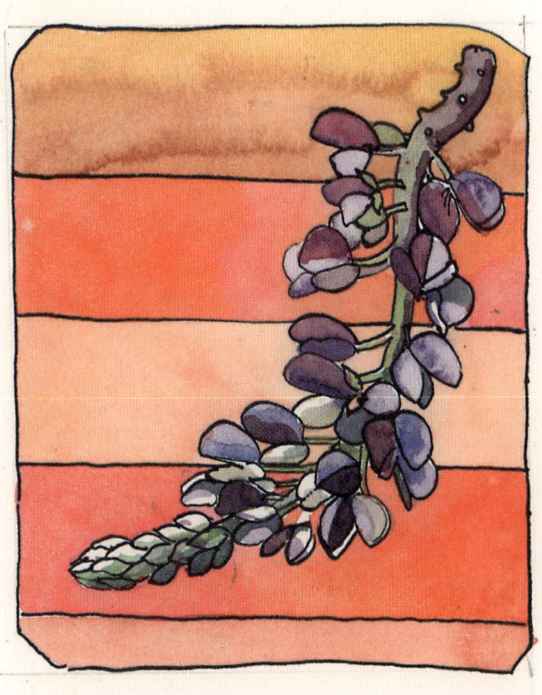

**B**

The lupins in versions *A* and *B* are identical, as are the stripes (or as similar as I could draw them!), but the colours in the first one have been inaccurately applied and are running over each outline and giving a very rough-and-ready effect. This detracts from the artwork's appeal, both overall and in close detail. In short, it looks messy.

**What to do and how to avoid**

Once again, the most important thing is to work slowly and carefully. I sometimes find that using an old and worn-out brush can also have this messy effect. If you must use an old one, it is even more important to slow down and watch that bold outline.

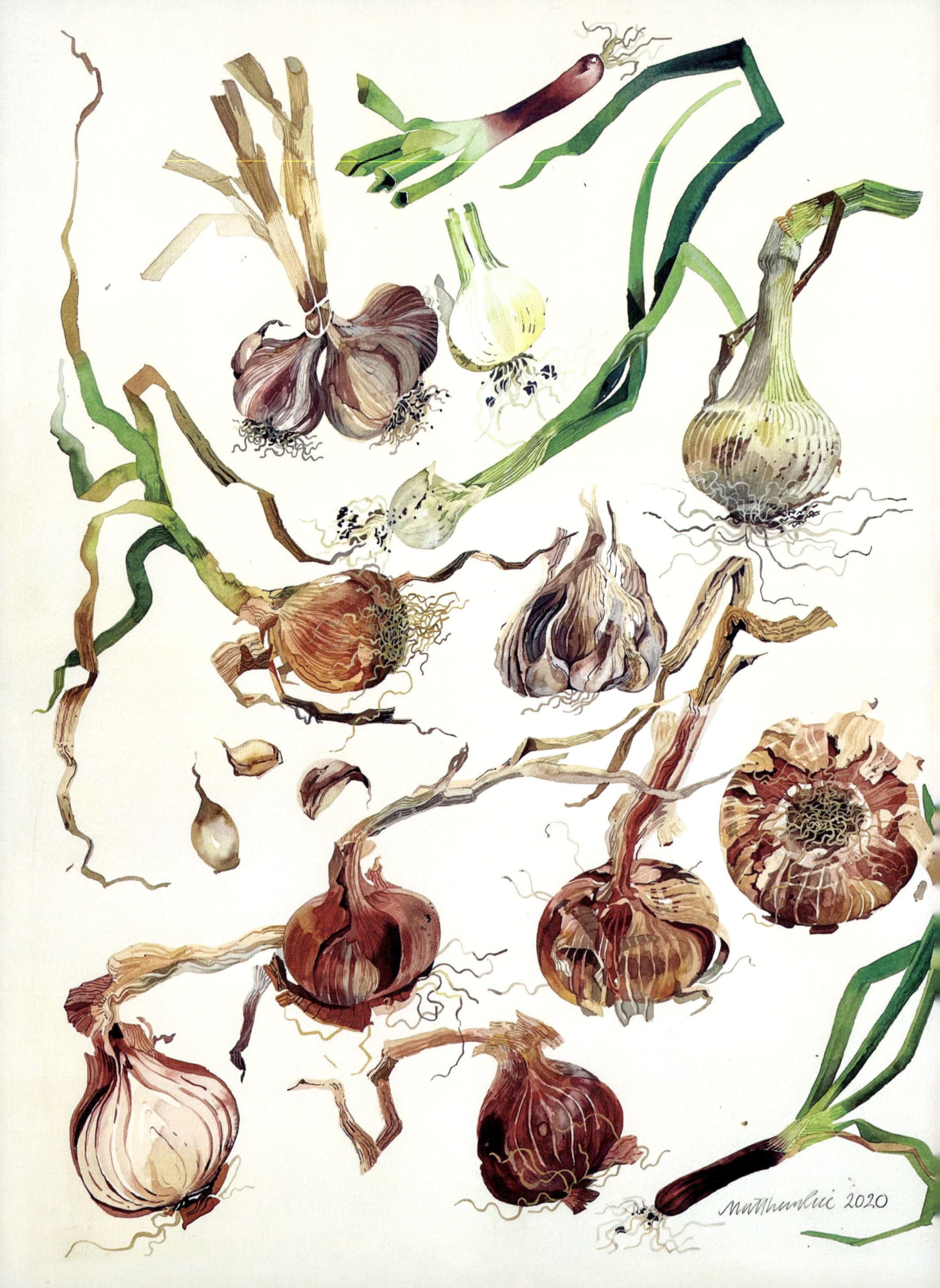
2020

# THREE GOOD THINGS TO REMEMBER

## ONE

We've already noted the old adage that a carpenter must measure twice and cut once. That look-before-you-leap stricture is just shorthand for recommending that you take decision-making *slowly* and think about every line: where it starts and to which point it leads. It seems almost irresistible to rush as if, by making a dash for it, it will somehow work. That doesn't work with parking the car, and it isn't advisable for drawing either. Bold draughtsmen like Quentin Blake, Gerald Scarfe, Oskar Kokoschka, Maggi Hambling and Catherine Goodman seem to do this, but do they really work in a rush? Perhaps that is just an impression. And even if they can produce these dynamic marks at speed, it doesn't follow that we can all do it. I recently started a series of piano lessons. Having played all my life, I had realized that my skill levels have remained the same for 40 or even 50 years. I have already learned a lot (and changed my playing), but by far the most important lesson has been a change of pace (and volume) – slowing down my playing, and while doing so making less of an infernal noise, has been a revelation (not least to the people who work in my studio, which they share with two big pianos). I now revel in the diminished volume and pace, trying to make each note and each harmonic progression more telling. This is totally analogous with a similar ordering of one's drawing. The highly developed and skilled bravura brushstrokes of the Chinese masters may be well out of reach, but there is a similar aim, which is to make each mark count.

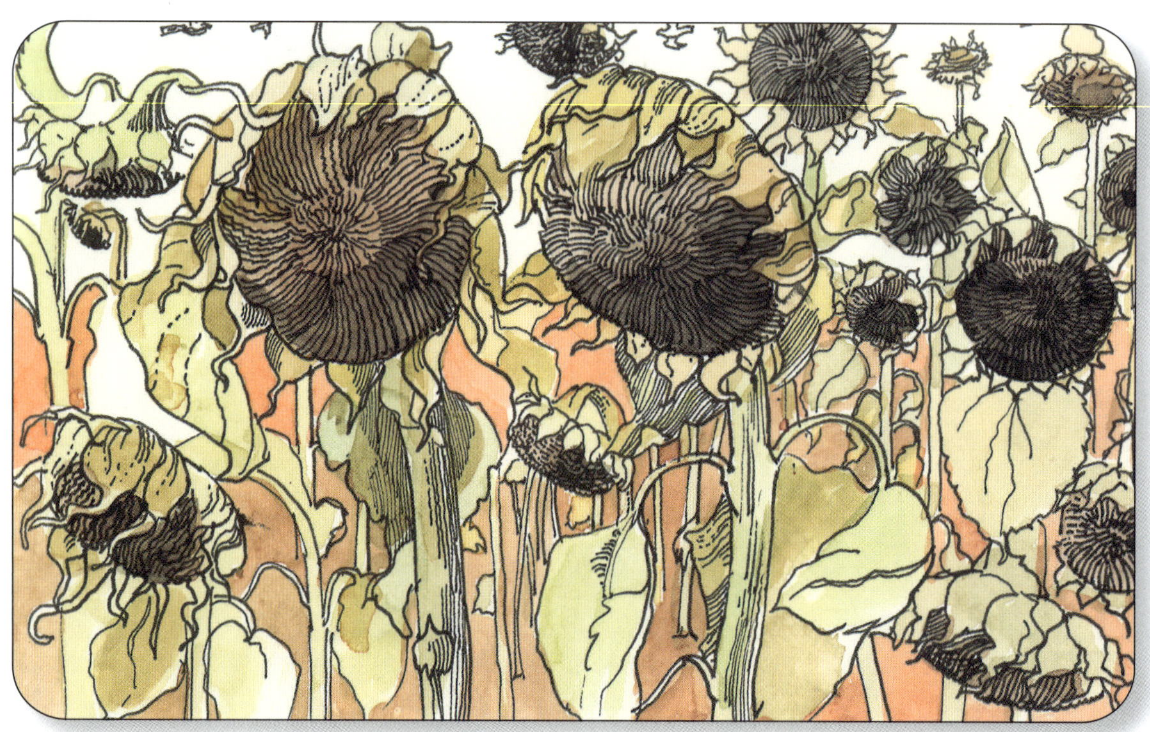

## TWO

Consider before you start a drawing what you are trying to draw. If, for example, you are looking at hens in the orchard, are you thinking of their silhouettes against the green grass, their dynamic actions as they scrape for insects, or the complex patterns of their plumage? Are you drawing one hen or a group? It's this initial process without a pen in your hand that leads to a satisfying picture. Even drawing the roughest sketch first can fix in your mind what scale you will work at or give you a clue as to what you might need to look at more carefully. Like typing in the postcode of a destination on Google Maps (or even looking at an actual map), your plan, even if it is only in outline, is essential to a successful outing. Just switching on the car and driving into the blue yonder is unlikely to pay dividends. While most people wouldn't do that on a journey, it's not unusual for artists of every ability (and I am a prime culprit here) to try to do this conceptual thinking with pen and paper already in hand. Unless you're striding off into the world of abstract expressionism (not the subject of this particular book), thinking up a picture, choosing a view and conceiving an idea *first* is a better bet.

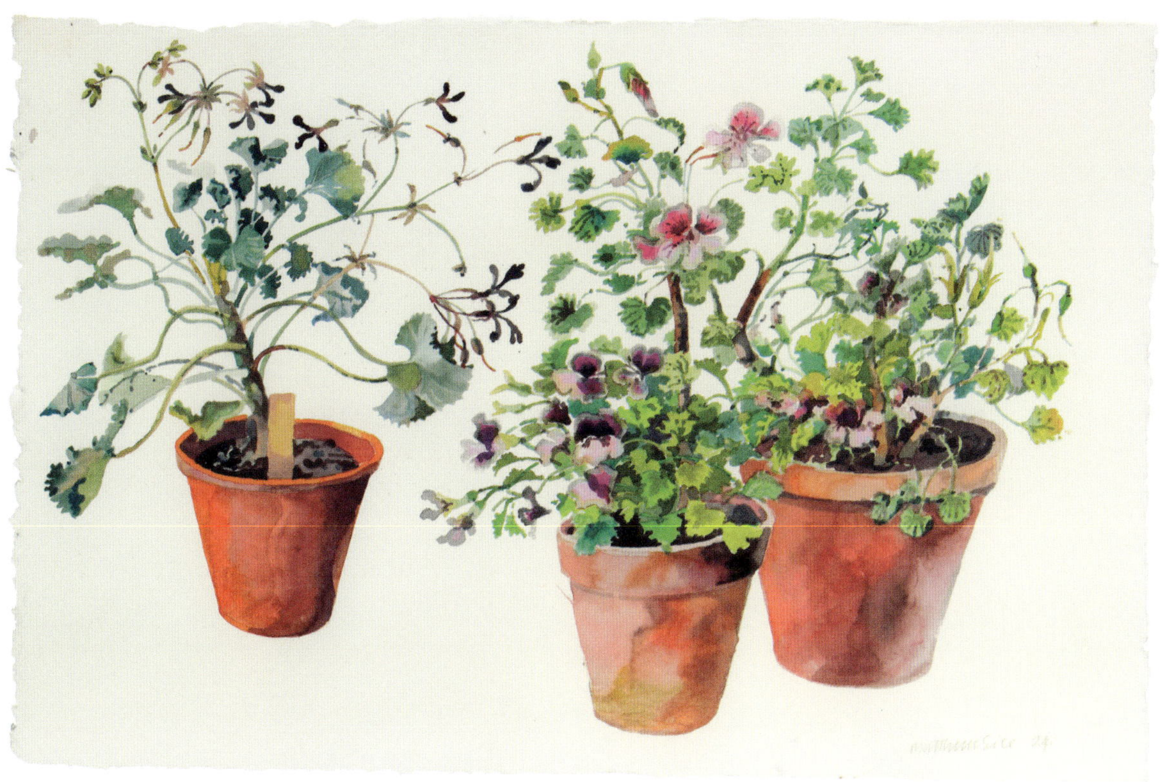

## THREE

Time spent in reconnaissance is rarely wasted. Go quiet and get your mind and equipment together. Free up an hour and don't answer the phone (sometimes I work in silence, sometimes with a talking book droning at my side). Arrange yourself comfortably on a chair or sit against a wall... wherever works. It's difficult enough to draw without awarding oneself a cramp-inducing bad posture or indeed just sitting too far away from one's subject. It's strange how often I have found someone straining to see what they are trying to draw because they have opportunistically plumped for a perch on a wall that is entirely in the *wrong place*. And, sad to say – and I have worked this out over years of fighting my own garrulous character – drawing is a solo activity. You might be among friends, drawing in a group or in a life class or studio, but the actual activity is *solo*. You cannot draw without concentration, or rather, your drawing will be immeasurably less good. Peeling back the layers of distraction (leaving the phone at home; not even listening to that talking book!) pays dividends and allows you to move forwards and not just tread water.

# SKETCHBOOKS

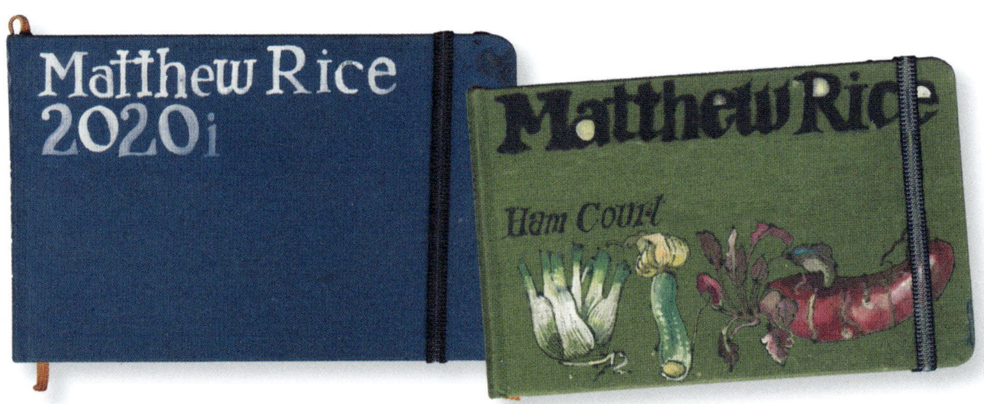


Loose drawings get lost. It's as simple as that. The sheets of paper scatter on the breezes of one's home and life and are gone, and so the sketchbook came to exist. In the days of the medieval sketchbook, paper was a luxury material and one that warranted serious attention. Binding it in covers was worthwhile, and in an age when imagery was sparse, making drawings as a record of the world, for reference and to further understanding, were a vital function of the artist. The wonderful sketchbook of the fourteenth-century artist Giovannino de' Grassi is kept in the Civic Library in Bergamo in northern Italy. His drawings of animals, many of which would never have been seen by the worshippers in the churches he decorated, are as real and resonant today as they were in the fourteenth century and have been preserved by being bound in leather covers six hundred years ago. Leonardo da Vinci similarly left some (rather charmless) cat and dog studies along with many hundreds of pages that trace his extraordinarily searching mind's travels and recorded his discoveries and inventions anatomical, scientific or astrological. Rarely charming and always fascinating, his fine penwork and neat writing make these perhaps the best known of the genre. Similarly, the Renaissance and Baroque architects of Europe knew the value of the sketchbook when working out preliminary drawings for their designs or for recording the classical models for their new designs. John Ruskin recorded Gothic Venice, too.

There are a number of wonderful facsimile sketchbooks published: one by Samuel Palmer has a whole series of the most beautiful landscapes and individual trees that are not drawn in his very mannered (but beautiful) style but are in fact just sensitive pen drawings of enviable accuracy and charm. David Hockney's Yorkshire landscape sketchbook is bold, bright and dynamic and a thing of utter beauty, with page after page filled with paintings of the rolling Yorkshire Wolds. The sheep sketchbook of the painter Henry Moore is a sketch-monograph focused on

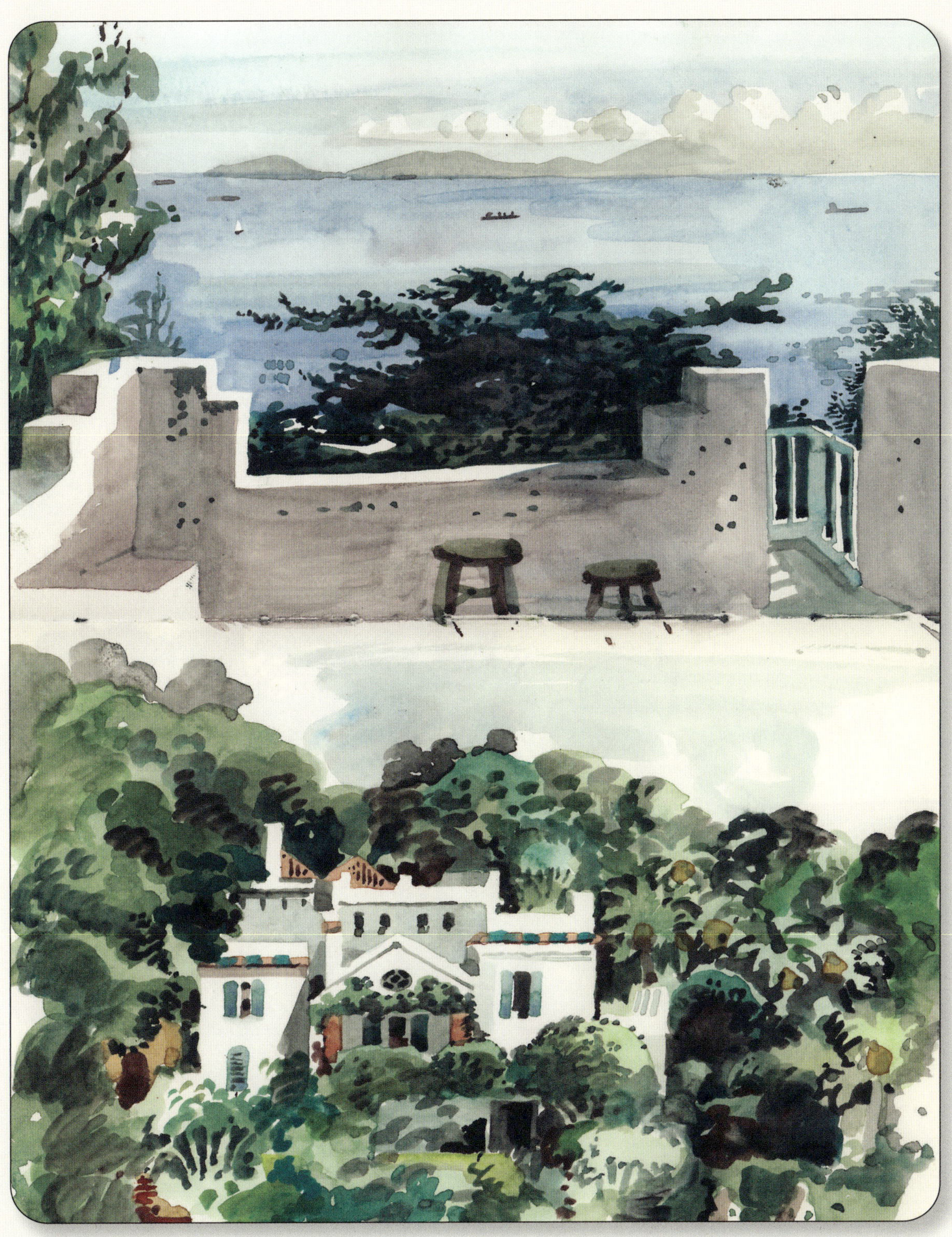

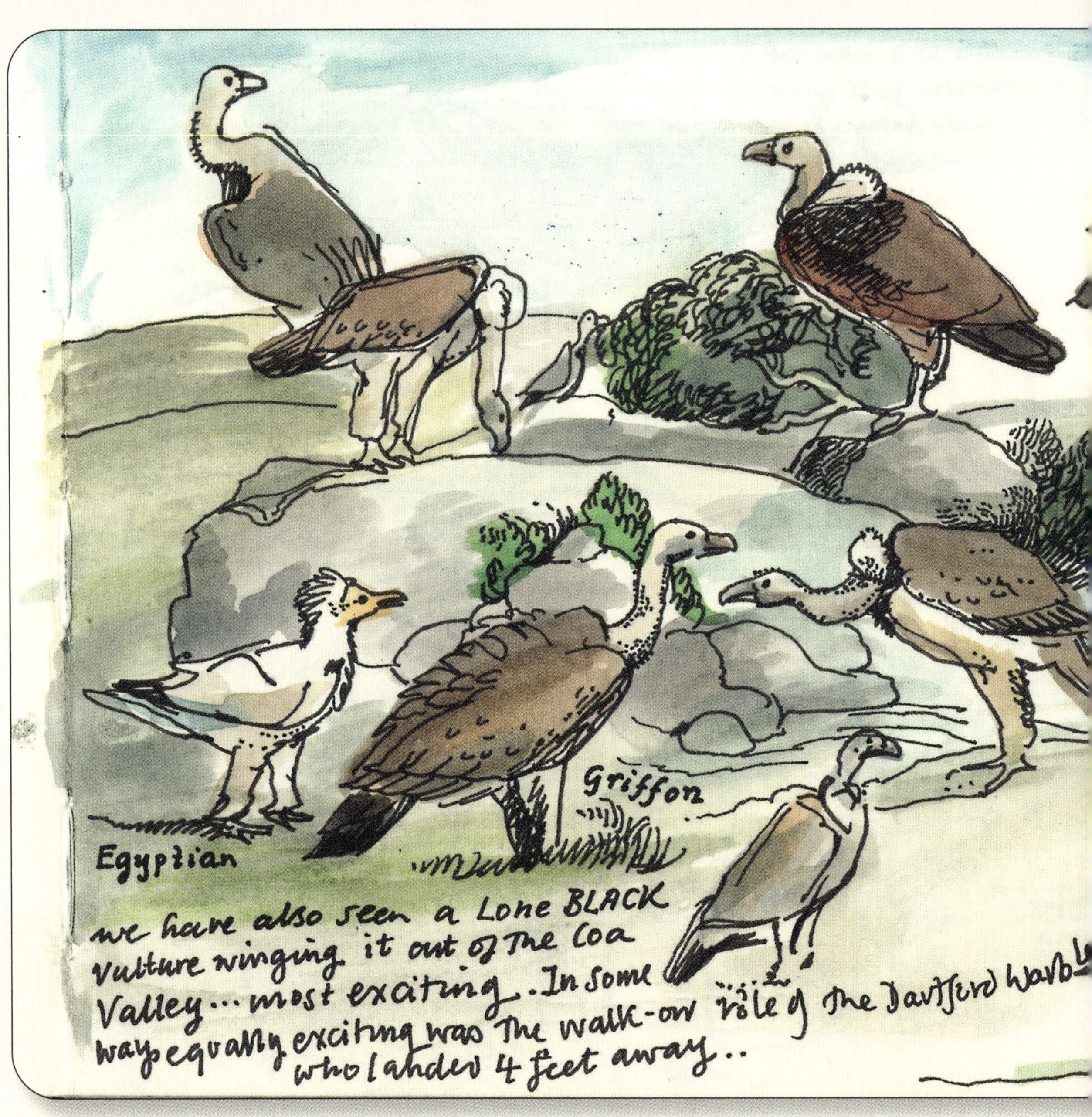


Drawings of a memorable day watching vultures eating a dead donkey as part of a conservation project in Portugal.

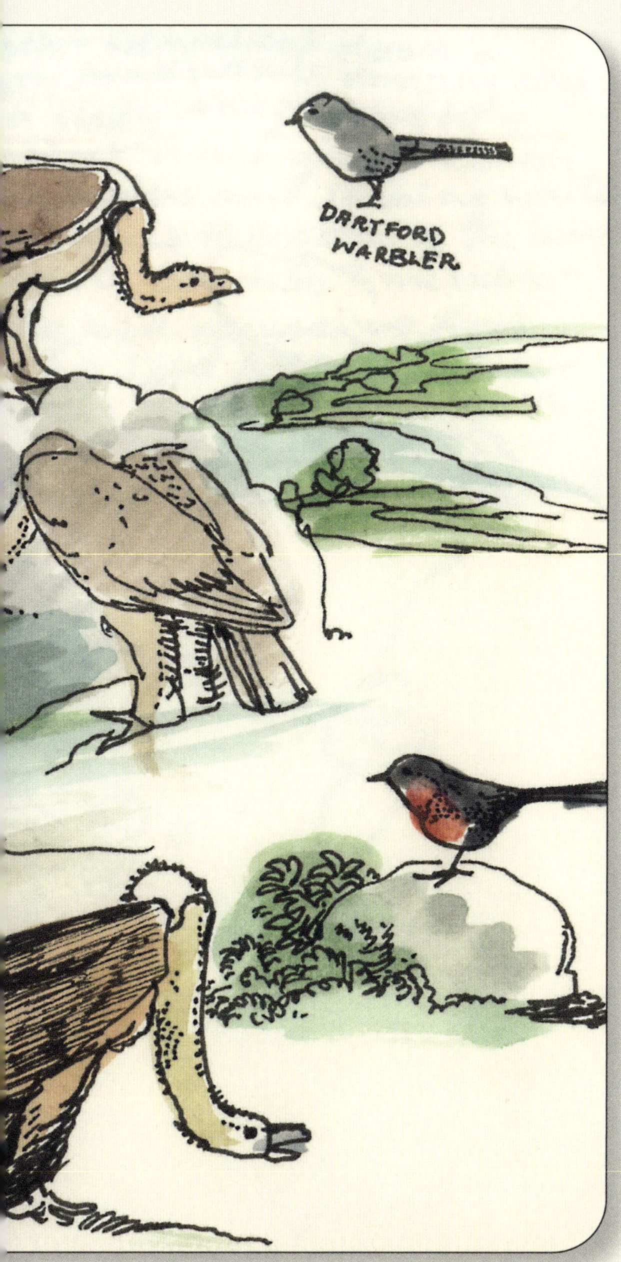


(but in no way limited in appeal by) sheep. He explores in pen and ink the softly disguised anatomy of the unshorn sheep, the undulating wool tracing their underlying anatomy.

There are many more in print, for we have a fascination with the sketchbook. It seems to allow us to see directly into the thoughts of an artist, avoiding the mediation of technique or of highly developed period style and the preconceptions of conventional compositions. There is an accessibility about a sketchbook that is particularly appealing to the viewer, while for the creator there is similarly a lack of reticence. The sketchbook drives away or at least dilutes artist's block. Because the blank page of a sketchbook is so much smaller than a canvas or sheet of paper, and is also just one of one hundred such pages, it becomes a less daunting place to tackle even a complicated subject.

This idea – that a sketchbook is the place in which to explore your subject – has been understood for centuries and remains the case today. Keeping a sketchbook is like a diary, a visual journal of the life and surroundings of the drawer. Whether you are drawing the most domestic and everyday details or the more remarkable views seen on holiday, keeping a sketchbook provides a place to do this that enshrines that series of drawings and elevates them. They become a record and something specifically describing one person's experience.

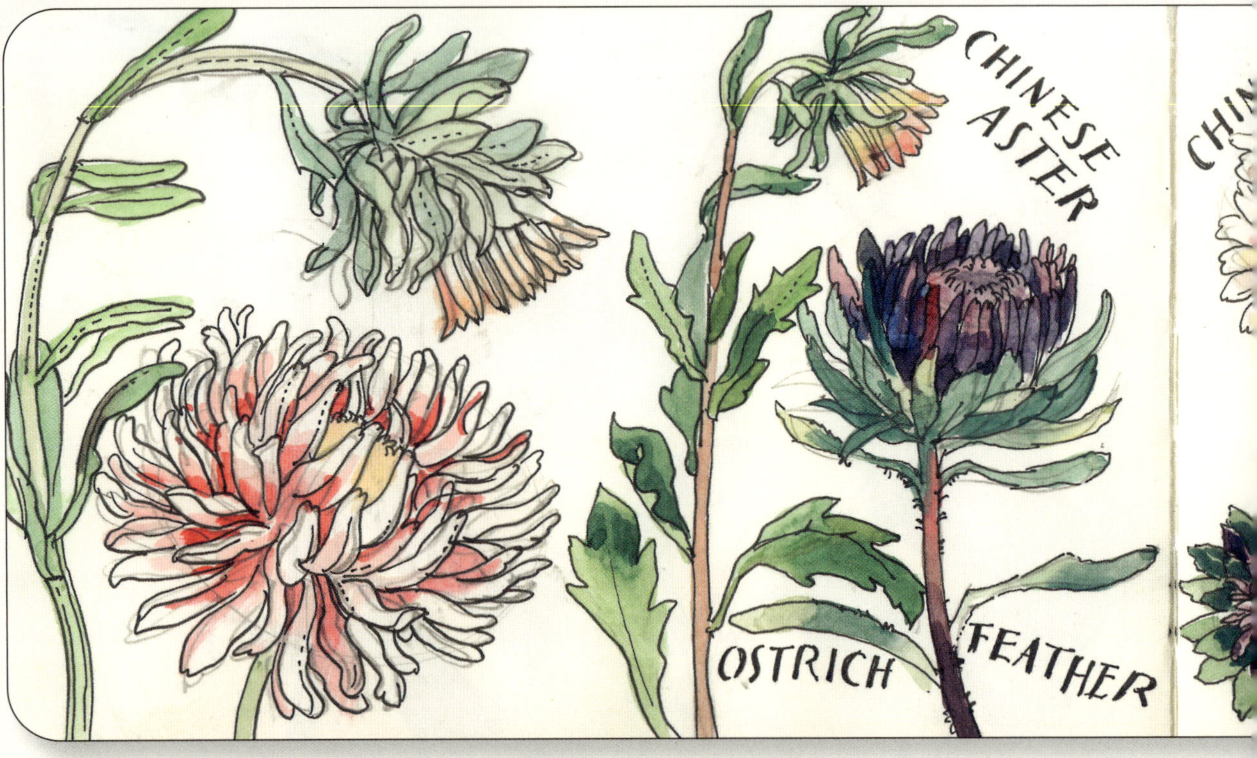

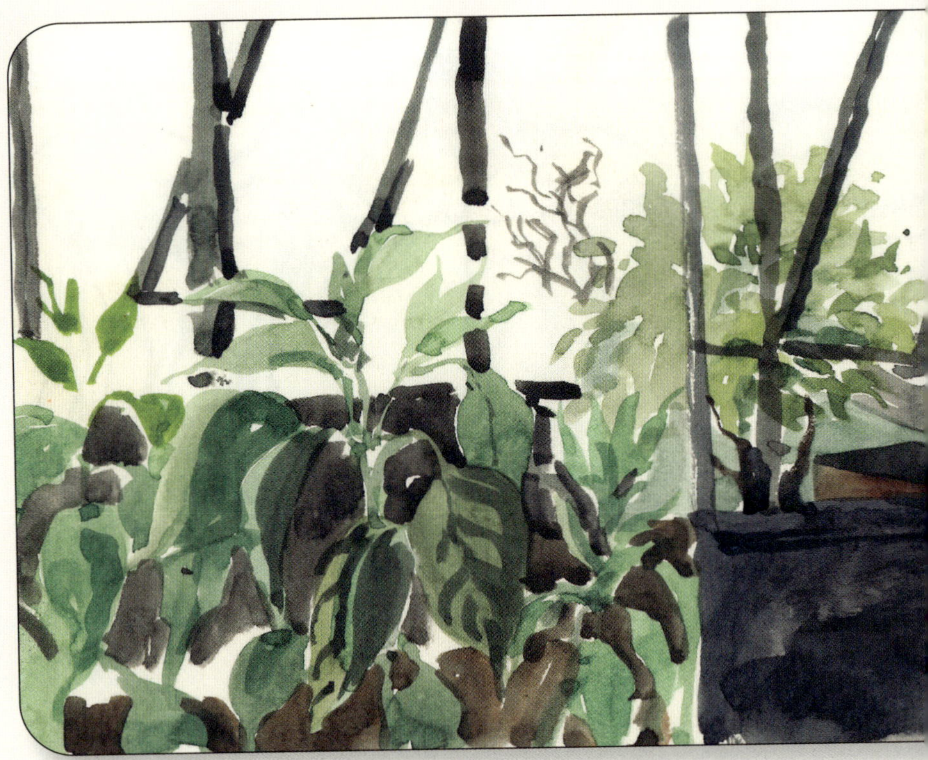

A more than usually detailed lockdown drawing of my daughter Kitty, while she was drawing in the greenhouse.

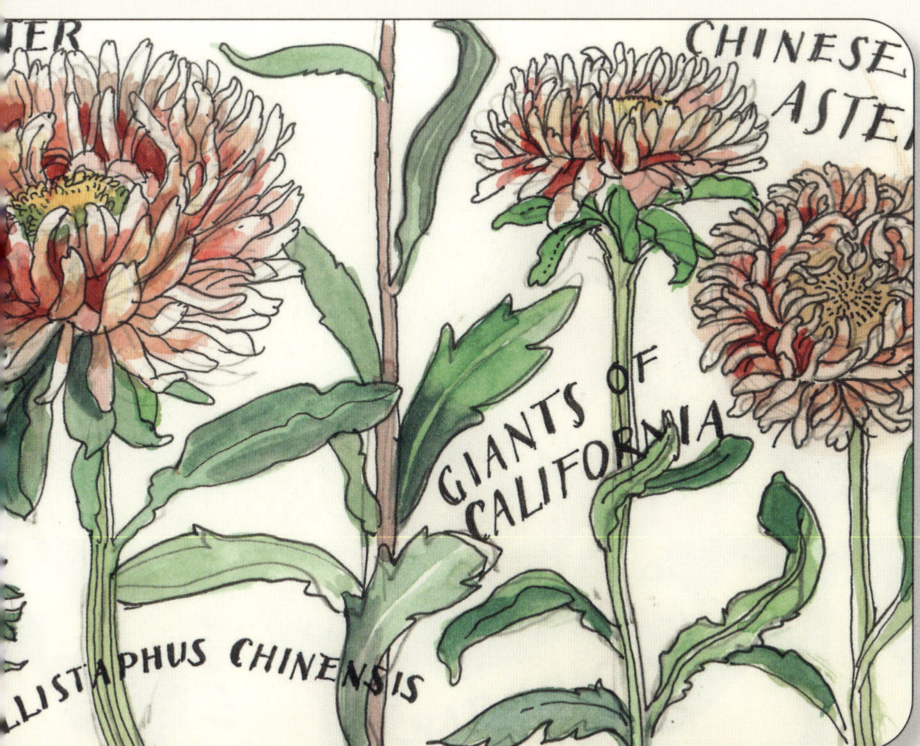


Record of my short-lived passion for Chinese asters.

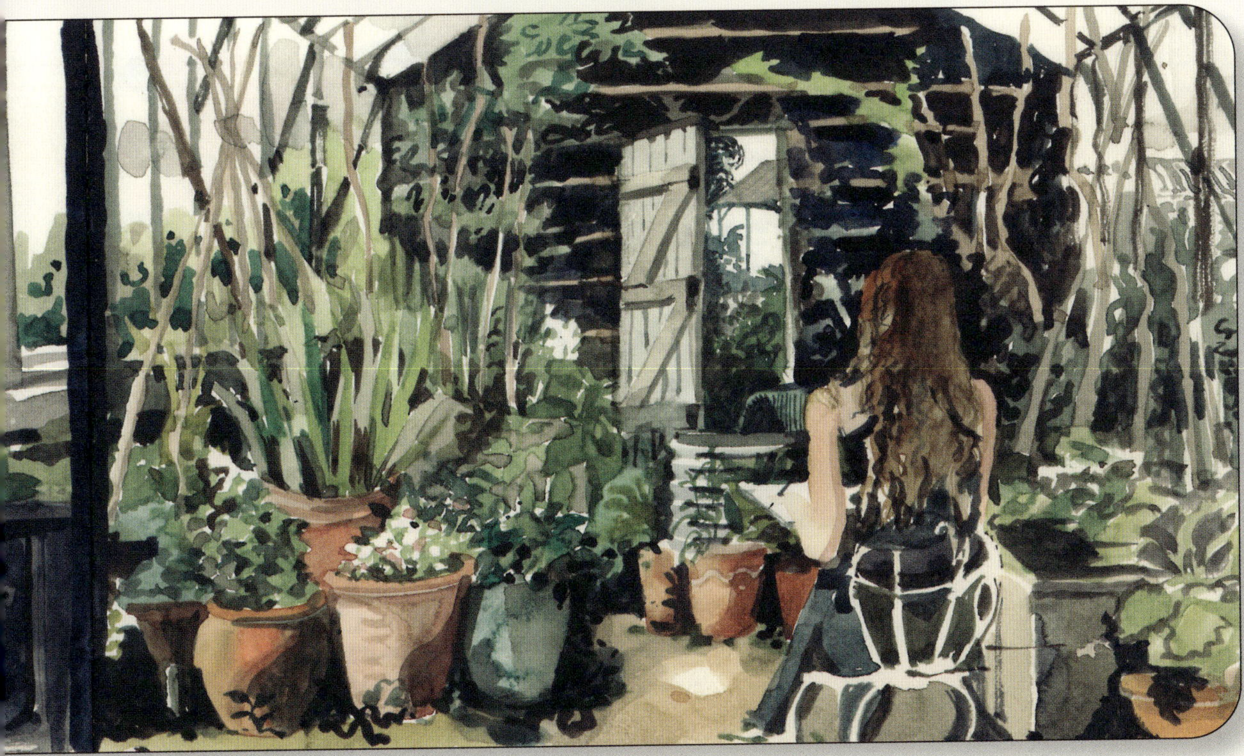

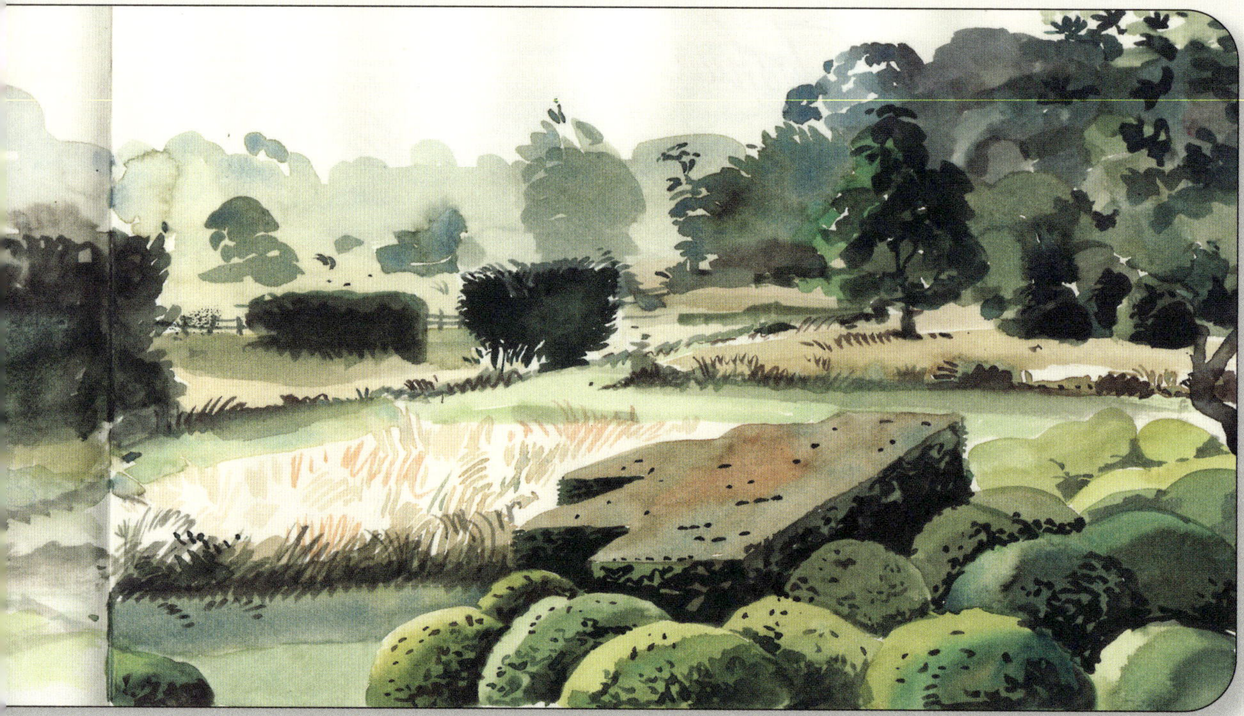

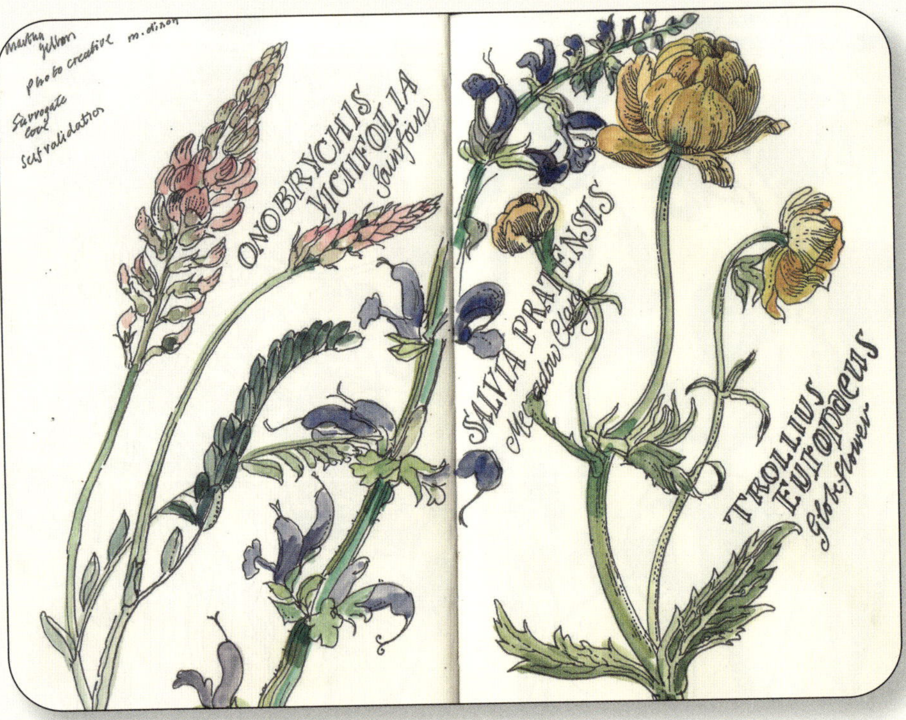
ONOBRYCHIS VICIIFOLIA
Sainfoin
SALVIA PRATENSIS
Meadow Clary
TROLLIUS EUROPAEUS
Globeflower

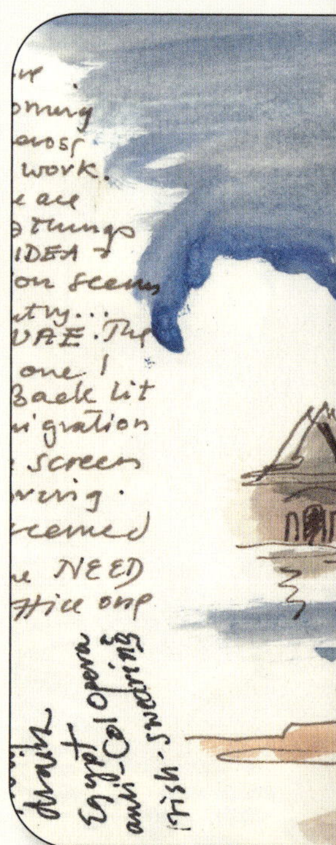

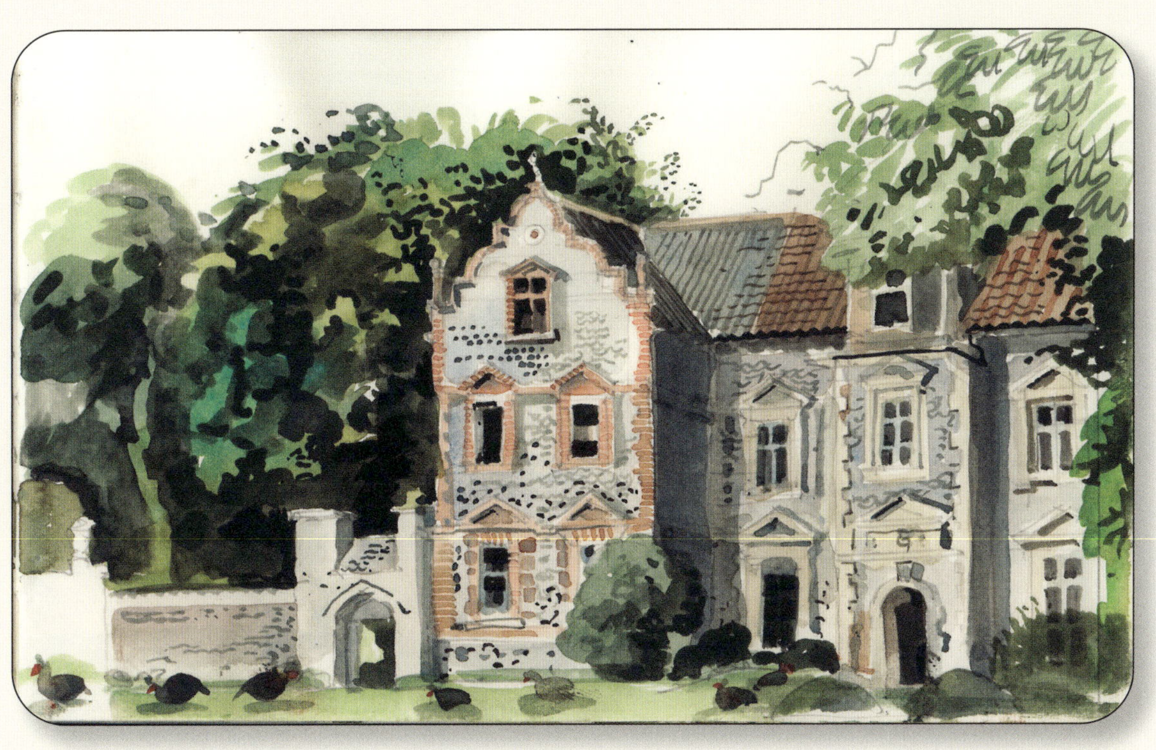

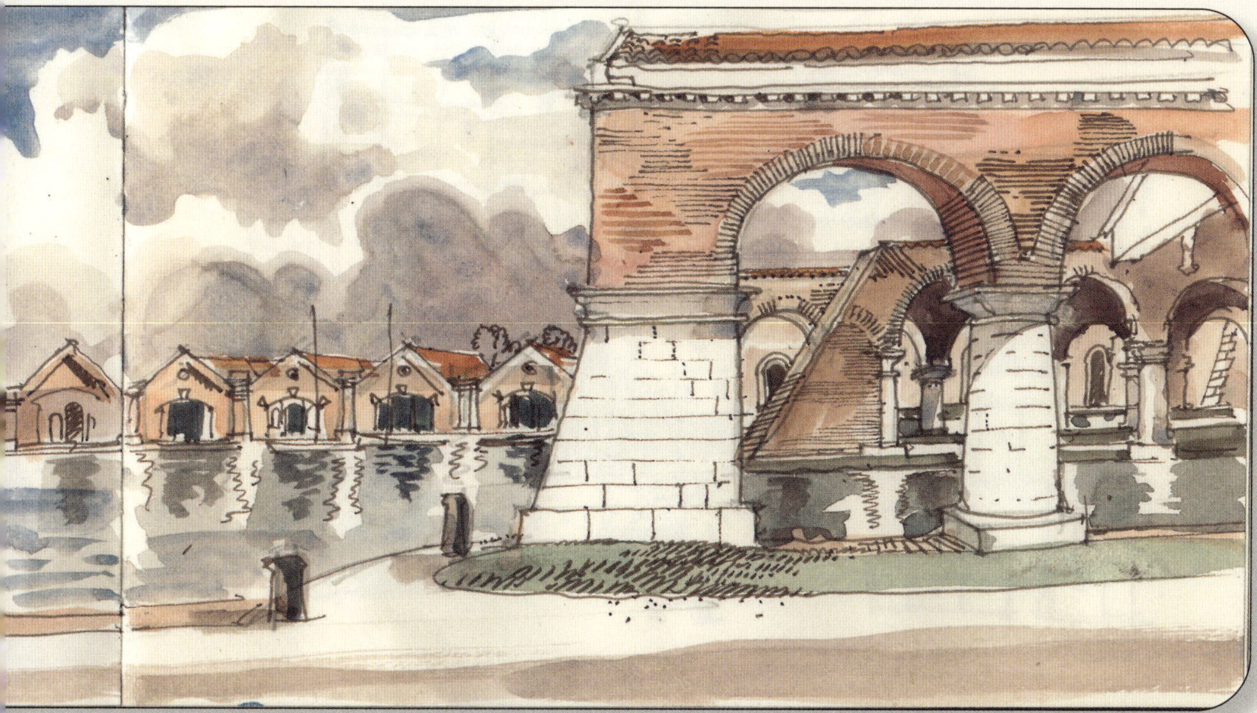

*Paint slowly! Don't rush lines or washes. There's no hurry. Make every line count.*

While for some artists the sketchbook is an end in itself, it also frequently serves as a workbook, as a place to experiment and to plan more evolved work – in fact, a book of sketches in which, hidden from view, a series of solutions can be explored in miniature while the artist or architect or designer decides in which direction they will take a problem.

One format of the sketchbook that has had rather too much emphasis is the kind produced by school art students encouraged, mainly by a rather plodding syllabus, to record their explorations while also including railway tickets, crassly traced exhibition postcards and decorative frames on each uninformative page. This has emerged in the last 40 years (it was not part of my education) and is due for retirement, as it uses up time that might be more usefully employed looking and drawing!

My sketchbooks track about 40 years of my life (if you exclude juvenilia). They continue the series of my father's sketchbooks begun in 1948, so it is quite a long period recorded that stretches from trips to Paris when taxis were horse-drawn, through journeys on barges along the Thames, to weekends in Venice or afternoons in the greenhouse just last week. My choice of sketchbook has developed from thick, shiny white pages through softer cream cartridge paper to most desirable books of bound Arches watercolour paper. I think these are perhaps a bit expensive for everyday use but delicious to draw with pen and ink in.

## A FEW USEFUL TIPS FOR EVERYDAY SKETCHBOOKS THAT DOUBLE UP AS YOUR NOTEBOOK

1. Some simple housekeeping: draw from one end (the beginning) and write notes from the back. This means that the dreary bits are grouped together and need not be looked at again when they cease to be topical.

2. Unless you have a lot of time to spare, which, during a visually stimulating holiday, seems rarely to be the case, draw on the spot and colour in when you have a moment later on. Preferably, this would be on the same day when the image is fresh in your memory.

3. Try to make some pages that are painted all over. A coloured wash varies the pace of the book and makes it more interesting to look at.

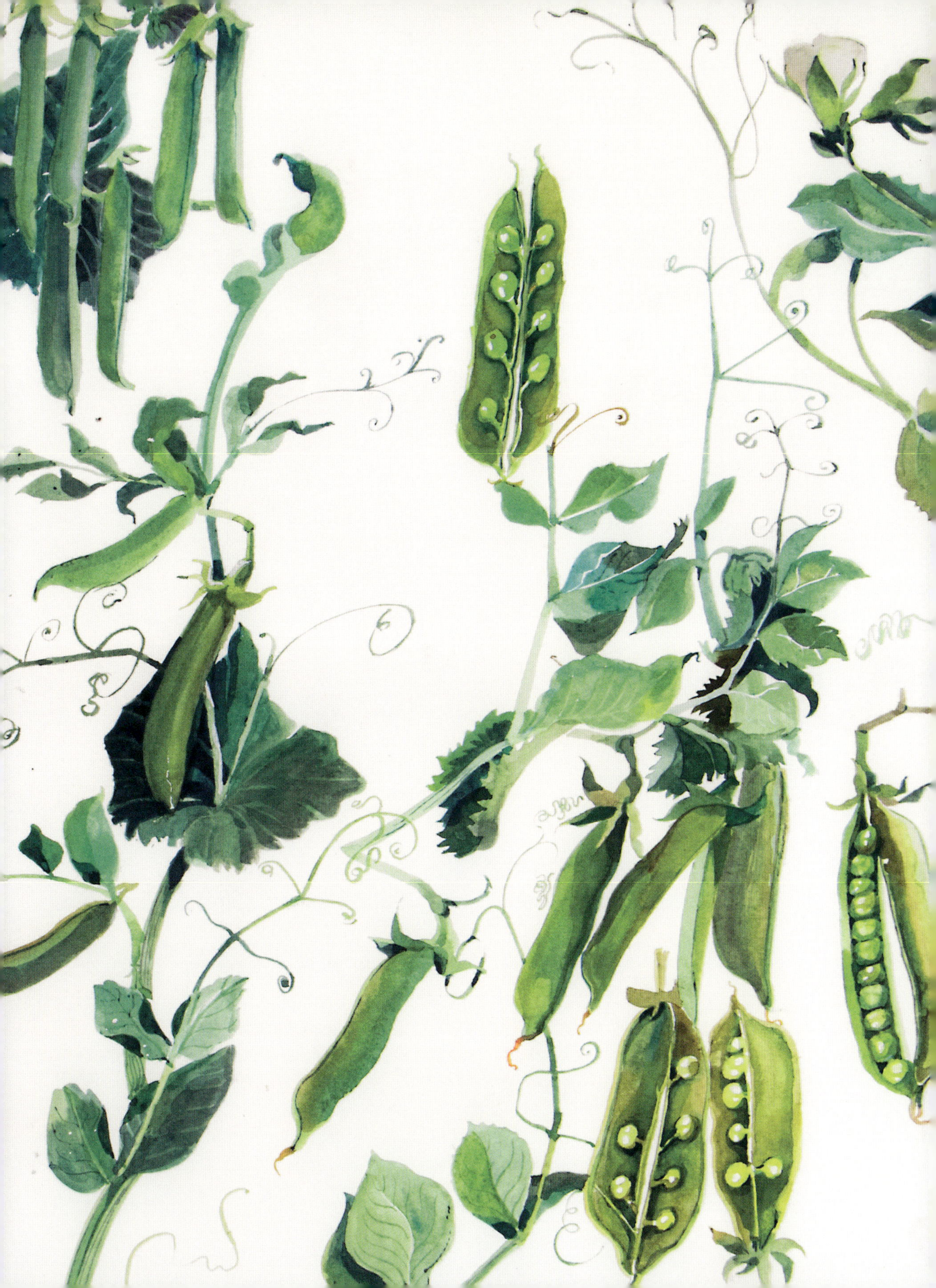

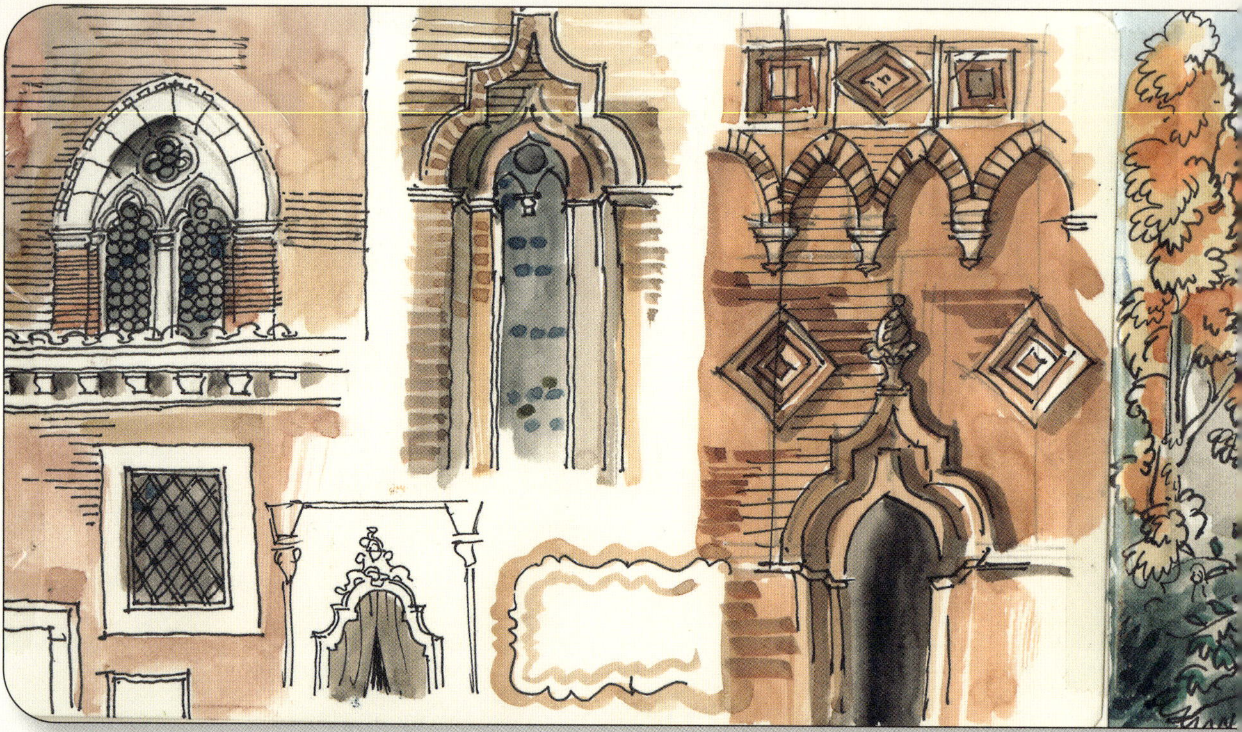

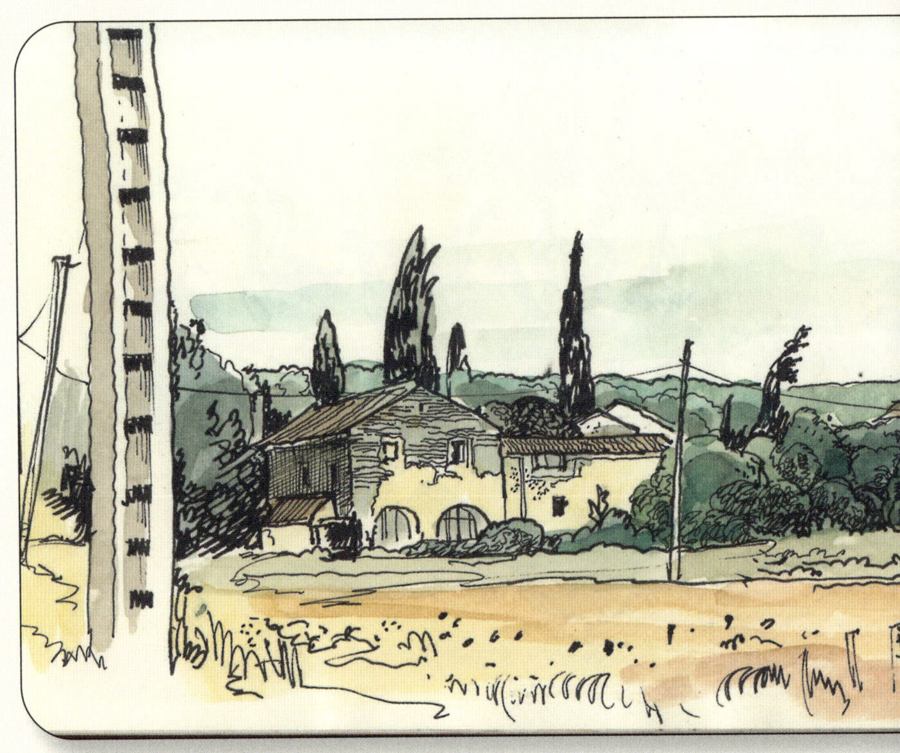

A southern landscape, painted while staying with my friends Desmond and Harriet at Flaux, France.

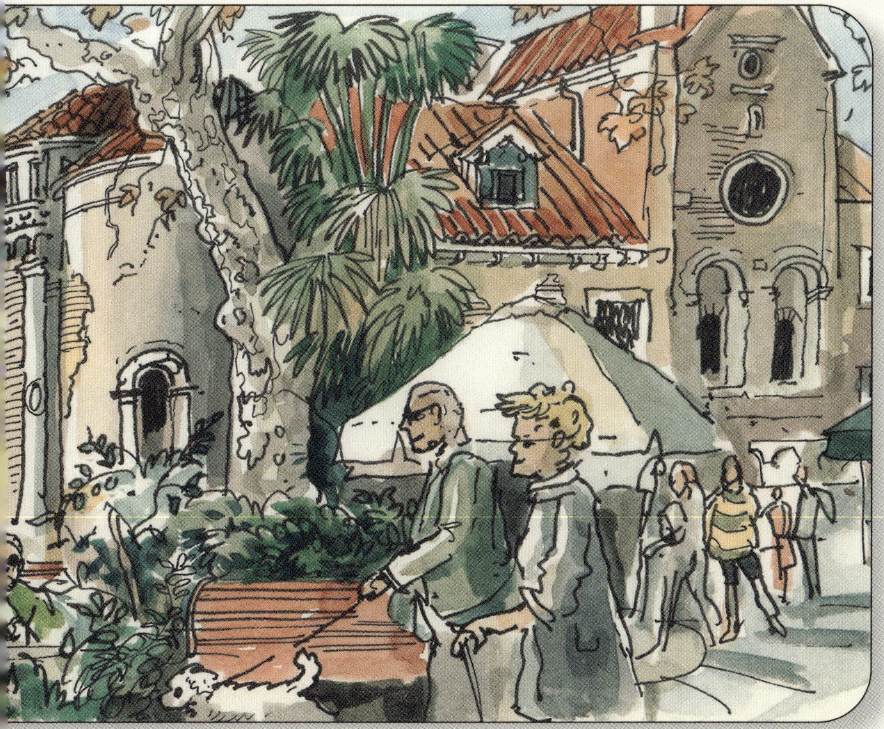

One of hundreds of little Venetian drawings.

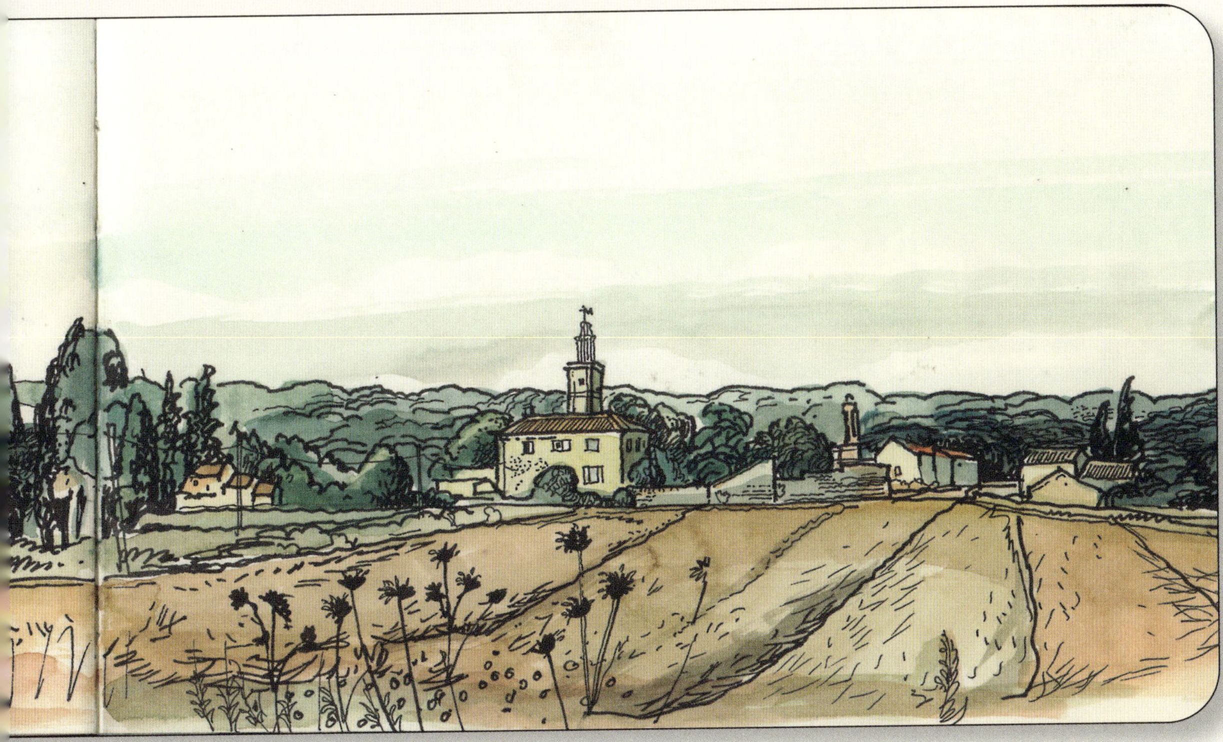

# DAILY PRACTICE

Two years ago, I began a new habit: to draw a picture every day – a picture that would be the same size and format, and that would in some way reflect the day on which it was drawn. It began with a Happy New Year card on Instagram and has been a consistent rule ever since. It has turned into a task undertaken with an almost monkish regularity and indeed with joy – not something I had intended but instead an evolved practice. Now, at the time of writing, some 500 days later, this has become a surprising corpus of work and one in which, from time to time, new work ideas and treatments have emerged that have percolated into my wider work.

I very rarely approach this daily task with anything other than pleasure, even when, as oftentimes happens, the job is begun late in the day. I picked a size (initially 6cm × 6cm and, more recently, a more generous and liberating 10cm × 10cm) that made the job quick. I usually spend about half an hour on each picture, only very occasionally being lured into a more sustained project, so it is essentially a painted note, a postcard. The point of it is to stick to a rule, one that is self-imposed but that has become a moment of the day when other work or conversation pauses. It would be indulgent and self-aggrandizing to make too much of a fuss about this as something with some amorphous higher purpose. It has none and is no more than a personal regimen that has produced a lot of small pictures. But as their number slowly grows, and for as long as each one is a work in miniature (subject and composition, colours and line), it has some validity as a record, a visual diary of my surroundings. Drawing gets worse the less you do. That sounds obvious, but it is the case that this happily improves with practice.

This project is not so special. Many people do this: fill a sketchbook, a drawing a day, or perhaps track the changing seasons in a view in which change is so slow as to be almost invisible. As it happens, it sits in the middle of my wider work, sometimes reflecting or influencing other projects. As I am as much a designer as a painter, the inclusion of the date as an intrinsic part of the composition is part and parcel of each day's picture.

I recommend some similar daily project, maybe initially for a month only. But be warned! It is highly likely that once begun, the work will continue, and you will find yourself tied to this peaceful daily half hour.

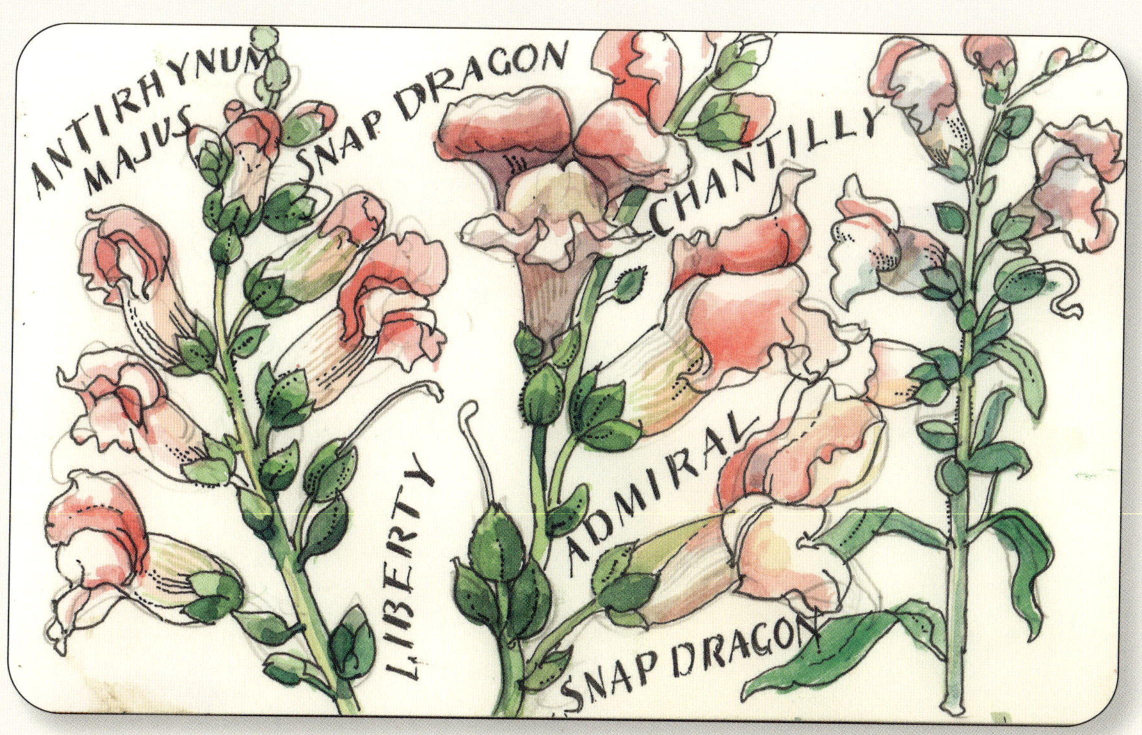
ANTIRHYNUM
MAJUS
SNAP DRAGON
CHANTILLY
LIBERTY
ADMIRAL
SNAP DRAGON

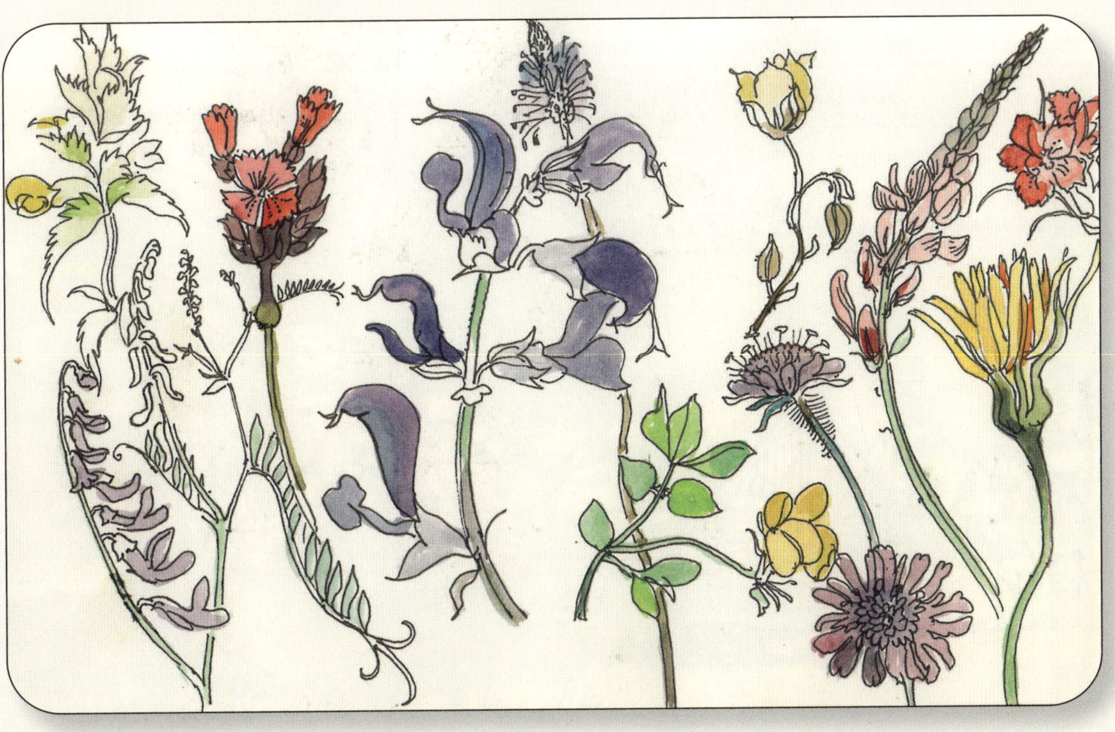

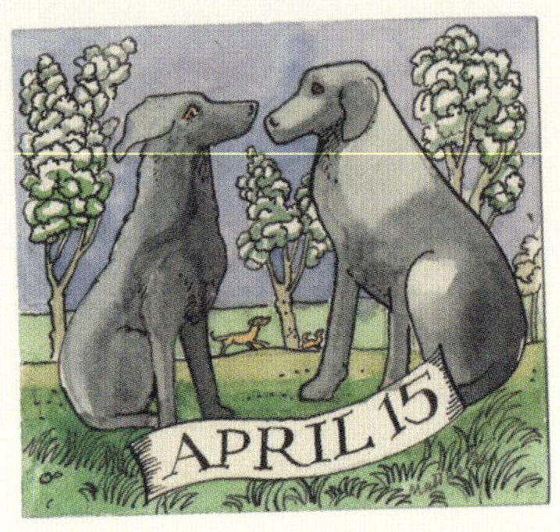


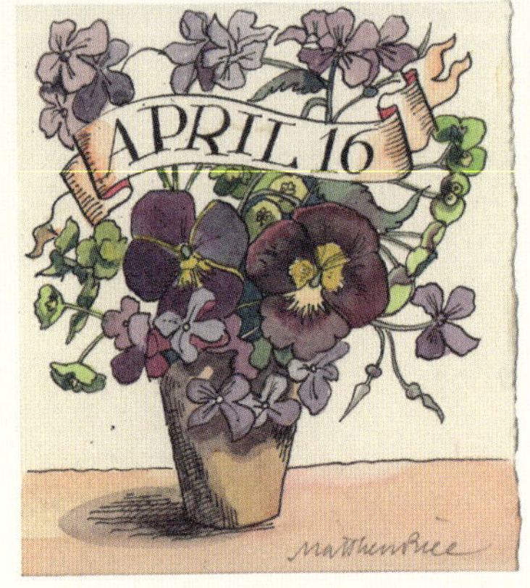


A selection of 'daily card' drawings, from a series that I began in January 2024, and which continues as a daily discipline.

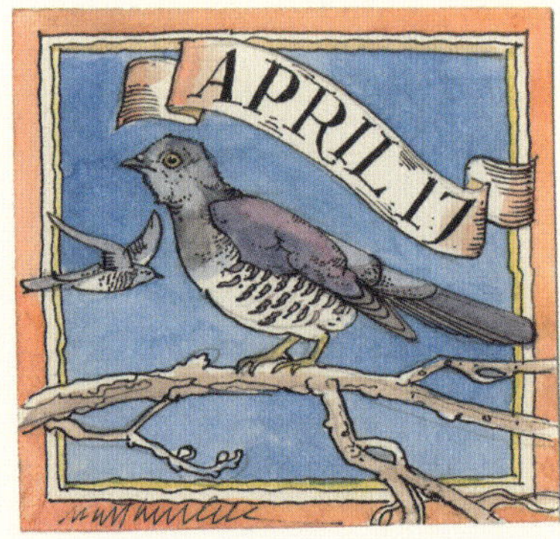


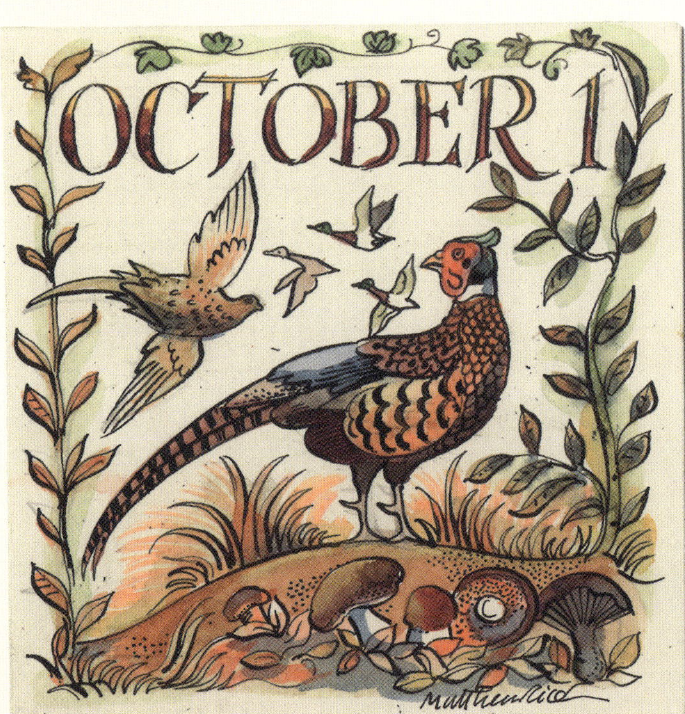


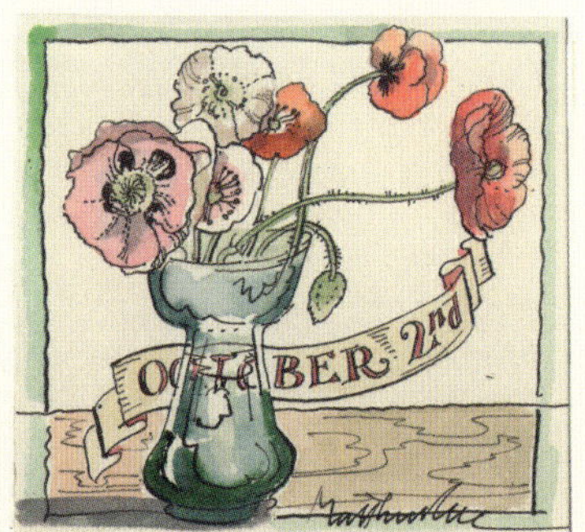


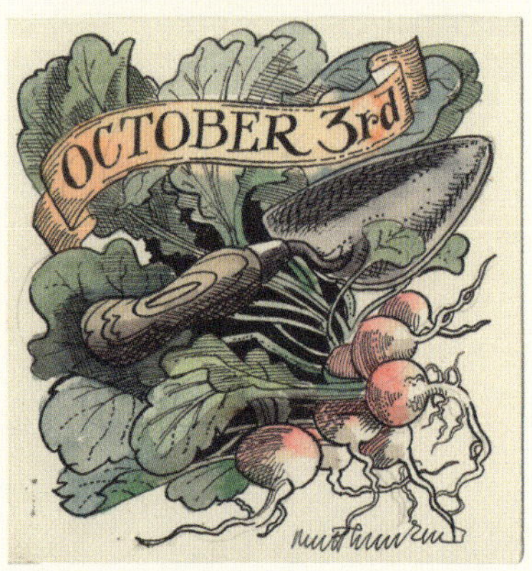


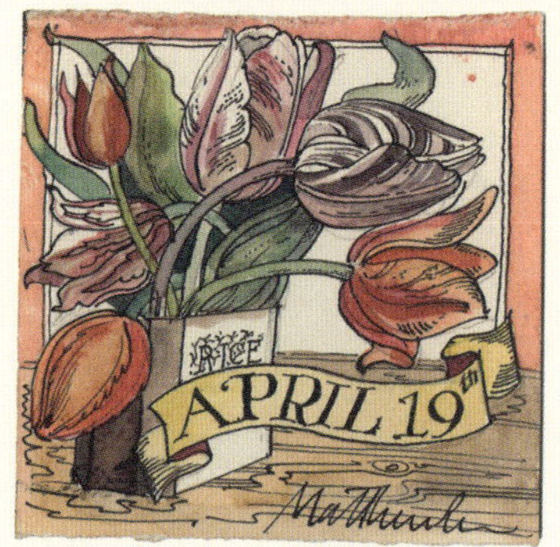


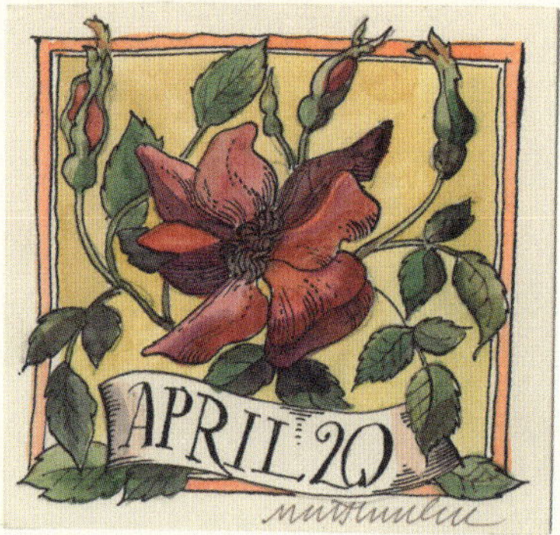

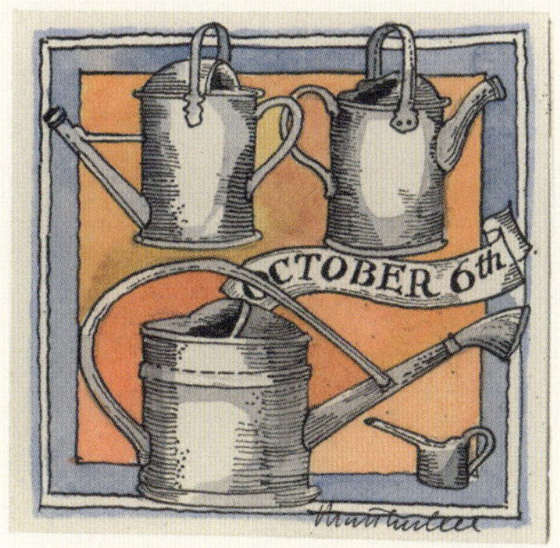
OCTOBER 6th

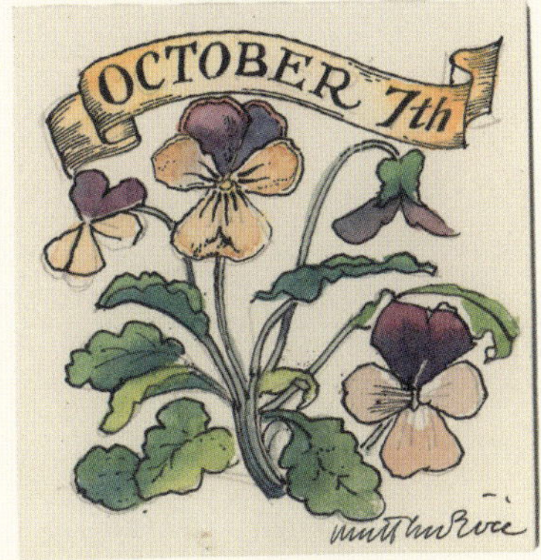
OCTOBER 7th

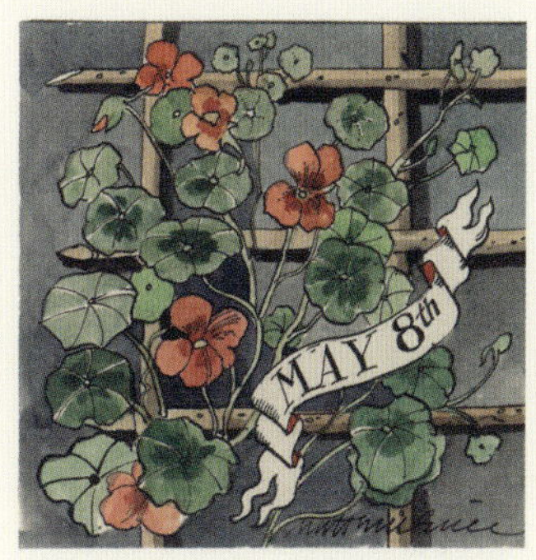
MAY 8th

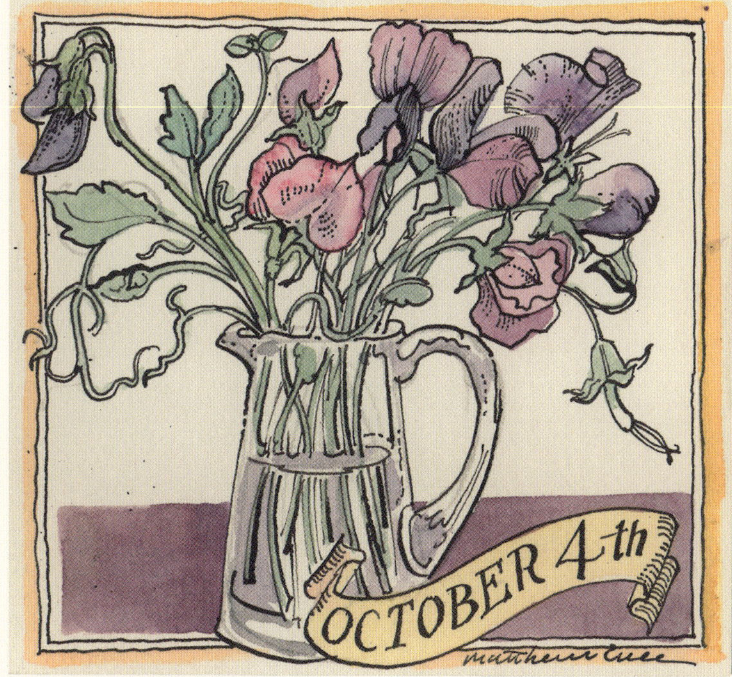
OCTOBER 4th

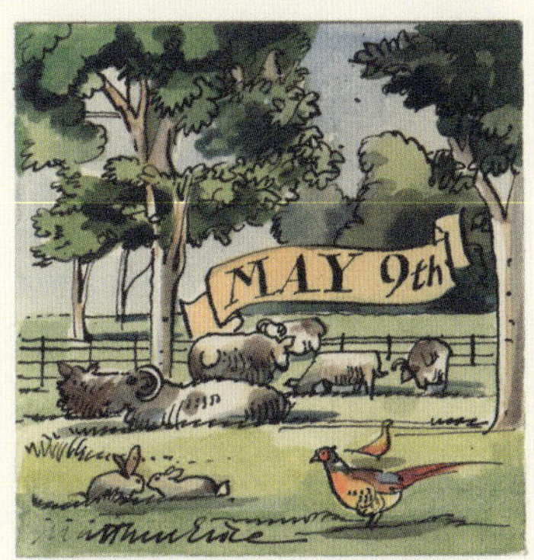
MAY 9th

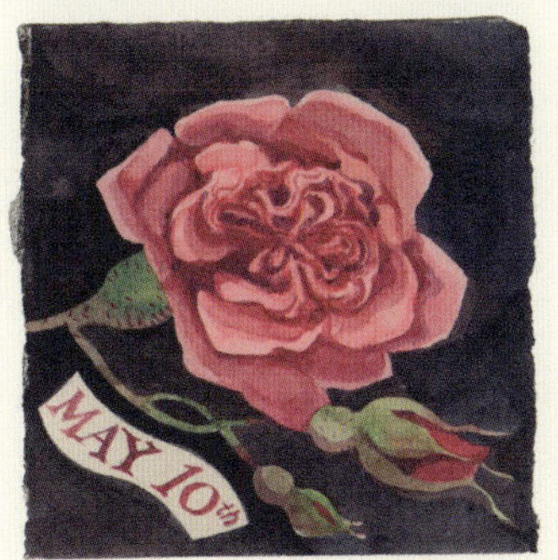
MAY 10th

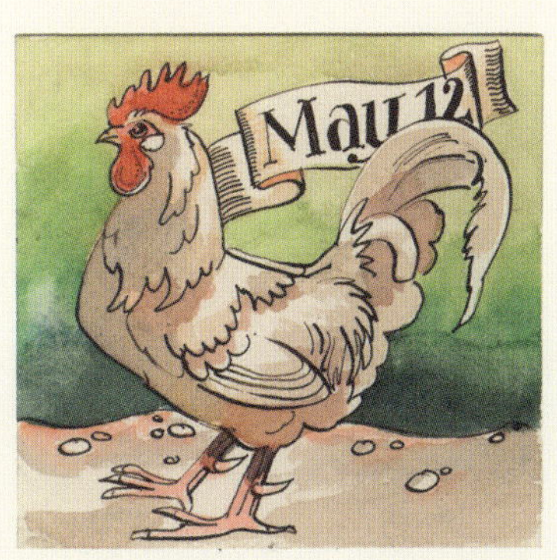
May 12

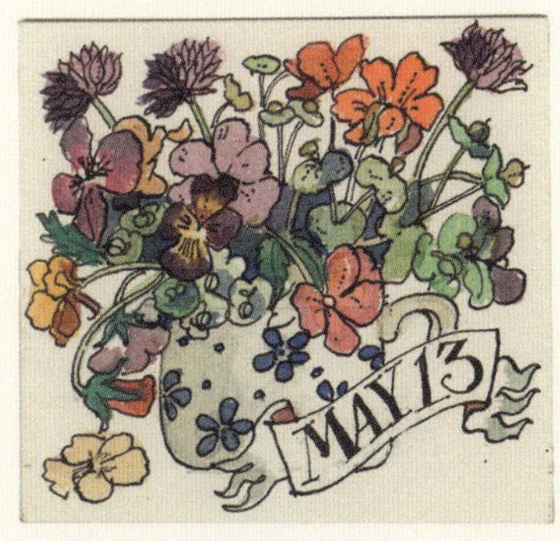
MAY 13

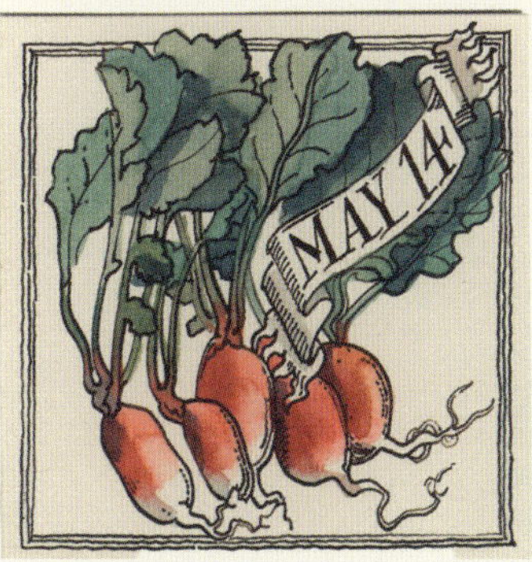
MAY 14

An Hachette UK Company
www.hachette.co.uk

First published in Great Britain in 2026 by Ilex,
an imprint of Octopus Publishing Group Ltd
Carmelite House
50 Victoria Embankment
London EC4Y 0DZ
www.octopusbooks.co.uk



Additional picture credits:
p24: Photo Scala, Florence
p27: Archivart/Alamy Stock Photo
p28: Smith Archive/Alamy Stock Photo

Portrait of Matthew on back cover flap © Tom Pilston
Portrait of Matthew on p8 © Phineas Sajous

Distributed in the US by Hachette Book Group
1290 Avenue of the Americas, 4th and 5th Floors,
New York, NY 10104

Distributed in Canada by Canadian Manda Group
664 Annette St., Toronto, Ontario, Canada M6S 2C8



ISBN 978-1-84091-908-0
eISBN 978-1-84091-909-7

A CIP catalogue record for this book is available from the British Library

Printed and bound in China

10 9 8 7 6 5 4 3 2 1

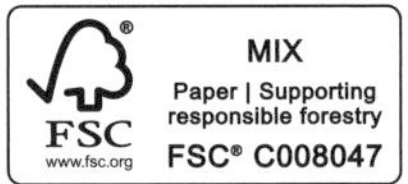